The Multitasking Mind

To Tom —

With my compliments

— David

OXFORD SERIES ON
COGNITIVE MODELS AND ARCHITECTURES

The Multitasking Mind

Dario D. Salvucci and
Niels A. Taatgen

OXFORD
UNIVERSITY PRESS
2011

OXFORD
UNIVERSITY PRESS

Oxford University Press, Inc., publishes works that further
Oxford University's objective of excellence
in research, scholarship, and education.

Oxford   New York
Auckland   Cape Town   Dar es Salaam   Hong Kong   Karachi
Kuala Lumpur   Madrid   Melbourne   Mexico City   Nairobi
New Delhi   Shanghai   Taipei   Toronto

With offices in
Argentina   Austria   Brazil   Chile   Czech Republic   France   Greece
Guatemala   Hungary   Italy   Japan   Poland   Portugal   Singapore
South Korea   Switzerland   Thailand   Turkey   Ukraine   Vietnam

Published by Oxford University Press, Inc.
198 Madison Avenue, New York, New York 10016
www.oup.com

Oxford is a registered trademark of Oxford University Press

Library of Congress Cataloging-in-Publication Data

Salvucci, Dario D.
The multitasking mind / Dario D. Salvucci, Niels A. Taatgen.
p. cm. — (Oxford series on cognitive models and architectures)
Includes bibliographical references and index.
ISBN: 978-0-19-973356-9 (hardback)
1. Human multitasking. 2. Time management. I. Taatgen, Niels A. II. Title.
HD69.T54S25 2010
650.1'1—dc22
2010026119

9 8 7 6 5 4 3 2 1

Printed in the United States of America
on acid-free paper

To Laura and Steffi

Preface

This book presents the theory of *threaded cognition*, a theory of the workings of the multitasking mind. The collaboration leading up to this book began in 2005, when each of us was developing a separate computational account of human multitasking (Salvucci, 2005; Taatgen, 2005). Our individual approaches had some successes, but also some limitations, inspiring us to work together to find a more complete theory that unified the best aspects of each approach. This work led to our first description of threaded cognition (Salvucci & Taatgen, 2008) focused on concurrent multitasking—doing multiple tasks at the same time. Using this work as a basis, we further developed an account of sequential multitasking—alternating between multiple tasks, such as during an interruption—and revisited Niels' account of multitask learning to reframe it in the context of the new theory. This book aims to describe threaded cognition, its theoretical foundations, and its applications to empirical phenomena in a single, accessible volume.

Because our central purpose is to present the theory of threaded cognition, the book does not attempt to cover comprehensively the bountiful research efforts related to multitasking and its conceptual cousins (attention, cognitive control, etc.). Other recent volumes (e.g., Kramer, Wiegmann, & Kirlik, 2007; Wickens & McCarley, 2007) have served this purpose admirably, and we did not wish to duplicate these efforts. Also, the book is not intended to be a trade book with very broad but high-level coverage of multitasking phenomena. Nevertheless, it is critical that we relate our theory both to existing research and to everyday issues and questions. We have thus structured the book to include these aspects: each chapter begins with general questions about practical issues, and ends with some answers to these questions as derived from our theory. Each chapter also includes a self-contained section that connects the theory to closely related research in that chapter's topic area.

We have written this book primarily for a scientific audience, particularly researchers and students in the areas of cognitive psychology, computer science, and human factors and ergonomics. At the same time, the book is also intended for researchers and practitioners in applied domains, especially in the broad domains of transportation human factors and human–computer interaction. As may be evident from the table of contents, we have tried to emphasize the theory in the context of application domains by alternating book chapters between theoretical components, and applications to illustrative domains. Finally, we also hope that the book will be of interest to general readers with a scientific background, and/or those with a deep curiosity for the workings of the mind and the nature of human multitasking.

We owe many debts of gratitude to the great many people that inspired this research and helped to see this work come to fruition. In terms of research, the ACT-R theory (Anderson, 2007) is clearly the central foundation for our own work, and we are indebted to John Anderson and many members of the international ACT-R community for their guidance, comments, and assistance with implementation and testing. The research efforts of Erik Altmann, Greg Trafton, Dave Kieras, Dave Meyer, and Chris Wickens have also been an important influence on our own work, and the work of Jelmer Borst was a critical foundation for the theory. Dan Bothell has generously helped with coding issues related to the ACT-R architecture. We are also very grateful to Paul Bello and Susan Chipman at the Office of Naval Research (#N00014-03-1-0036, #N00014-09-1-0096, #N00014-08-10541), Ephraim Glinert at the National Science Foundation (#IIS-0426674, #IIS-0133083), and Jerome Busemeyer and Jun Zhang at the Air Force Office of Scientific Research (#FA95500710359) for their steady guidance and support.

For the book itself, Catharine Carlin, Valerie Patruno, Stefano Imbert, and colleagues at Oxford University Press have been a pleasure to work with throughout the publishing process. We sincerely thank them for their many efforts in bringing this work to fruition. We also thank Frank Ritter for his valuable guidance; Stu Card, Pete Pirolli, and Alex Kirlik for their advice on the book-writing process; and Brad Best, John Lee, Mike Schoelles, and one anonymous reviewer for their many helpful comments and suggestions.

D.D.S.: I would also like to express my sincere thanks to colleagues and student collaborators at Drexel University, who supported this work and helped to flesh out a number of complementary ideas; to Duncan Brumby, whose collaboration inspired a novel perspective on multitasking that greatly benefited this work; to Bonnie John and her research team, whose collaboration shaped our own research on proto-typing and evaluation tools; to former colleagues at Nissan Cambridge Basic Research, who steered the early research on driver behavior; to the Henrietta Hankin Library for a comfortable work environment during my sabbatical; to Jill and Ron Moyer for their encouragement and a weekly home office away from home; to my parents for their ever-present love and support; to my children for helping me to understand the benefits of interruption and distraction; and to Laura, for the thousand little things that make it all possible and for showing me what multitasking is all about—I love you.

N.A.T.: Good research often requires a good team of people, and I have been lucky to have had very talented people working for and with me both in Pittsburgh and in the Netherlands. In both places, Jelmer Borst has been a Masters and now Ph.D. student on the project of multi-tasking, and his research is one of the cornerstones of this book. My collaboration with Hedderik van Rijn also spans both places and involves, among many other topics, the perception of time, an underestimated factor in cognition. In Pittsburgh, several very talented people worked on the projects discussed in this book: Ion Juvina on the many issues of control and individual differences in multitasking, and Daniel Dickison, David Huss and Stefan Wierda on the FMS project. Many people in the ACT-R group were stimulating and supportive of my research. I don't mind mentioning John Anderson once more, but also Christian Lebiere, Dan Bothell, Andrea Stocco, Jennifer Ferris, Jon Fincham, Scott Douglass and Lynne Reder. Thank you all!

Within the Netherlands I would like to thank Sander Martens for teaching me everything about the Attentional Blink, and the people of the Cognitive Modeling group, who have always remained supportive during my absence: Leendert van Maanen and Fokie Cnossen. John Michon deserves special thanks, because he got me interested in cognitive modeling in the first place. In addition, I have eventually picked up two of his main interests, time perception and driving. My final thanks are for Steffi, without whom at least my part of this book would never have been written, but to whom I am grateful for so many other things that her bringing me to Pittsburgh seems almost insignificant.

Contents

The Multitasking Mind

1

A Unifying Theory of Multitasking

Standing at the corner of 32nd and Market Streets in Philadelphia, signs of our multitasking world are all around. Two Drexel University students have an animated chat while walking through a crowd, waving to friends and navigating around others on their way to class. Another student hurriedly checks her voice mail while looking for oncoming cars at the traffic light. The woman in the Lexus sedan changes lanes while slowing down at the light, all the while chatting on a cell phone. The two food vendors, impossibly crammed into their tiny mobile cart, take orders from seven different customers while filling the orders first-come, first-served. A parking officer, standing at an expired meter, listens to the car owner's pleadings while writing him a parking ticket. And we, your dutiful authors, move our attention from person to person, jotting down notes as we watch each multitasking scenario unfold before us.

Just as in this street-scene microcosm, multitasking pervades our everyday lives. Office workers juggle phone calls, email, paperwork, and meetings. Parents feed, clothe, shuttle, entertain, and otherwise look after their young ones. Farmers perform daily duties of feeding and milking while doing long-term planning for planting and harvesting. Carpenters saw, drill, nail and screw while continually checking for structural strength and integrity. Taxi drivers check in with dispatchers while talking to passengers and navigating through traffic. Doctors and nurses talk to patients while examining them and diagnosing their ailments. Examples of every-day multitasking abound.

In part, multitasking is thrust upon us by the ever-changing technology and increasingly hurried nature of today's world; at the same time, we ourselves contribute to the multitasking frenzy through countless actions in our everyday lives. For example, a recent study of employees at an information technology company (Gonzalez & Mark, 2004) examined the average continuous, uninterrupted amount of time spent on a variety of common office tasks: talking on the phone, managing email, reading paper documents, interacting with colleagues, and so on. Except for formal meetings, the employees spent an average of only 3 minutes per task before switching to another task. Although half of those switches represented external interruptions such as the phone ringing or an email arriving, the other half represented self-initiated switches including making a phone call or leaving the desk. So not only do we multitask at an extremely high level, we ourselves are at least partly to blame for our own multitasking craziness.

That is not to say that multitasking is a bad thing. Multitasking often allows us to perform tasks efficiently and effectively; office workers, par-ents, and doctors would be hard-pressed to do their work if they were forcibly made to focus on a single task for an extended period of time. However, there are also environments in which our multitasking may be dangerous if not lethal. For instance, consider the world of today's typical automobile driver, navigating congested roadways while interacting with similarly congested in-vehicle environments filled with onboard gadgetry and mobile devices. Drivers in the United States, for example, accumu-late over 3 trillion miles of driving per year, and these drivers have become more distracted than ever. One study (GMAC, 2006) reports that 40% of drivers talk on cell phones while driving, 24% of younger drivers aged 18–25 send text messages, and 20% select songs on an iPod while driving. Multitasking thus has become commonplace in an environment where our safety, and that of others, is continually threatened by our desire to multitask.

The challenges of living in a multitasking world are numerous and complex. The technological challenges have been an ongoing focus of the engineering community, and to this point we have a range of fabulous new technology unimaginable only a few decades ago. However, many of the difficult challenges raised by multitasking are not technological ones, but rather scientific and societal ones. The scientific challenge reduces to a single, central question: What is the nature of human multitasking? Research has explored this central question from many angles, using both tried-and-true methods of empirical study and more recent methods of computational modeling and simulation. The many results from these fields are now converging to paint a rich picture of human multitasking behavior. In this book, we present our own theory of human multitasking that aims to unify the many disparate areas of multitasking research under one theoretical framework. At the same time, using this framework, we aim to provide a rigorous but accessible account of the latest scientific views of how humans multitask.

Only with a better scientific understanding of human multitasking can we seriously address the associated technological and societal challenges. Technological developments can and should be guided by knowledge of how users interact with the technology—for example, when deciding whether a new type of desktop alert is too annoying, or whether a new type of in-car navigation system is too unsafe. Given new technology and a scientific understanding of multitasking, we as a society can then make informed decisions about whether and how this technology should be used. Although the technological and societal aspects of multitasking are not central themes in this book, we will occasionally interject these issues as they arise, to more fully consider the context of the scientific issues. Our hope is that, by focusing on scientific understanding of multitasking, we can inform and guide future work that more closely addresses the technological and societal challenges of our multitasking world.

The Scientific Challenge of Multitasking

What is the nature of human multitasking? Why do we multitask? How do we multitask? And, for two or more specific domains, how well do we multitask? Sometimes, multitasking can feel extremely easy—so easy that we hardly realize we're multitasking. Talking while walking, showering, or eating a meal often feels effortless. We can mix a bowl of ingredients while reading a recipe, wave at neighbors while whistling on the porch, listen to the radio while pulling weeds in the garden—all without feeling overworked. We may be interrupted by a phone call, doorbell, or email, or we may interrupt ourselves to find something, or to talk to someone; in these cases, even if it takes a second or two to recall and resume the interrupted task, it typically (especially after brief interruptions) does not feel taxing or straining. In some cases, it almost seems that people have a compelling need for multitasking, exemplified by people chatting on cell phones or listening to iPods while doing just about anything—sitting on a train, walking to work, driving a car—that offers even a bit of spare mental processing time.

At other times, multitasking can feel difficult, excruciating, or down-right impossible. Some scenarios may be difficult primarily because two tasks require the same body part, like trying to interleave typing and mouse movements (both require the right hand), or trying to drive while scanning an onboard navigation device (both require vision). But multi-tasking in the head is often more intense, and more difficult to work around, than multitasking of the hands or eyes. One good example is trying to read while others are talking: the cognitive, and more specifically linguistic, workload of both tasks creates interference and makes the dual-task scenario difficult. The frequent and sometimes lengthy interruptions in an office setting can lead to losing one's place in a task. And numerous other work environments, such as that of an air traffic controller, include such strenuous multitasking that frustration and stress can become serious concerns.

Many factors affect the difficulty of multitasking. Practicing one or more of the component tasks is the most obvious way to ease the burden. For example, for a person learning to play piano, every placement of a finger on a key requires mental effort for a beginner; but soon the transla-tion of notes to finger placements becomes easier and routine; then the musician learns to play with both hands and chords with multiple fingers. Then, when a piece is well-practiced, the motor execution becomes straightforward and the musician can spend more mental effort on higher-level aspects such as dynamics and interpretation. The amount of practice needed to achieve expertise in a domain may be lengthy and intense, such as the years of training needed for air traffic controllers to become fully certified.

While practice helps us to multitask, one fascinating trait of our multi-tasking skill is that we can perform arbitrary tasks together, even those we have never tried previously to combine. Consider two tasks that most people have never performed together, such as washing dishes and doing mental arithmetic: although it may not feel easy, especially at first, we typically find that we can indeed succeed at performing both tasks together. Nevertheless, one task may interfere with performance of the other: Does our arithmetic become slower or more error-prone while we wash dishes, or does our dishwashing become slower or less effective while we perform mental arithmetic? Granted, perhaps getting answers to these specific questions may not be all that important. But exploring such questions can further our understanding of our innate multitasking skill, and can guide us in finding answers to similar questions in important everyday domains (e.g., multitasking while working at a computer, walking, or driving) that affect our daily lives.

Multitasking is—like many aspects of the human system, such as language, vision, and problem solving—a basic human skill that we perform on a routine basis, and yet have great difficulty explaining and understanding, even though we perform it so well. As such, the study of multitasking requires that we step outside of ourselves to examine its true nature through rigorous scientific inquiry. Our scientific approach in this book, namely the specification of a unifying theory of multitasking, aims to accomplish this and shed light on the nature of human multitasking—both its many wondrous capabilities, and its many fascinating limitations.

Threaded Cognition: A Unifying Theory of Multitasking

This book describes a theory of human multitasking that we call *threaded cognition*. At its core, threaded cognition states that multitasking behavior can be attributed to multiple threads of thought running simultaneously. Just as sewing threads interweave strands of material through a fabric, or Internet forum threads interweave messages related to a conversation topic, cognitive threads interweave independent tasks through the mind, and result in multitasking behavior. Each cognitive thread represents an independent task goal that a person is currently trying to perform; after hearing the phone ring, you might start independent tasks of finishing the sentence you were speaking, looking for the phone, and guessing who might be calling, each of which could be considered an independent thread. The independence of cognitive threads is the key to our multitasking ability; namely, the ability to take single-task skills and combine them as needed to accomplish a higher-level goal. At the same time, depending on the nature of the particular task threads, multitasking interference can arise that hinders the progress of one or more of the tasks. Threaded cognition attempts to formalize task behavior and the potential sources of interference in order to account for multitasking phenomena, and to augment our understanding of human multitasking more generally.[1]

Threaded cognition builds on a vast array of previous research over the past many decades on multitasking behavior. This previous research has taken many forms, in terms of both the particular domains being studied and the methodologies with which they are studied. One of our major goals in this book is to unify these many efforts under a single theoretical framework, spanning as large a range of domains as possible while utilizing as many methodological tools as possible in our analysis. To this end, we have found it useful to characterize the study of multitasking along three distinct continua, each of which illustrates how sometimes disparate research efforts can be considered along the same conceptual continuum. We describe these continua below, and conclude by clarifying our approach to multitasking in the context of these three continua.

The Multitasking Continuum: From Concurrent to Sequential Tasks

As a first step to our exploration of human multitasking, we would like to bring some order to the broad range of activities that encompasses what we mean by "multitasking." One useful way to characterize multitasking activities views each activity in terms of the time between task switches, or the typical time spent on one task before switching to another. Figure 1.1 illustrates this characterization on a timeline ranging from sub-second intervals to intervals of several hours or more. In doing so, we define a multitasking continuum that we can use to categorize and reason about particular multitasking activities.

On the left side of the multitasking continuum, we find multitasking activities for which people switch tasks at sub-second intervals up to every few seconds. We call behavior at this end of the continuum *concurrent multitasking*, because each task progresses either simultaneously or with very short interruptions. Concurrent multitasking activities, as described

---

1. Computer scientists will note another meaning of "threads" as independent computer processes executing concurrently. Although these computational threads share some features with the cognitive threads described here (e.g., relative independence of processing, potential conflicts and bottlenecks), the brain and the computer are distinctly different, and we would caution against drawing too strong an analogy between the two.

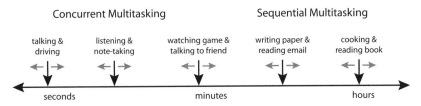

Figure 1.1. The Multitasking Continuum. From Salvucci, Taatgen, & Borst (2009), Copyright 2009 Association for Computing Machinery. Adapted with permission.

earlier, are extremely common in our everyday routines. For example, we often talk while walking, eating or driving, and both tasks generally progress with little to no interference. Even when one task prevents the other from progressing (e.g., chewing prevents talking), the interruption is brief and the interrupted task soon resumes its progress. As another example, listening while taking notes in a lecture or meeting can be done concurrently with fairly frequent switches (say, every few seconds) between the two tasks.

On the right side of the continuum, we find multitasking activities for which people switch tasks after lengthy periods of execution on only one of the tasks. We call behavior at this end *sequential multitasking*: although there may be some overlap between tasks during switching periods (e.g., when a person finishes typing a sentence before picking up a ringing phone), each task receives focused attention during most of its allocated execution time. Our office-worker domain represents a classic example of sequential multitasking: the worker might focus on writing a paper for several minutes to hours before switching to another task, perhaps later resuming the original interrupted task. We could imagine another example involving cooking while reading a book: a person spends an hour preparing a casserole dish, places it in the oven, and switches to reading until the dish is ready.

While the distinction between concurrent and sequential multitasking is a useful one, it is by no means clear-cut. Consider a situation in which a person is watching a baseball game while talking to a friend: if the person talks continually while closely monitoring the game, we would consider this behavior to be concurrent multitasking; then again, if the person only talks between innings, the behavior more closely resembles sequential multitasking. In fact, our example of talking while driving might be considered sequential if the driver only talks at traffic lights, and our example of cooking and reading might be considered concurrent if the person reads while cutting vegetables. Thus, as we refer to the concurrent-versus-sequential distinction throughout this book, it is important to remember that each category represents only a rough range along the multitasking continuum, and that specifics about particular tasks, as well how those tasks are performed at each instance, heavily influence where they fall along the continuum.

A fair-minded reader may then ask, why make the concurrent-versus-sequential distinction at all? First, much of the previous research done on multitasking has focused exclusively on either concurrent or sequential multitasking. On the one hand, basic research on concurrent multitasking has examined the fine-grained details of a "cognitive bottleneck" in the performance of concurrent simple laboratory tasks (Byrne & Anderson, 2001; Hazeltine, Teague, & Ivry, 2002; Meyer & Kieras, 1997; Pashler, 1984; Schumacher et al., 2001; Welford, 1952). Applied research has also tried to understand dual-task interference and workload in domains such as driving (Alm & Nilsson, 1994, 1995; Brookhuis, De Vries, & De Waard, 1991; Lee et al., 2002; McKnight & McKnight, 1993; Senders et al., 1967; Strayer & Drews, 2004), aircraft piloting (Kantowitz & Casper, 1988; Parasuraman, Sheridan, & Wickens, 2000; Wickens, 2002b), and game playing (Lebiere, Wallach, & West, 2000; Ritter & Wallach, 1998).

On the other hand, basic research on sequential multitasking has focused on performance of alternating simple tasks and the costs of switching that arise therein (Altmann & Gray, 2002, 2008; Rogers & Monsell, 1995; Rubinstein, Meyer, Evans, 2001; Sohn & Carlson, 2000). Applied research has often framed sequential multitasking in terms of task interruption and resumption, again in diverse domains such as human–computer interaction (Bailey & Iqbal, 2008; Cutrell, Czerwinski, & Horvitz, 2000; Czerwinski, Cutrell, & Horvitz, 2000; Iqbal & Bailey, 2005, 2006; Monk et al., 2004, 2008; Trafton et al., 2003), aviation (Dismukes, Young, & Sumwalt, 1998; Latorella, 1999) and emergency room care (Chisholm et al., 2001). Unfortunately, there has been surprisingly little crosstalk between these areas of study, particularly across the concurrent–sequential "boundary" (as artificial as it may be). As a matter of exposition, we present our own theory in terms of each of these categories because it allows us to relate our theory more easily to this previous research. Nevertheless, in keeping with the unifying spirit of the theory, we will discuss how to merge the treatments of concurrent and sequential multitasking into a unified view that best reflects the space of multitasking as a continuum, rather than two distinct categories of behavior.

The Application Continuum: From Laboratory to Applied Tasks

The second continuum with which we can characterize the study of multitasking is what we call the *application continuum*. Multitasking research has focused on task domains and paradigms that range from basic psychological tasks to complex applied tasks, and everything in between. The application continuum represents, for a particular studied domain, the extent to which the domain is conceptually close to and relevant for some everyday task scenario. In the depiction of the application continuum in Figure 1.2, common tasks are considered applied and appear on the right side of the continuum. In contrast, highly controlled and greatly simplified tasks, as might be performed in the psychology laboratory, are much less applied and appear on the left side. Between these extremes lies a

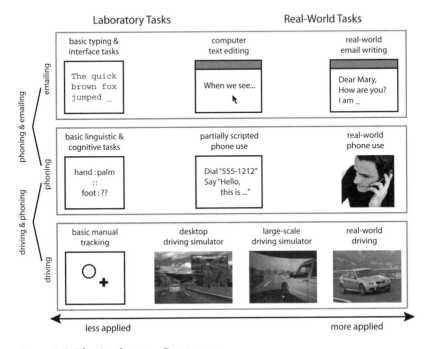

Figure 1.2. The Application Continuum.

range of domains that could be considered both applied in some respects, and not applied in other respects.

To illustrate this idea, let us consider examples across the application continuum. The top area of the figure shows sample tasks related to the common task of writing and sending email, shown on the right side in the applied area of the continuum. At the laboratory end of the continuum, we can consider basic tasks that have investigated people's ability to use a standard computer interface, such as those examining the speed and accuracy with which people type or make mouse movements. In between, we have tasks that have been studied in the laboratory but involved more realistic behavior than simply typing a word or moving a mouse; for example, the task of computer text editing has been studied in a controlled laboratory setting, but involving a number of realistic aspects of computer use (Bovair, Kieras, & Polson, 1990; Polson & Kieras, 1985; Rosson, 1983; Singley & Anderson, 1987).

The middle area of Figure 1.2 shows three analogous tasks for the domain of using a phone, including dialing and conversation. At the less applied end, we can consider basic linguistic and cognitive tasks that investigate very specific abilities to construct concepts and phrases—for example, our ability to analogize between complex concepts (Holyoak & Thagard, 1989; Salvucci & Anderson, 2001), or to recall a list of numbers for dialing (Anderson & Matessa, 1997). Grounding these core processes in the particular setting of phone use, we can imagine scripted phone-use tasks that do not actually involve dialing and conversation, but simulate the real tasks sufficiently for some purpose; for example, user-interface designers may test behavior on a partially-functional prototype of a dialing interface (Pew & Mavor, 2007). Finally, the applied phone task would involve dialing in a completely natural way (e.g., using either a keypad or an address book) and would allow for natural conversation between caller and callee.

The bottom area of Figure 1.2 includes tasks related to the domain of driving. At the leftmost extreme, we could identify a host of basic-research domains that relate to the real driving task, such as a manual tracking task in which a person tries to keep a moving cursor within some target boundaries (Wickens, 1976). At the rightmost extreme, the real-world driving task—control of a vehicle with the goal of traveling to a destination—is a fabulously complex task with many multitasking components (controlling the vehicle, monitoring other vehicles, deciding on a route to the destination, performing secondary tasks, etc.). In between, we can identify more realistic tasks that do not yet reach the complexity of the full-fledged driving task. In particular, as a less costly and safer alternative to real driving, a large class of studies have utilized computer-based driving simulators to collect driver performance data. These simulators fall along an application continuum in their own right: they range from game-like desktop systems, to larger simulators with projection screens and more realistic controls, to multimillion-dollar simulators with a realistic vehicle, moving base, and surround projection with as much realism as technology can provide. The more complex simulators thus provide a more realistic driver experience at the expense of (sometimes extravagant) manufacturing and experimental setup costs in time and money. At the rightmost extreme lie studies which indeed involve driving in a real vehicle.

Given these three sample domains and their variants across the application continuum, we can easily imagine combinations of tasks that embody less applied or more applied forms of multitasking. More often than not, studies combine tasks that both reside in roughly the same slice of the continuum: two laboratory tasks (e.g., a basic cognitive choice task while tracking) or two applied tasks (e.g., unconstrained phoning and driving) are combined and performed together. Many studies are performed in a controlled setting with an experimenter providing directions or instructions—for instance, a study of dialing a phone while driving in a simulator in which an experimenter occasionally asks the driver to perform this secondary task (e.g., Reed & Green, 1999; Salvucci, 2001a). Other studies simply observe and analyze natural behaviors directly in their naturalistic setting (e.g., Neale, Dingus, Klauer, Sudweeks, & Goodman, 2005), collecting data from drivers performing exactly those tasks that they would normally perform in the course of their everyday lives. However, both tasks need not reside in the same slice of the continuum, and a number of research efforts have combined simplified forms of one task with more realistic forms of another. For example, some work on driver distraction has utilized real driving with laboratory tasks such as a serial-addition task (Brookhuis, De Vries, & de Waard, 1991). Such studies aim to study how "cognitive distraction" affects driver performance, and thus try to constrain the cognitive load placed on drivers to best control the experimental setup. On the other hand, some work has involved realistic, unconstrained conversation while driving, but with data collected in a driving simulator (Drews, Pasupathi, & Strayer, 2008). In this case, the critical goal was to study realistic conversation with the (reasonable) assumption that effects in the simulator correlate well to effects in a real vehicle (see, e.g., Reed & Green, 1999).

Thus, all points along the continuum provide different tradeoffs among the desire for practical applicability, the particular investigational focus of the study, and the overhead costs of developing and running the study. The basic-research studies focus on very particular components of the human system and allow us to understand the individual contributions of these components. Basic research on multitasking has appeared in many contexts, such as under broad headings of "attention" and "executive control processes" (e.g., Baddeley, 1986; Kahneman, 1973; Kramer, Wiegmann, & Kirlik, 2007; Logan, 1985; Meyer & Kieras, 1997; Norman & Shallice, 1986; Posner & Petersen, 1990). Applied studies of multitasking and workload in particular domains provide us with a broader understanding of how these components integrate and result in the complex behaviors associated with common tasks (e.g., Dismukes & Nowinski, 2007; Kantowitz & Casper, 1988; Mitchell, 2000; Strayer & Drews, 2004; Wickens, 2002b). Ideally, our theoretical efforts should aim to account for as wide a range as possible along the application continuum—after all, the empirical phenomena, whether laboratory or applied, arise from a single system, the human system. In addition, a solid theoretical framework also provides a way to unify ideas across the continuum by integrating lower-level theories into higher-level ones (Anderson, 2002; Gluck & Pew, 2005; Gray, 2007; Newell, 1990; Pew, 1974). As will become evident in subsequent chapters, our approach to studying multitasking involves a bootstrapping effort in which we simultaneously evaluate theories against empirical results, gathered from as many points as possible along the application continuum.

The Abstraction Continuum: From Milliseconds to Months

The multitasking continuum and application continuum provide two ways to characterize a task domain being studied in terms of the frequency of multitasking, and the applied nature of the task. The *abstraction continuum* speaks to the theories that we develop about these task domains, as well as the particular data and measures used to validate these theories. In essence, we can study any given domain at different levels of abstraction, corresponding to the levels of behavior in which we are most interested. What are these levels of abstraction, and how do they impact our study of multitasking?

Allen Newell (1990) famously described human behavior as residing along a range of "time scales of human action," as shown in Figure 1.3. Newell divided the time scales into four "bands of cognition": the Biological Band for neural and physiological processes at the sub-second level, the Cognitive Band for actions and unit tasks (see Card, Moran, & Newell, 1983) lasting a few seconds, the Rational Band for tasks ranging from minutes to hours, and the Social Band for long-term behavior (days, weeks, and beyond). Newell and others (Anderson, 2002; Pew, 1974) have argued that in the study of human behavior, larger tasks can be decomposed into smaller component tasks, allowing us to develop theories of component tasks and then work on unifying them into larger theories of the higher-level tasks. The figure shows the three sample task domains related to email, phone, and driving tasks. For instance, in the email task, we can build on the physiological processes at the left extreme of the continuum, and integrate these into domain-relevant movements such as moving a mouse or pressing a key. These basic interface actions can be composed into unit tasks—commonly repeated tasks on the order of several seconds, such as deleting an email message or searching for text. Further still, we can compose these unit tasks into larger-scale tasks, like responding to all new email, and at the rightmost extreme we have the highest-level goals related to maintaining a sense of community with family, friends, and colleagues.

Considering task domains at different time scales provides us with the power of abstraction: focusing on aspects we deem most interesting for the domain, and abstracting over (ignoring) those aspects less relevant to our purposes. When developing theories of behavior at a chosen time scale, we typically focus on data and measures that best quantify behavior at that time scale. These measures are shown along with sample tasks in Figure 1.3. Returning to the email example, if we were primarily interested in understanding behavior at the level of basic interaction with the email application, we might collect data in the cognitive band—by recording, for instance, all mouse clicks and keystrokes along with the time at which they occurred. If we were more interested in larger-scale issues, such as how frequently a user wrote email over the course of one day, it may suffice to collect coarser-grain data—for example, the number of times the user switched to the email application and how long, on average, they used the application before switching away. When considering two tasks in a multitasking scenario (such as talking and emailing, or driving and dialing, as shown), the measures for the individual tasks are

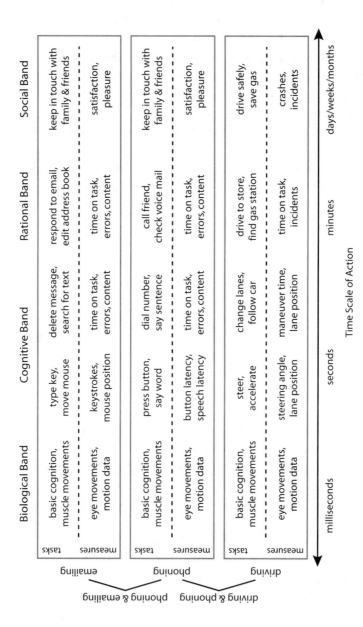

Figure 1.3. The Abstraction Continuum (based on Newell, 1990).

essential for determining the effects of multitasking; we might, for instance, measure driver performance while driving alone, and compare this to performance while dialing a phone number, thereby gauging the effects of dialing on driving.

In fact, abstracting over time is only one method of abstraction, and there are often other ways of formulating a theory with respect to the level of approximation needed or desired. Consider a computer user moving a mouse pointer to an onscreen target object. A useful engineering approximation might simply take an average time for all mouse movements across a range of common user tasks: Card, Moran, and Newell (1983) derived an estimate of 1.1 seconds, an approximation that does not require specification of the distance to the target. As a more specific formulation using distance, we can use (one form of) the well-known equation known as Fitts' law (MacKenzie, 1992):

$$MT = a + b \log_2 \left(\frac{D}{W} + 1 \right)$$

This equation states that movement time (MT) is a function of D, the distance to the target, and of W, the width of the target in the direction of movement; because W appears as a denominator, the equation thus states that the thinner the object, the longer the movement time. (The values a and b are constants that do not change with the target.) While Fitts' law is an extremely useful description of movement time, it does not account for the fact that two-dimensional target objects have a width and height. Additional research (e.g., Accot & Zhai, 2003) has suggested that Fitts' law can be reformulated in terms of both target width and height. And we might easily imagine a host of variations on this theme, taking into account, for example, changes that might arise as a function of mouse hardware characteristics, software differences that change the pointer's movement characteristics, the user's visual acuity, and so on. Deciding which theory is "best" depends wholly on its purpose; namely, finding the most important factors that may influence behavior, and abstracting over the other factors to find the most useful approximation of behavior.

All of these issues play into our development of a general theory of multitasking. Ideally, we would like to account for tasks all along the abstraction continuum, with a theory that provides detailed predictions at all levels of abstraction—but in practice, this is not possible. Indeed, individual research efforts have focused on behavior within a narrow slice of the abstraction continuum; even Newell's (1990) "unified theories of cognition" focused on the cognitive band, with, as he deemed, much less relevance to the other bands. At the same time, research efforts focused on one time scale often draw on general understanding from other time scales; for example, research on user behavior in the cognitive band may build on known characteristics of brain function in the biological band, and research on driver performance in the cognitive band might have implications for safety at the social band. Like Newell, we will primarily emphasize the cognitive band of behavior, with frequent excursions in the rational band. Nevertheless, we will also base our ideas on known aspects of the biological band and draw out implications for social band as much as possible, with the hope that these looser connections can be further developed in future research.

Representing the Theory in a Computational Cognitive Architecture

The rest of this book presents the theory of threaded cognition, and how it can account for a range of task domains across the multitasking, application, and abstraction continua. The question remains, however, of how to express the theory and codify it as a tool for understanding and predicting multitasking behavior. The underpinnings of any theory lie in the experimental work that, generally speaking, reveals the overall level of multitasking interference between particular tasks. For example, empirical studies have explored whether a simple visual–manual task (seeing and typing) interferes with an aural–vocal (listening-and-speaking) task—a case where tasks do not overlap in terms of physical resources (eyes and hands versus ears and mouth), but do overlap with respect to cognitive resources needed by each task (to be described in Chapter 2). Experimental results typically address the presence or absence of such interference (did each task affect the other during multitasking?) and, if present, the size of the interference effect (how much did each task affect the other?).

Building on these empirical results, some theories aim to express multitasking interference in quantitative terms. For example, Wickens' (1984, 2002a, 2008) multiple-resource theory characterizes dual-task interference in terms of four dimensions: stages (perceptual/cognitive, response), sensory modalities (auditory versus visual and others), codes (visual versus spatial), and visual channels (focal versus ambient). Using his theory and associated methodology, one can create a matrix of values that represent the interference across these dimensions and, in the end, a single numeric value that represents overall interference. Such a theory can be very useful for capturing the basic effects of multitasking at a high level, when accounts of behavioral event sequences and/or domain-specific measures (e.g., time on task, errors, etc.) are not needed.

A more detailed description of multitasking behavior examines how behavior unfolds over time. Such a description, often called a *process model*, characterizes behavior as a temporal sequence of events, and is often depicted along a timeline or box diagram making this sequence explicit. Figure 1.4 shows a possible box-diagram process model for a simple choice task that we will explore further in Chapter 2. In a visual–manual version of this task, the person sees a visual stimulus and presses an associated key in response. Previous research (e.g., Pashler, 1994) has characterized behavior in this task as a 3-stage process of stimulus perception, response selection, and response execution, illustrated by three boxes in the upper portion of the figure. This model is straightforward in the single-task case, and when considering a dual-choice scenario with two choice tasks performed simultaneously, the model helps to understand interference effects. The bottom portion of the figure shows an aural–vocal version of the choice task, in which an audible stimulus evokes a verbal response. As will be discussed in Chapter 2, the two tasks can proceed independently for the most part, because of their use of distinct perceptual and motor channels; however, the "select response" stage can produce interference between tasks because both tasks require cognitive processing at the same time, causing the second task to be delayed at point (A). Such interference can be neatly represented and visualized in these types of box-diagram process models. More complex box-diagram representations, such as those provided by CPM-GOMS (John, 1990; see also Gray, John, & Atwood, 1993; John & Kieras, 1996) and similar frameworks (e.g., Freed, 1998), allow for explicit specification of the cognitive, perceptual, and motor processes in a schedule chart, from which an analysis can derive the critical path, and thus the total processing time, for the task.

While a box diagram can depict the temporal processing of behavior at a gross level, it has a number of limitations when addressing a complex task such as driving or air traffic control: behavior can easily span many seconds to minutes or hours, making depiction of the full timeline infeasible;

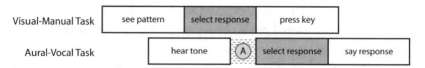

Figure 1.4. Box diagram of a dual-choice task, with a response-selection bottleneck at point A.

the perceptual stimuli change continually, creating a complex dependency between the person's behavior and the changing state of the interactive system; and standard measures of interest for the task, such as vehicle lane position (in driving) or gaze frequencies for visible aircraft (in air traffic control), may be difficult or impossible to predict. In other words, a box diagram abstracts over the details of the underlying interaction, and for complex tasks, this abstraction sometimes does not provide the kind of detail (in terms of data and measures) needed to understand behavior and evaluate theories of behavior.

To address this issue, in a tradition dating back several decades to the onset of work in artificial intelligence, many researchers now develop computational process models to represent their theories of behavior. Very generally, a computational model is a formal description of behavior in a computational framework that can generate behavior through a computer simulation. In modern frameworks, the models typically interact with an actual task simulation, often the same simulation used to collect data from human participants in an experiment. For example, a model may obtain perceptual information as an onscreen interface changes, or may move the mouse and click on objects in the visible interface. When integrated into robotic systems (e.g., Trafton et al., 2006, 2008), computational models can also explore and act in the world via robotic perceptual sensors and motor actuators.

Our approach to multitasking centers on a major class of computational frameworks known as *cognitive architectures*. A cognitive architecture is a framework that facilitates the creation of computational models of behavior: given some task domain, the architecture allows for specification of a process model that performs the task, typically (as mentioned earlier) through interaction with a realistic simulation of the task. At the same time, the cognitive architecture incorporates a rigorous theory of human cognition and performance, including both the abilities and constraints of the human system. For example, a cognitive architecture typically includes some type of memory system that provides the ability to store and recall knowledge; at the same time, the architecture places constraints on this ability—for instance, by dictating how a piece of information decays in memory such that, after some time without rehearsal or retrieval, that information may be forgotten. Similarly, the architecture would include perceptual resources that acquire information about the external world, and motor resources that perform actions in the world—both with constraints to reflect these systems' limitations, such as an inability to see details outside the eye's fovea, or specification of motor movement times from one location to another.

Cognitive architectures have been used to model and account for multitasking behavior in a range of task domains. Table 1.1 includes a sampling of such models, some of which were explicitly intended to account for multitasking, others of which were intended to model behavior in some complex task and only implicitly accounted for multitasking as part of the work. One of our primary goals in this book is to learn from these efforts, and to generalize the underlying ideas into a unifying theory of multitasking. The cognitive architecture in which we have chosen to develop our work is the ACT-R cognitive architecture (Anderson, 2007; Anderson et al., 2004). We will describe relevant aspects of the ACT-R theory incrementally as they relate to our exposition detailing threaded cognition and the associated modeling efforts.

The instantiation of our theory in a cognitive architecture allows for expression of the theory at all the levels of description mentioned above. The theory can be boiled down to general predictions about the presence and amount of interference between two or more tasks; given some knowledge about the tasks at hand (e.g., the visual-manual and aural-vocal dual-choice scenario described earlier), it allows us to reason about whether we would expect interference between tasks and, roughly speaking, whether there would less or more interference than some other combination of tasks. When a process-model description is needed, the theory can be expressed with box diagrams that depict processing across stages of a task—which can be especially useful in determining overlapping processing between multiple tasks, a good indicator of interference. And, for complex tasks where more abstract methods are insufficient, our theory, in conjunction with the underlying ACT-R cognitive architecture, allows task models to run in simulation with actual task interfaces, and generate predictions of the same measures collected from human participants (see, e.g., Ritter & Young, 2001). We shift frequently throughout

Table 1.1.   A sampling of models developed in a cognitive architecture that incorporate aspects of multitasking behavior

Domain	Architecture(s)	Reference
Air traffic control (KA-ATC)	ACT-R	Taatgen & Lee, 2003
Air traffic control (AMBR)	ACT-R, D-COG, EPIC-Soar, iGen	Gluck & Pew, 2005
Aircraft maneuvering	ACT-R	Gluck et al., 2003
Aircraft piloting (TacAir-Soar)	Soar	Jones et al., 1999
Aircraft piloting	CI	Doane & Sohn, 2000
Aircraft taxiing	ACT-R	Byrne & Kirlik, 2005
Attentional blink	ACT-R	Taatgen et al., 2009
Driving	ACT-R	Salvucci, Boer, & Liu, 2001; Salvucci, 2006
Driving	QN-MHP	Tsimhoni & Liu, 2003
Driving	Soar	Aasman, 1995
Driving & phone dialing	ACT-R	Salvucci, 2001a, 2005; Salvucci & Taatgen, 2008
Driving & memory rehearsal	ACT-R	Salvucci & Beltowska, 2008
Driving & secondary task	QN-MHP	Liu, Feyen, & Tsimhoni, 2006; Wu & Liu, 2007
Dual choice	ACT-R	Anderson, Taatgen, & Byrne, 2005; Byrne & Anderson, 2001; Salvucci & Taatgen, 2008
Dual choice	EPIC	Meyer & Kieras, 1997
Dual choice	QN-MHP	Wu & Liu, 2008
Dynamic systems	ACT-R	Schoppek, 2002
Flight management system	ACT-R	Taatgen et al., 2008
Game playing (Unreal Tournament)	ACT-R	Best & Lebiere, 2006
Game playing (Quake)	Soar	Laird & Duchi, 2000
Game playing (Urban Combat)	ICARUS	Choi et al., 2007
Radar operation (Argus Prime)	ACT-R	Gray & Schoelles, 2003
Radar operation (CMU-ASP)	ACT-R	Anderson et al., 2004; Taatgen, 2005
Shooting & mathematical comprehension	ACT-R, IMPRINT	Kelley & Scribner, 2003
Tactical decision making & instruction following	ACT-R	Fu et al., 2004
Task switching	ACT-R	Altmann & Gray, 2008; Sohn & Anderson, 2001
Task switching	EPIC	Kieras et al., 2000
Timing multiple intervals	ACT-R	van Rijn & Taatgen, 2008
Tracking & choice	ACT-R	Salvucci & Taatgen, 2008
Tracking & choice	EPIC	Kieras & Meyer, 1997
Tracking & choice	EPIC-Soar	Chong, 1998
Tracking & choice	Soar, EPIC	Lallement & John, 1998
Tracking & decision making	EPIC	Kieras & Meyer, 1997

(based on Salvucci, 2005)

the book among all three of these levels, with the goal of providing both an overall feel for the theory's predictions and a rigorous description of the inner workings of its processes.

Looking Ahead

This book maps out the threaded cognition theory of multitasking in three major components. The first component focuses on concurrent multitasking, beginning with an introduction to threaded cognition in Chapter 2. The chapter provides an overview of the foundations of the mind's critical components (resources, chunks, and productions) as formalized by ACT-R theory, and then outlines the basic principles of threaded cognition, and provides examples from basic laboratory task domains. Chapter 3 continues the theme of concurrent multitasking by highlighting an application of threaded cognition to the important domain of driver distraction. After introducing driving as a single-task behavior, the chapter examines driving when combined with dialing a phone, to highlight perceptual-motor conflicts, and also when combined with memory rehearsal, to highlight cognitive interference. The chapter includes an overview of the challenges of driver distraction, and conclusions for what we might draw from the theory for this domain.

The second component centers on generalizing the account of concurrent multitasking to sequential multitasking. Chapter 4 discusses the central role of problem state—temporary information related to a task—in the conceptual transition from concurrent to sequential multitasking. It describes an account of task suspension and resumption based on memory processes, in which problem state is strengthened during interruption and recalled after completion of the interrupting task (based on Altmann & Trafton, 2002). Chapter 5 highlights the application of this theory to the domain of human–computer interaction. It particularly focuses on broadening the memory-based account to situations in which problem state must be reconstructed from the task environment. The chapter also describes an empirical study of deferrable interruptions that sheds light on how computer users delay task interruptions when possible.

The third component, embodied in Chapters 6 and 7, focuses on learning and skill acquisition, and their consequences for how multitasking behavior can change with practice. Chapter 6 introduces a theory of learning from task instructions that describes how these instructions are codified over time into procedural rules, thereby accounting for speed-up in performance, as well as diminished contention for declarative memory. The chapter illustrates the theory in a basic laboratory paradigm, as well as two tasks involving dictation and game-playing. Chapter 7 expands this account to sequential behavior in two more applied tasks involving simplified air traffic control, and interaction with a flight management system. This chapter also explores the idea of monotasking, and the difficulty of focusing on a single task in a multitasking environment.

The final two chapters tie together the many themes in the book, and place them in the larger context of theory and application. Chapter 8 outlines the implications of threaded cognition for interaction design, providing a set of design guidelines and user recommendations grounded in theoretical principles. It also describes a system for rapid prototyping and evaluation of in-vehicle interactive systems—an illustration of how the theory's behavioral predictions can be embedded into a user-friendly package intended for non-experts in cognitive modeling. Finally, Chapter 9 discusses the implications of threaded cognition in three important areas—individual differences, brain mapping, and metacognition—as first steps toward an even broader account of human multitasking behavior.

2

Concurrent Multitasking and Threaded Cognition

Let's say you are doing two things at the same time: walking and talking with a friend, listening and taking notes during class, changing and entertaining a baby, monitoring email while browsing the Internet. What task combinations would be more difficult, with one task continually interfering with the other? What combinations would be easier, with little interference between tasks? Are there any combinations for which you could achieve perfect time-sharing, with no interference at all between tasks? We now set out in search of answers to these questions.

The Multitasking Gedankenküche

Multitasking is often said to resemble the famous circus act of plate spinning: a performer spins plates perched atop thin sticks and, by moving from plate to plate and respinning each, keeps all the plates safely in the air. Perhaps a better analogy is that of a cook in a kitchen, making multiple dishes at the same time. Imagine a cook making a fish entrée, a pasta dish, and a cake all at the same time. For each item, the cook follows a series of steps to prepare the food: for the fish, the cook preheats the oven, then puts the fish in the oven for baking; for the pasta, the cook boils water, then cooks and strains the pasta; for the cake, the cook mixes the ingredients and then bakes the cake. Each step involves some resource (oven, stove, mixer), and performing some process (baking, boiling, mixing) on some food part of a dish (fish, pasta, cake mix). The cook is responsible for preparing the appropriate food and resource (e.g., putting pasta in boiling water), starting the process, waiting for the process to finish, and finally moving the food to the next resource (e.g., moving pasta to the colander).

Figure 2.1 shows how a cook might interleave the steps for all three dishes. The horizontal lines represent timelines for each resource (the cook her/himself, plus an oven, stove, and mixer), and the boxes show the processes as they proceed on each resource. The cook is the central resource, setting each process in motion (just like the circus performer spinning a plate), then allowing the process to run on its own. As such, the cook is very busy throughout the process, with only a brief rest at point A, waiting for the fish and pasta to finish cooking. In the meantime, the cook makes good use of parallelism—that is, the fact that the other resources can run their processes with little to no intervention on the cook's part—such as when the cook mixes cake batter while the oven preheats and the water heats to boiling.

Cooking, like multitasking, can experience resource conflicts when multiple tasks need the same resource at the same time. The cook her/himself can experience resource conflicts, like at point B in the figure, when the fish is done baking but the cook is in the middle of straining the pasta and needs to complete this step before removing the fish from the oven. Resource conflicts can also occur for the other resources: although the cake batter is ready for baking at point A, the oven is occupied by the fish, and the fish needs to finish baking before the cake can start baking (assuming the cake is baked at a different temperature) at point C. How do these resource conflicts affect the time needed to make all the food? Sometimes drastically, sometimes not at all: in this example, the pasta experiences no delays and completes in the same amount of time needed to make it by itself, the fish experiences slight delays due to the resource conflict at B, and the cake experiences long delays due to the resource conflict for the oven at C.

There are two ways we can think about the cook. We can view the cook as the central manager of the kitchen, with an important role in planning the optimal use of all the resources. This "managing cook" actively tries to minimize conflicts and suboptimal use of resources, as illustrated above. For example, the managing cook would postpone straining the pasta at point A, in order to remove the fish from the oven and

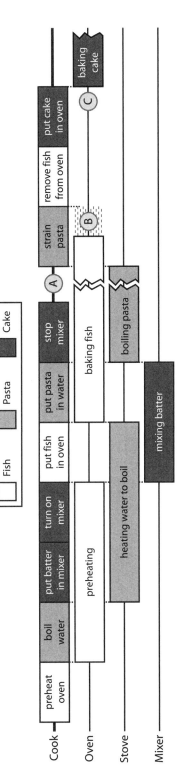

Figure 2.1. Process timeline for making fish, pasta, and a cake.

put the cake in first, minimizing the time the oven was not in use. We can also consider a cook who is just a cog in the whole system of the kitchen. This "mechanical cook" does no planning but instead simply responds to what needs to be done at a particular moment; as each dish requires some action, this cook attends to it as soon as possible and as soon as the needed resource becomes available. The mechanical cook still has a responsible job, because he has to select which dishes to make in the first place, and when to start preparing each dish—but once set in motion, things play out automatically.

In the view of threaded cognition, the multitasking mind is itself a wondrous Gedankenküche—"thought kitchen," to borrow Albert Einstein's turn of phrase (Venkataraman, 1994). The mind has a number of resources at its disposal; namely, resources that handle the complex processes of memory, vision and perception, physical movement, and so on. The mind's cook is a central cognitive resource that manages the other resources to produce goal-directed action. These resources can often work in parallel, threading processes across available resources, but the resources also may experience delays due to resource conflicts, just as our cooking example illustrates. All the while, the mind's kitchen produces its own kind of food, the food of thought and behavior.

Is the central cognitive resource a managing cook or a mechanical cook? It is tempting to think it is a managing cook, or homunculus—the little person in the brain that is as intelligent as the brain itself—perhaps because it is consistent with our ideas about free will and intelligence. As we will see, however, central cognition is in fact more like the mechanical cook. Threaded cognition is our attempt to formalize the cook, and the entire mind's kitchen, as a computational model, with the goal of better understanding multitasking behavior and performance.

Foundations: Resources, Chunks, Productions, and Models

The notion of processing resources in the mind has a rich history in the study of multitasking: researchers have long speculated on how best to codify the mind's various resources (Navon & Gopher, 1979; Wickens, 2002a, 2008), as well as its processes and potential processing bottlenecks (Broadbent, 1958; Keele, 1973; Newell & Simon, 1972; Pashler, 1984). For this purpose we lean heavily on a theory known as ACT-R (Anderson, 2007; Anderson et al., 2004), which for several decades has been one of the leading computational theories of human cognition. Figure 2.2 shows a diagram of ACT-R's formulation of the mind's processing resources. Around the diagram are various resources that correspond to the major cognitive, perceptual, and motor resources of the human system. For example, the declarative memory system, as we will soon discuss, provides the ability to store and recall information; importantly, the formulation of this system also incorporates its limitations, such as functions that determine how memories fade and are forgotten if unused. The perceptual resources (vision and audition) and the motor resource provide channels through which cognition can interact with the external world, acquiring information from perception and acting in the world through motor movements. As labeled in the figure, each of these resources can be associated with a particular brain region involved in the necessary processing. At the center lies the procedural resource—the central resource that coordinates the other resources to enact goal-directed behavior. These resources communicate with the procedural resource through buffers, or temporary storage areas that hold information to be passed between the resources.

The next two sections provide the foundational details on the two cognitive resources central to our multitasking theory; namely, the declarative memory resource and the procedural resource. As we draw examples from particular domains, we will also fill in further details on the other resources as needed. We should also note that each of these resources can produce "multitasking" in their own right. Vision, for instance, involves a massively parallel neuronal structure that can execute multiple visual tasks, such as tracking multiple moving objects (Pylyshyn & Storm, 1988). The motor system can perform multiple movements at the same time, some easily (walking, talking, and gesturing), and some with more difficulty (the classic trick of patting your head while rubbing your belly). Research focused on human vision, biomechanics, and so on, has generated an enormous literature on these types of (if you will) resource-specific multitasking. Our treatment here focuses on multitasking that coordinates across all the cognitive, perceptual, and motor resources—all of which are typically involved in the complex tasks that we aim to address.

Declarative Memory and Chunks

Declarative memory serves as the main resource for storage of information, allowing for access to the information while accounting for the effects of rehearsal, decay, and forgetting. Each individual unit of information is

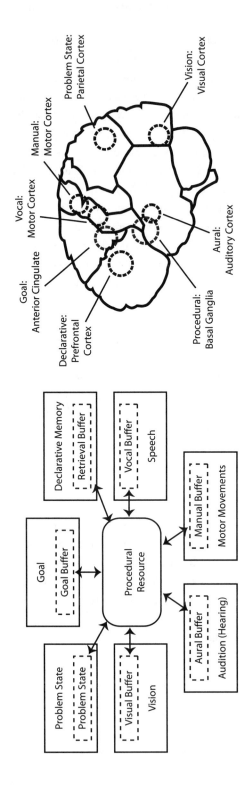

Figure 2.2. The mind's resources and their associated brain regions as specified by ACT-R theory.

encoded as a chunk of knowledge that is related to other chunks of knowl-edge. For example, we may represent each of the numbers "3", "4", and "7" as chunks in declarative memory, and then define a chunk representing the fact "3+4=7" that links to each of the number chunks. A vast set of chunks would also link to these number chunks: the multiplication fact "3×4=12" would also link to "3" and "4" (but not "7"), while the telephone area code "347" would link to all three numbers, but represent a different type of fact. As depicted in Figure 2.3, this linking between chunks results in a massive, highly interconnected network of chunks that represents the mind's information storage center.

Of course, we would not expect to dissect the brain and find numbers and addition facts in the cortex. So what is a chunk, anatomically speak-ing? A chunk might best be thought of as a pattern of neural activations, distributed across a region of the brain rather than located in a strictly defined location. Computers use patterns of bits to represent informa-tion: In the ASCII encoding of the English alphabet, the binary pattern "1001101" represents the character "M". Similarly, our brains can repre-sent concepts as a complex pattern of neural activity that, taken as a whole, can be interpreted as a particular concept such as "3+4=7". Some theories that strive for a closer biological implementation do indeed rep-resent concepts in computational neural networks and related frame-works (O'Reilly & Frank, 2006; Rumelhart & McClelland, 1986); in fact, the ACT-R framework has itself been implemented as a neural network (Lebiere & Anderson, 1993). For our purposes, however, the precise makeup of these neural patterns is not particularly important to our

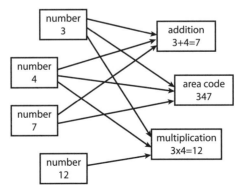

Figure 2.3. A network of a small set of chunks in declarative memory.

understanding of multitasking, and thus a chunk is a useful abstraction that allows us to focus on the more important aspects of multitasking—namely, what information is passed among resources, rather than how this information is biologically encoded.

Declarative memory not only serves as the central storage for chunks of information, but also provides retrieval processes to recall information when requested. A retrieval request comes in the form of a partial chunk pattern: if memory received a request of "3+4=_" it would attempt to return the chunk that best fits this request. For most adults, for whom such chunks are well learned and easily retrieved, the memory recall process is fast and error-free; for children learning these facts, the process would take more time, and/or may introduce errors (e.g., mistakenly retrieving a sum of "8"). ACT-R theory incorporates detailed equations that govern how memory and recall change over time and with practice. We will provide further details in a later chapter when examining memory in the context of sequential multitasking.

While the chunk is the basic unit of declarative memory, chunks are used not only for memory but across all resources. More specifically, all communication between resources uses chunks to pass information, with each resource's buffer serving as the temporary storage for information-passing. For example, when the visual resource encodes a visual input, it converts the input into a chunk representation, and places the chunk in the visual buffer. This chunk is then used by the procedural resource to perform actions on this information. Similarly, requests for motor movements are done by placing a chunk representing the request (e.g., "type the letter A") into the manual buffer, after which the manual motor resource processes the request and executes the movement. Critically for multitasking, the current goal to be achieved (e.g., "drive to the store") is also represented by a chunk stored in the goal buffer. Chunks can represent the broad spectrum of information that people utilize on a minute-by-minute basis, such as the fact that the Louvre is in Paris, or that you don't like seafood, or that your sister is looking for a new job, or that you had eggs for breakfast this morning. Thus, chunks are central to the representation and communication of information across the mind's resources.

Procedural Skill and Productions

The central resource in the mind, the procedural resource, is the primary engine for our thoughts and behavior. Whereas declarative memory stores static information as chunks, the procedural resource stores units of procedural skill called *production rules* or simply *productions*. A production can be thought of as a single step in a larger procedure that advances the current state of the mind (and environment) toward some goal. More specifically, a production gathers information from the other resources and then, based on this information, sends new information to the resources—with all communication occurring through the various resource buffers. This procedural step is often called a *production firing*. Typically, some task goal (e.g., reading, typing, driving, etc.) would be associated with a number of productions, each of which represents a unit of skill that, when combined, help to achieve the task goal.

Consider a person shopping on the Internet, typing the digits of a credit card number into a web browser to complete an order. We might encode this basic skill as two productions—one that visually encodes the next number to be typed, and another that types this number into the computer. These two productions, along with the state of the resources before and after production firing, are illustrated in Figure 2.4. The numbered panels in the figure unwind the process as follows:

(1) Initially, the only information in the resource buffers is the current goal to type a credit card number;

(2) the first production "read next digit" starts the process of visual encoding;

(3) the visual resource then works to encode the digit, and finally

(4) places a chunk representing the digit in its buffer;

(5) the second production "type digit" takes the digit from the visual resource and passes it to the manual resource to initiate typing; and finally

(6) the manual resource executes the typing movement.

Note that state (6) is very similar to state (1) except for the manual resource being busy, and thus if there are more digits to be typed, the 2-production process can repeat.

Just as a chunk is an abstraction of a pattern of neural activity, a production is an abstraction of a transformation of these neural patterns. One might imagine, looking at Figure 2.4, that the connections in these diagrams are high-bandwidth neural connections that transfer patterns from one brain region to another. The procedural resource, then, defines the transformational connections by which certain patterns over the resource buffers are translated to subsequent patterns over the same buffers.

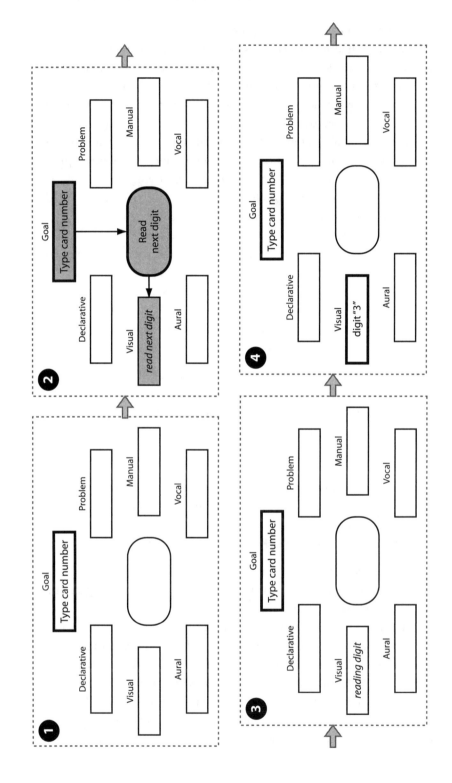

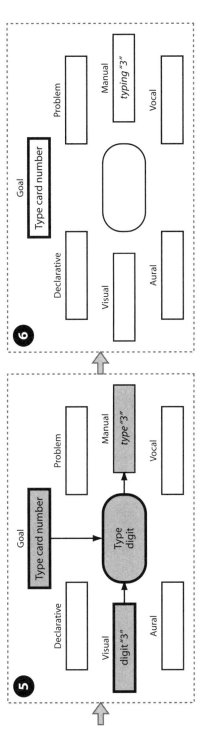

Figure 2.4. Resource states and production firings for reading and typing a credit-card digit.

Computational simulations of this type of neural pattern transformation have explored various ways in which the brain might enact these mechanisms (e.g., O'Reilly & Frank, 2006; Schneider & Chein, 2003). Again, as for chunks, we do not require a precise (real or simulated) anatomical implementation of productions for our study of multitasking. Nevertheless, the fact that neural-like computations can approximate production-like processing gives us faith that these more abstract mechanisms are realizable and plausible in the neural cortex.

The presence of a goal chunk is critical to both the scalability of the mind's skill acquisition, and the mind's ability to multitask. We would expect the mind to contain thousands, or more likely millions, of such productions for all the tasks that may arise in the world. The goal chunk activates the productions that are relevant to the current context (see also Norman & Shallice, 1986; Cooper & Shallice, 2000); without it, the system would become highly undirected and simply reactive to its current environment. (Imagine the variety of productions that become active when the visual resource sees a word—reading silently, reading aloud, choosing the labeled object, etc.—that, without the directive of a goal chunk, might all try to execute in tandem.)

We should also note that our illustrative representation of credit card entry is very much oversimplified. For example, we may have two very different sets of productions for people who can type digits without looking at the keyboard and those who cannot; people who need to look would require use of the visual resource while typing, and their typing times would likely be longer than those for no-look typists. As another example, many people would not type digits singly but rather memorize a group of digits (e.g., "4783") and type out the entire group as one burst—changing the dynamics of both the visual resource usage and the process times themselves. Nevertheless, our simple analysis here offers a straightforward representation of behavior with which we can illustrate multitasking behavior.

While the visualization of a production in Figure 2.4 can be useful in showing the information flow between resources, we are often interested in the timing of the various processes and how they might conflict, since this knowledge is critical for multitasking behavior. With this in mind, another way to visualize a production's operation is in terms of a process timeline, just as we did for our cooking analogy. Figure 2.5 shows a process timeline for these same productions executing one after

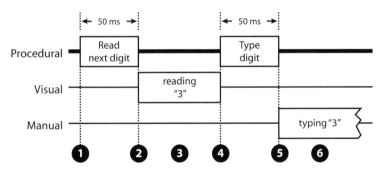

Figure 2.5. Process timeline for reading and typing a credit-card digit. Numbered states 1-6 correspond to states in Figure 2.4.

the other, and the numbers in the figure correspond to the numbered states in Figure 2.4. One nice property of such a timeline is that the resource usage is plainly evident in the figure: for much of the time, many of the resources remain idle and might be used for other purposes, and clearly this will be important as we develop our understanding of multitasking.

The timing of resource processes such as visual encoding, typing, and so on depend critically on the nature of both the process and the task at hand. This book will describe the relevant portions of ACT-R's perceptual and motor resources as needed. For the procedural resource, there is a solid estimate of the time needed for one production to execute: 50 milliseconds (ms). The evidence for this estimate comes from theoretical and modeling studies of literally hundreds of task domains that have used this estimate to account for behavior (see Anderson, 2007, and Meyer & Kieras, 1997, for a sampling). It is important to note that 50 ms is a relatively short period of time—shorter than many perceptual actions, and much shorter than most motor actions. As a consequence, the procedural resource, even with its central role in cognition, is typically not the primary bottleneck in behavior, though we will soon explore situations in which it can become a bottleneck in both laboratory and applied tasks.

Cognitive Models of Task Behavior

The mind's resources, chunks, and productions, as outlined above, are assumed to be the building blocks of human cognition—particularly at the cognitive band of behavior (Newell, 1990).[1] This representation defines a framework in which we can specify behavioral knowledge for particular task domains. Returning to our example of Internet shopping, we might attempt to specify all the knowledge that goes into buying something online. We would first specify chunks to represent the static elements of the domain, such as the web site to visit, the item to buy, etc. Then, we would specify the skill knowledge as productions—for example, as productions that search for information about an item (Fu & Pirolli, 2007), place the item in a virtual shopping basket, then purchase the item by entering name, address, credit card, and other information. All together, this knowledge would comprise a cognitive model of this task domain.

Let us look at three cognitive models that we can use as examples to describe and analyze threaded cognition. The three models represent behavior in three very simple tasks, in which a person perceives a stimulus and performs an action in response. The three tasks are as follows:

- Type a card number: As we have seen, these two productions see a credit card digit and type the digit.
- Answer a phone call: The person hears a sound, and after encoding the sound as a ringing phone, reaches to pick up the phone.
- Respond to a question: The person hears a sound, and after encoding the sound as a 1-word question, says one word in response.

For each of these tasks, we can define a cognitive model with two productions: one that perceives the stimulus (visual or aural), and one that performs the response action (manual or vocal). These productions are illustrated along with their associated process timelines in Figure 2.6. We have already detailed the workings of the model of typing a card number. For the two tasks involving listening, both tasks begin with the aural resource detecting a sound, and a single production that notes that a sound has been detected and initiates the aural process to encode the sound (i.e., figure out what it is). When encoding has finished, the production *answer phone* fires, if the sound is a ringing phone, and initiates

---

1. There are certainly holes in this assumption—for instance, the notable downplaying of emotional factors in cognition and behavior—but we aim to demonstrate that many aspects of multitasking arise from the implications of this assumption.

the motor action of picking up the phone. If the sound is the spoken question, "Coffee?" the production *respond to question* fires and initiates a verbal response, "Yes." (This production is certainly not intended to be a model of language understanding and decision making, though this behavior may be present in true coffee addicts.) In the single-task case shown in these timelines, the behavior of the models is very straightforward. In the next section, as we further examine threaded cognition, we will see how these straightforward models play out in various dual-task combinations.

Threaded Cognition

The cook in our "thought kitchen" was making three dishes at the same time (fish, pasta, cake), where each dish required a specific sequence of steps to complete the final dish (see Figure 2.1). As such, each dish can be thought of as an independent process that could be made easily on its own (as the only dish) or combined and interleaved to be made in conjunction with other dishes. Similarly, the mind works on its own "dishes," namely the various task goals that a person would like to accomplish. Whatever the task goals—walking and chewing gum, listening and notetaking, talking and driving—they can also typically be performed independently or combined into multitasking behavior. The behavior in service of each task goal is an independent thread, and together these threads form the basis of our multitasking behavior.

Threaded cognition attempts to formalize the notion of threads and how they execute and interleave during multitasking. Conceptually, threaded cognition attempts to account for the interference between two or more tasks—the sometimes large interference for two highly conflicting tasks, the sometimes small or no interference for two less conflicting tasks. Computationally, given cognitive models of two or more individual tasks, threaded cognition allows for concurrent execution and simulation of these models, quantifying between-task interference in terms of performance of individual tasks, and overall performance.

We can formalize threaded cognition as a set of four principles that build on the notions of resources, chunks, and productions described above. We now examine these principles in detail.

Threaded Processing Principle: Cognition can be represented as a set of active threads, each associated with a current task goal.

Production for Perception

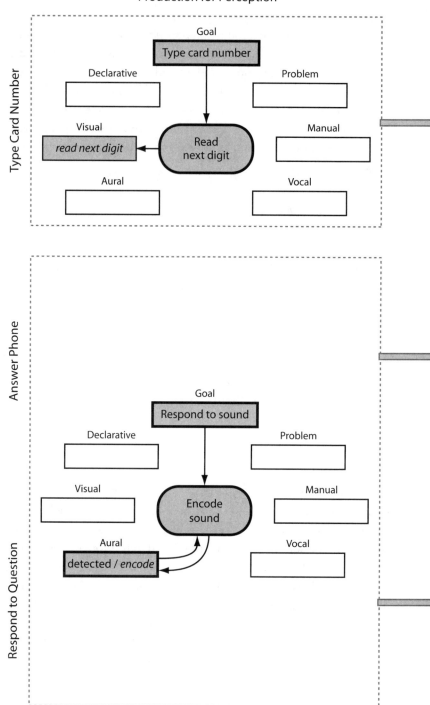

Figure 2.6. (continued)

Production for Response

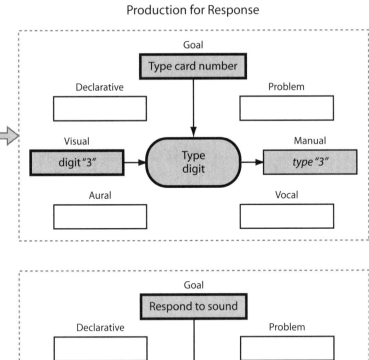

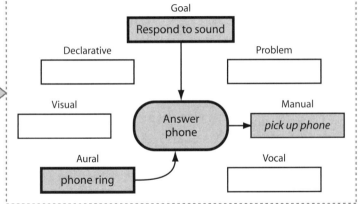

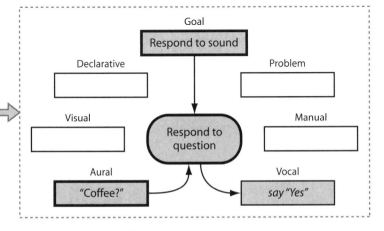

Figure 2.6. (continued)

Process Timelines

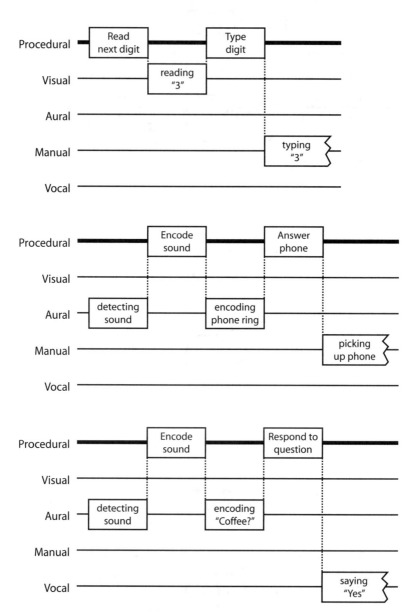

Figure 2.6. Productions and process timelines for typing a credit-card number, answering a phone, and responding to a simple question.

Our central tenet is that cognition can be characterized in terms of threads that represent independent streams of thought. Each thread is associated with some task goal, such that the thread executes to achieve this desired goal as part of the given task. Simple tasks, like in our example of typing a credit card number, can be thought of in terms of a single thread; complex tasks can be represented as a group of threads that collectively work toward a higher-level goal, with each thread focusing on a unique subcomponent of the larger task. For example, driving and air traffic control are both complex, dynamic tasks that involve many subtasks, such as monitoring the environment for situation awareness, and controlling cars or planes safely to their destinations. Nevertheless, even seemingly simple tasks may invoke multiple threads: when a person listens to someone dictating a phone number, they must hear the spoken numbers as well as rehearse the entire sequence, each of which could be characterized as a distinct task thread.

A threaded perspective on cognition offers a very natural account for the flexibility of human multitasking, because independent threads are combined or separated in whatever way is needed for the task at hand. Even for complex tasks that might involve multiple task threads, people can often perform subtask threads individually without other threads—for instance, a driver who knows the route well can concentrate on controlling the vehicle, but in an unfamiliar environment, the driver can start an independent thread to determine a best route. In fact, in times of high workload, task threads can sometimes even be allocated to another person: the same driver in an unfamiliar place can ask a passenger to find a best route when the driver needs to concentrate on navigating through busy highway traffic. Threaded cognition thus posits that people can easily start, execute, and stop threads of behavior to adapt dynamically to a changing environment.

To ground the concept of a thread computationally, we can place it in the context of the resources, chunks, and productions discussed earlier. Specifically, instead of having a single goal activate relevant productions, we define a goal set—a set of currently active goals—and have the goal set activate relevant productions for all currently active tasks. This formalization agrees nicely with the idea that starting and stopping threads is a conceptually easy process, in that starting a thread simply involves adding its associated goal to the goal set, and stopping the thread simply involves removing the associated goal from the set. It also allows us to define a thread more formally as all processing (across all resources) performed in service of a particular task goal.

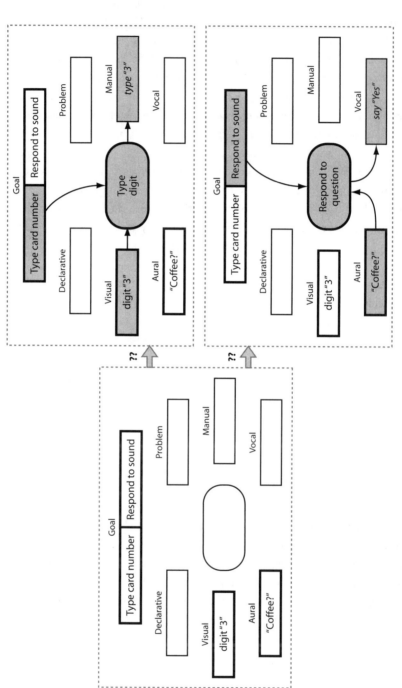

Figure 2.7. Possible production firings for typing a card number and responding to a question in a dual-task condition.

The idea of maintaining a goal set is straightforward, but its realization in terms of resources and processes poses a challenge. Consider a situation in which a person tries to type a card number and respond to a question at the same time. The left side of Figure 2.7 shows the goal set that includes doing both tasks, as well as a possible state of the buffers: the person sees a "3" and also hears the question, "Coffee?". Given this state, the right side shows two productions that could fire—the upper panel for typing the digit, and the lower panel for responding to the question. What does the person do next? At one extreme, we might imagine that productions for all active goals execute simultaneously; unfortunately, this scheme does not predict the types of interference we do indeed find in multitasking behavior (as we will see in the upcoming analysis of basic dual-choice experiments). At the other extreme, we could imagine focusing only on one goal until completion of the goal; this scheme would work for these very simple tasks illustrated here, but would not generalize to most complex tasks (e.g., imagine a driver dialing an entire 10-digit phone number before looking back up to the road). The remaining principles help to flesh out how threaded cognition finds the middle ground between these two extremes.

Resource Exclusivity Principle: All resources execute processes exclusively in service of one task thread at a time.

One of the core principles of threaded cognition, derived from the underlying ACT-R theory, is that each resource exclusively serves one task thread at a time. This principle may seem surprising given the brain's massive connectivity, which would seem to favor parallel processing across the resources. In fact, the principle does allow for (and indeed we would expect) parallel processing within individual resources—for example, within the visual and manual resources. Instead, the principle states that a resource can handle only one request at a time (e.g., encoding a visual object or typing a key), and by extension, the resource can only serve a single task thread at any given time. In terms of our sample dual-task scenario in Figure 2.7, resource exclusivity posits that both productions cannot fire simultaneously, because the procedural resource is constrained to serve only one of the active threads.

The exclusivity principle is closely related to various psychological theories that place capacity limits on processing resources (Just, Carpenter, & Varma, 1999; Wickens, 2002). Such theories define a set of resources and a total capacity (either per resource or across all resources), and then behavior for a given task would occupy some percentage of the processing capacity. Exclusivity is a stricter version of the capacity approach that assumes all-or-nothing use of each resource by a task thread. Exclusivity greatly simplifies analysis, in that it easily generalizes to all resources; in contrast, a capacity approach must be more carefully defined for certain resources that have a serial bottleneck and cannot be divided according to percentages (e.g., a finger that can move to only one location, or a vocal system that can say only one thing). While our notion of exclusivity is an approximation of the real system (ignoring, for example, the possibility of cascaded processing: McClelland, 1979), we will show that this approximation goes a long way in capturing multitasking behavior: parallelism across multiple resources and within each resource, counteracted by seriality in each resource serving one thread exclusively, nicely accounts for both the power and limitations of multitasking.

Figure 2.8 depicts three dual-task scenarios that illustrate how the resource exclusivity principle constrains multitasking behavior. The exclusivity principle is clearly evident in the procedural resource for all three scenarios, with productions firing one at a time rather than simultaneously. Panel (a) shows a dual-task scenario that involves typing a card number and answering a ringing phone. In this case, because both tasks use the manual resource, the phone-answering task must wait at point A for the typing task to finish typing a digit; only when the first motor movement is complete can the production for the second motor movement (answer phone) proceed. Panel (b) depicts a scenario with concurrent tasks of typing a card number and responding to a spoken question; thus the tasks have no perceptual or motor conflicts (visual–manual use for the first, aural–vocal for the second). Nevertheless, as the process timeline illustrates, the second task can still experience a conflict for the central procedural resource at point B: encoding of the sound finishes during another production firing, and thus the response task must wait until completion of this firing. It is also possible that, in some situations, the timing of productions allow for no conflicts on the procedural resource, as in panel (c). In this case, the person achieves perfect time-sharing, and both tasks execute as quickly as they would if they were a single task.

Resource Usage Principle: Threads acquire and release resources in a greedy, polite manner.

The third principle of threaded cognition describes how and when threads acquire and release resources for their needed processes. The most straightforward way to think about acquisition of a resource—that is, when the thread initiates a request to the resource—is that a thread

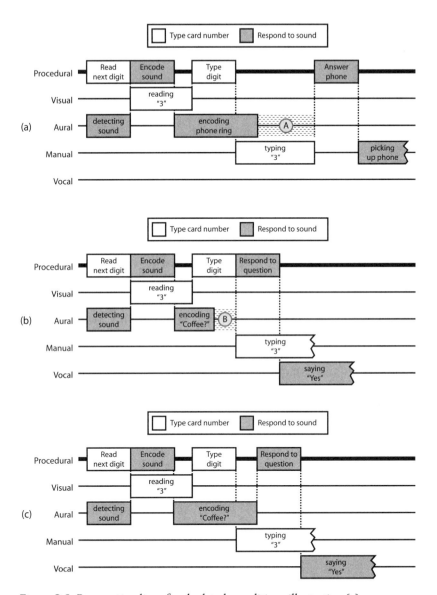

Figure 2.8. Process timelines for dual-task conditions illustrating (a) a resource conflict for the manual resource at point A, (b) a resource conflict for the procedural resource at point B, and (c) no resource conflicts for perfect time sharing.

acquires the resource in a greedy manner. As soon as it can initiate the request, it proceeds and makes the request. A more sophisticated way to handle resource initiation would be to plan ahead and optimize the sequence of upcoming steps. For example, consider again the example of typing a credit card number. After typing one digit, the recall of the next digit will likely happen much more quickly than the typing motor movement, and thus the thread will need to wait for the motor resource to become free. Instead of requesting the memory recall immediately, the thread could, if desired, wait until later, and time the request such that it finishes at the same time as the previous motor movement (perhaps allowing other threads to proceed more efficiently). Threaded cognition favors the greedy approach because it requires no intelligent planning. In that sense, it better coincides with our notion of the procedural resource as a "mechanical cook" that goes ahead with processes whenever possible, without the overhead of higher-level planning.

The release of a resource can be thought of along similar lines. If threaded cognition were an intelligent coordinator of threads, it might examine whether a thread just used a resource and needs it again in the near future, thereby allowing it to "keep" the resource (i.e., maintain a lock on its processing and not allow other threads to proceed on that resource). Again, sticking with the notion of a mechanical cook, threaded cognition posits that threads release resources in a polite manner—releasing the resource as soon as that resource has finished its task and has delivered results, if any (e.g., a encoded visual object), to the procedural resource. In fact, politeness arises naturally from the underlying ACT-R theory: process results are placed in a buffer (e.g., visual object in the visual buffer), and removed when used by a production. Thus, a resource is released as soon as (1) processing has completed, and (2) any results have been used and the resource buffer is now empty.

We should note that threaded cognition's mechanistic stance on multi-task processing does not mean that people do not engage in intelligent reasoning about how to sequence and execute tasks—there is no doubt that they do. However, threaded cognition posits that a simple, greedy, polite mechanism for interleaved processing is the common case for basic multitasking skill, and that these other, higher-level metacognitive multi-tasking processes should be thought of as being founded on this basic skill.

Conflict Resolution Principle: When multiple threads contend for the procedural resource, the thread with the highest urgency is allowed to proceed.

The one scenario not addressed by the first three principles involves conflicting requests for the procedural resource—that is, when two or more threads want to fire a production at the same time, as illustrated in Figure 2.7. Threaded cognition states that in this situation, the thread with the highest urgency is allowed to execute on the procedural resource. One straightforward way to formalize urgency is in terms of the amount of time since the thread fired its last production, thus allowing the least-recently-processed thread to proceed. This scheme ensures that all threads have equal opportunity to progress in their respective tasks, and avoids "starving"[2] any thread of processing time—thus achieving balanced processing across threads.

A slightly augmented scheme would allow a thread to dictate its own urgency simply by specifying the next time at which it would like to proceed. If each thread's next time is equal to the time immediately after it last fired a production, this scheme reduces to the least-recently-processed scheme above. However, it also allows threads to run less frequently, if possible, for a given task. For example, a driving thread on an empty road, or a memory rehearsal thread for a list that is very easy to recall (say, 3 digits) may not need constant processing, but rather could specify a need to proceed only 0.5 or 1 second after the last firing (Salvucci, 2005). We do not need to augment the simple threaded mechanism to allow for this scheme, however; instead, we can utilize a temporal mechanism that extends the ACT-R theory (Taatgen, van Rijn, & Anderson, 2007; van Rijn & Taatgen, 2008), and allow this mechanism to control the timing for a thread.

Examples from the Laboratory

The four principles of threaded cognition lay out the basic theory of concurrent multitasking. We now explore how the theory works in two simple but illustrative laboratory tasks. The first task, the dual-choice task, has a long history of associated research. Studies of dual choice date

---

2. As computer scientists will note, terms such as "threads" and "starving" evoke the analogy to computation and computer hardware. We exploit this analogy to the extent that it helps to understand how the mind performs its own brand of threaded processing, with the caveat that clearly the implementation details (and their limitations) differ greatly between the computer and human systems.

back at least to the 1930s–1950s (Telford, 1931; Welford, 1952), when researchers began investigating how simple reaction-time tasks might be delayed in a dual-task scenario. The second task, the manual tracking task, has been examined as an example of dual-task limitations in a longer continuous task (as opposed to the typically subsecond burst of response in the dual-choice task). Below, we outline the threaded cognition account of these tasks before moving on to the highlighted applied task of driving in the next chapter.

Dual Choice

The basic dual-choice task combines two simple-choice tasks in a concurrent way, and forces the person to make the two choices simultaneously, or almost simultaneously with a short delay between tasks. Three variants of the individual choice tasks are:

- Visual–Manual: The person sees a visual stimulus with three or four positions, and an "O" in one position, and presses a finger on the right hand corresponding to the position of the "O" (e.g., pressing index finger for the stimulus "O – –" or "O – – –").
- Aural–Manual: The person hears an aural stimulus as a low, medium, or high tone and presses a finger corresponding to the tone.
- Aural–Vocal: The person hears an aural stimulus as a low, medium, or high tone and says an associated phrase in response (e.g., saying "one" for a low tone, "two" for a medium tone, or "three" for a high tone).

Note that these three tasks are highly controlled variants of the three sample tasks discussed earlier (typing a card number, answering a phone, and responding to a question). As illustrated in Figure 2.8, two simple concurrent tasks interfere if their resource demands overlap in time. In order to detect interference, researchers often use a dual-task paradigm in which they compare dual-task performance to single-task performance. If someone is as fast on a task when it is presented concurrently with another task, as when the task is presented alone, and likewise for the other task, then there is evidence of no interference. This is exactly what Schumacher and his colleagues (2001) found in an experiment in which participants performed concurrent visual–manual and aural–vocal choice tasks, the two tasks with no perceptual–motor resource conflicts. It took participants on average 282 ms to do the visual–manual task by itself, and 283 ms when it was concurrent with the aural–vocal task. Similarly, participants needed on average 447 ms for the aural–vocal task alone, compared to 456 ms for both tasks in parallel (with, not surprisingly, no statistical difference between the two values).

If we look back at Figure 2.8, threaded cognition has two accounts for dual tasks with no perceptual–motor conflicts—one with interference (Figure 2.8b), and one without (Figure 2.8c). The difference between the two accounts is the timing of the various perceptual–motor processes, and when they complete their actions. Fortunately, for a task as simple as the choice tasks above, the ACT-R theory provides good processing-time estimates for all the critical resources. As noted earlier, a production takes 50 ms to fire. Reading the visual stimulus takes by default 85 ms (though a more sophisticated theory of eye movements and encoding is also available: Salvucci, 2001b). Estimates for other peripheral resources have been taken from research done by Kieras and Meyer in the context of their EPIC architecture (Meyer & Kieras, 1997), and can be traced back to even older work by Card, Moran and Newell (1983). Based on that research, we estimated that determining the pitch of a tone takes around 200 ms—much longer than the visual processing. A final assumption, derived from the Kieras and Meyer work, is that tone detection has an onset time of 50 ms; that is, it takes the aural resource 50 ms to detect the presence of a tone (before encoding what that tone is). Byrne and Anderson (2001) originally modeled Schumacher's results in ACT-R, but we will present our version of it here, which is very similar to theirs. Figure 2.9a shows the timeline of that model, which is very similar to Figure 2.8c. It is important to note that there is noise in the timing aspects of all resources involved; for example, detecting the pitch of a tone may take 200 ms on average but can vary from trial to trial.

The reason why perfect time-sharing occurs in this experiment, at least according to the model, is that the production firings that initiate responses (or *response-selection steps*, as they are generally called in the literature) do not overlap in time. Schumacher and colleagues, and later Hazeltine, Teague and Ivry (2002), have tried various experimental manipulations to ensure that the response-selection steps occur at the same time. In Schumacher et al.'s (2001) Experiment 3, they made response selection harder by introducing an incompatible mapping. For example, participants had to respond to the pattern "– – – O" by pressing the index finger (of the right hand) instead of the pinkie; this response is

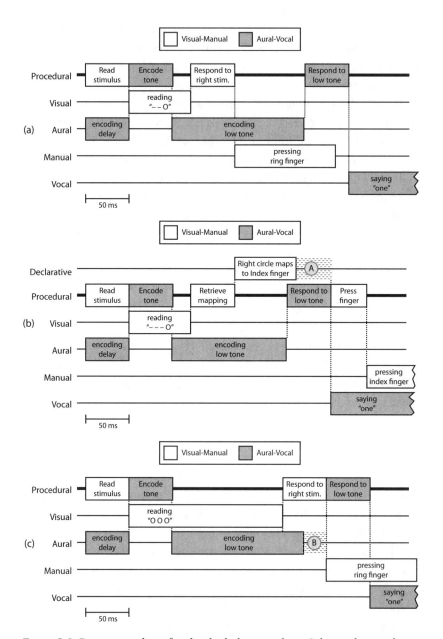

Figure 2.9. Process timelines for the dual-choice tasks in Schumacher et al. (2001) and Hazeltine et al. (2002): (a) perfect time sharing, (b) conflict in the incompatible-mapping experiment at point A, and (c) conflict in the difficult visual stimulus experiment at point B.

an incompatible mapping, because the rightmost stimulus corresponds to the leftmost response (of the fingers used in the experiment). As expected, this manipulation increased response times considerably, from approximately 280 ms in their first experiment to 470 ms. The manipulation also introduced interference: dual-task response times were no longer the same as single-task response times.

When Schumacher et al. analyzed these data in more detail, they found substantial individual differences. About two-thirds of their participants showed only small amounts of interference, on the order of 30 ms. The remaining third showed much larger interference, on the order of 150 ms. Figure 2.9b shows how threaded cognition can account for the group with small amounts of interference. The assumption in this model is that the incompatible mapping cannot be made directly by a production, but that the mapping must be retrieved from declarative memory. As a consequence, the "press finger" and "respond to tone" productions often overlap in time. In the example in the figure, the response to retrieving the mapping between the index finger and the right circle is delayed (point A in the figure) because the procedural system is still executing the "respond to low tone" production. As a result, the response time on the visual–manual task will be slower than it would have been in a single-task condition. Given the variability in the timing of the different resources, interference could also have affected the aural–vocal task, or it could have been absent altogether. This means that, on average, the interference effect is approximately half the duration of a production firing, or 25 ms (Anderson, Taatgen & Byrne, 2005). This model cannot explain the one-third of participants with a substantially larger interference. One concern about these artificial dual-task experiments is that some participants seem to treat the two tasks as a single combined task; these participants might impose additional order constraints on how resources are used, effectively reducing efficiency. In a later chapter we will look at the phenomenon of *attentional blink*, which can be explained by unnecessary order constraints on subtasks.

Hazeltine et al. (2002) tried to produce a similar effect by making the visual component of the visual–manual task more difficult, using a bright circle among circles of lesser intensity to mark the target position. In our account of this revised task, we assume that the visual resource needs more time to process the stimulus (Figure 2.9c). The result is similar to Schumacher's manipulation, making it more likely that the response-selection steps of each choice task coincide. Figure 2.9c shows an example of interference (point B) in the aural–vocal task, which arises because the procedural system is still busy executing the "respond to right stimulus" production. Thus, our account suggests that the aural–vocal task would slow down by roughly half a production firing (25 ms) on average; indeed, Hazeltine et al. found that the aural–vocal task slowed down by an average of 19 ms (while the visual–manual task slowed down by a non-significant 1 ms). This suggests that processing the visual stimulus is still faster than processing the tone, but not always fast enough to avoid interference. Hazeltine et al. (2002) performed other experiments to force the two response-selection steps to coincide, with similar outcomes. Anderson, Taatgen and Byrne (2005) have modeled these variations in a way similar to that described here, further supporting a threaded account.

One thing shown by these experiments is that it is very hard to produce observable interference in the procedural resource. Most tasks include some amount of "slack time" in the procedural resource, and given that the firing time of a production is only 50 ms, interference can be on the order of tens of milliseconds and therefore very difficult to detect. Other resources are much better candidates to produce interference, like the manual resource in Figure 2.8a. We should also note that these dual-choice studies required multiple training sessions to achieve almost perfect time-sharing; before that level of training is reached, participants exhibit not only slower overall performance but also much more dual-task interference. Later in the book (Chapter 7), we describe how this interference is not caused by the procedural resource, but instead by declarative memory: As long as a task is not fully practiced, declarative memory is needed to determine the next action, and if we have multiple threads that correspond to new tasks, cognition can experience heavy contention for the declarative memory resource. This idea also corresponds to the general finding in skill acquisition, that people are much better at carrying out tasks in parallel if they are sufficiently practiced in these tasks.

The findings on perfect (and almost-perfect) time-sharing may be surprising in that they seem at odds with the phenomenon known as the psychological refractory period (PRP) effect. Like dual-choice experiments, a PRP experiment consists of two relatively simple tasks. However, the two tasks are not presented at the same time, but with a variable interval between them called the *stimulus onset asynchrony* (SOA). Moreover, participants are instructed to respond to one of the two tasks before responding to the second. For example, placing the visual–manual and aural–vocal tasks within a PRP paradigm, the experiment could present the aural stimulus first, followed by the visual stimulus after the SOA time period, and require that participants give the verbal response (to the aural stimulus) before the manual response (to the visual stimulus).

Figure 2.10 shows a typical trial and result of a PRP experiment, plotted as the reaction times of both tasks against the SOA. The figure is an abstracted version of the results from a PRP experiment from Schumacher et al. (2001), using the same aural–vocal and (easy) visual–manual task discussed earlier. The reaction times for Task 1 are independent of SOA, because participants are instructed to give priority to that task; thus, the appearance of the Task 2 stimulus does not affect performance on Task 1. The reaction times for Task 2, however, vary with SOA (with reaction times measured from the moment the Task 2 stimulus is presented,

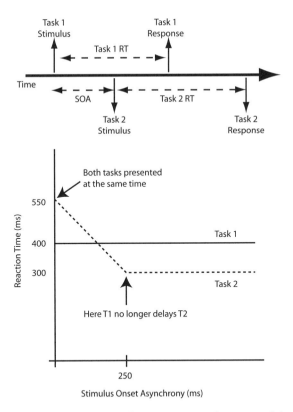

Figure 2.10. Schematic that shows the time course of a PRP trial (top), and schematic of typical results of a dual-task psychological refractory period (PRP) experiment (bottom).

not the start of the trial). If the SOA is very long, Task 2 begins after Task 1 has finished, and thus Task 2 can be viewed as a single task. The example in the figure shows that the single-task times are 400 ms and 300 ms for Tasks 1 and 2, respectively, corresponding to their reaction times at the longest SOAs. The interesting segment is when the SOA is less than 250 ms. If the SOA is 0 ms, in which case both stimuli are presented at the same time, the reaction time for Task 2 is 550 ms: this time is longer than the single-task time (550 vs. 300 ms), showing an effect of interference from Task 1. However, this time is also shorter than the combined single-task times (400+300=700 ms), showing that Task 2 benefited from being in a dual-task condition. With increasing SOA, the interference decreases linearly until it finally reaches zero at an SOA of 250 ms.

Why is there a substantial interference in this PRP task, even though the same tasks led to perfect time sharing in the dual-choice experiment? The answer lies with the fact that, in the PRP paradigm, participants are explicitly instructed to give priority to Task 1. Now, if we were to believe in an intelligent homunculus doing the scheduling, we could make sure that the Task 1 thread is always given appropriate priority, and that the manual response is initiated just after the vocal response is initiated. As a consequence, the manual response would come just after the vocal response, which would mean that with a SOA of 0 ms, the total reaction time for Task 2 would be just over 400 ms—much less than the actual 550 ms. The mechanistic scheduler from threaded cognition does not have the luxury of arbitrary scheduling; once the threads are initiated, there is no way to control them. A straightforward interpretation of the PRP task suggests a simple account: At the start of a trial, participants initiate a thread only for Task 1, and then, when the procedural processing for Task 1 has finished—when the vocal response is initiated—the Task 1 thread initiates a thread for Task 2. This simple account produces the results shown in Figure 2.11, which depicts both experimental results (solid lines) and the model results (dashed lines).

The dual-choice task is an important one because it uses two extremely simple concurrent tasks to explore the nature of the "cognitive bottleneck." Even for tasks using different perceptual and motor modalities, there exists a shared cognitive process that results—sometimes—in interference. Threaded cognition accounts for the level of interference that arises in particular dual-choice scenarios (i.e., PRP), while also accounting for the lack of interference that arises in other dual-choice scenarios (i.e., perfect time-sharing).

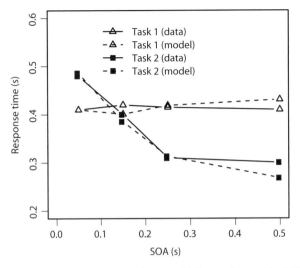

Figure 2.11. Dual-task response time, human (Schumacher et al., 2001) and model. From Salvucci & Taatgen (2008), Copyright 2008 American Psychological Association. Adapted with permission.

Tracking and Choice

The dual-choice task involves two very short tasks in a concurrent scenario that lasts about one or two seconds of total time. To complement this task, we now examine a tracking task in which a person provides continuous input to a moving system, allowing us to explore some effects of multitasking behavior as it unfolds over a longer period of time. This tracking task, a simpler variant of more complex tasks (Dixon, Wickens, & Chang, 2005; Kaber & Endsley, 2004; Wickens, 1976), is illustrated in Figure 2.12. The cursor, depicted as a crosshair onscreen, is randomly perturbed by a forcing function (i.e., pushed in different directions). Meanwhile, the participant in the experiment uses a joystick or mouse (with the right hand) to attempt to center the cursor within the given target area. In one version of this task, Martin-Emerson and Wickens (1992) used easy and hard conditions corresponding to the amount of force generated by the forcing function, making it easier or harder to keep the cursor centered in the target area. Also, in a dual-task condition, they introduced a simple choice task to be done concurrently with tracking: An arrow would appear at some distance down from the target area—the stimulus offset—and the participant would provide an appropriate

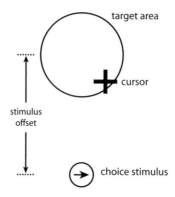

Figure 2.12. Tracking and choice task.

response (with the left hand) corresponding to arrows pointing in the left or right direction.

Our cognitive model representing the tracking task (Salvucci & Taatgen, 2008; see also Chong, 1998; Kieras et al., 2000; Lallement & John, 1998) is only moderately more complex than that for the choice task. In fact, the tracking task can be thought of as repeated iterations of a 2-step process in which the person finds the location of the cursor and then initiates a movement to the center of the target area. This tracking model is depicted in the white boxes in Figure 2.13. The process of

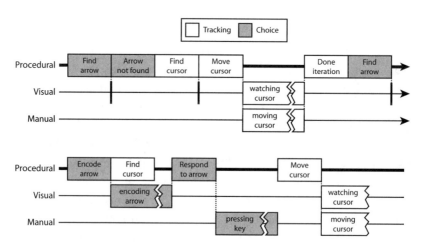

Figure 2.13. Tracking and choice process timeline.

finding the cursor requires only that the visual resource access the location of the cursor (without the need to fully encode the object), which happens instantaneously in the ACT-R theory, and thus there is a trivial amount of visual processing related to this step. The second step of moving the cursor engages both the manual resource for the actual movement, and the visual resource for visually guiding the movement. The tracking model includes a final step that notes the end of the current iteration when the manual and visual resources become free, and starts another iteration. For the choice task, the model has a second task thread that continually looks for the arrow stimulus. When it is found, the model simply encodes the arrow visually, and then responds manually, just as was done for the visual–manual choice task presented earlier.

To understand multitasking performance in this task, it is important first to understand performance in the choice task itself. Figure 2.14 shows how choice response time is affected by the stimulus offset (measured in degrees of visual offset from the target area center). Regardless of tracking condition, response time clearly increases as the stimulus

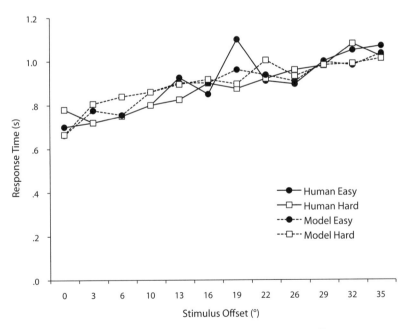

Figure 2.14. Choice response time as a function of stimulus offset. From Salvucci & Taatgen (2008), Copyright 2008 American Psychological Association. Reprinted with permission.

moves farther from the target area. The model's prediction of this effect comes from the visual resource, specifically the theory of eye movements and visual encoding integrated into the ACT-R cognitive architecture (Salvucci, 2001b). In essence, a visual object farther from the eye's line of gaze requires more time to encode, and thus the model produces the linear correlation between response time and stimulus offset.

More importantly for our interest in dual-task interference, how does stimulus offset affect tracking performance? The most important aspect of the model is the contention that arises for the visual and manual resources. Because tracking relies on fast repeated iterations (roughly 350 ms per iteration), any disruption to this pattern will affect tracking performance; in essence, a slower rate of iterations leads to decreased performance. As is clear in Figure 2.13, the choice task occupies both the visual and manual resources for a certain amount of time, thus not allowing the tracking thread to proceed until the choice response has been completed. In addition, the longer visual encoding time further disrupts

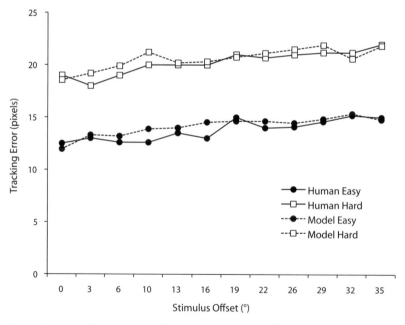

Figure 2.15. Tracking error as a function of stimulus offset. From Salvucci & Taatgen (2008), Copyright 2008 American Psychological Association. Reprinted with permission.

tracking and decreases performance. Putting this all together, Figure 2.15 shows the effect of stimulus offset on tracking error, which is measured by the average distance of the cursor from the target area center. Because visual encoding time for the choice task increases with stimulus offset, the longer encoding leads to longer delays for the tracking task, thus increasing tracking error. In addition, while the easy tracking condition (not surprisingly) leads to smaller errors than the hard condition, the steady increase as a function of stimulus offset is evident in both conditions.

In reality, the task of manual tracking is much more complex than the laboratory task described above would imply (see Ricard, 1994, for a bibliography). Nonetheless, our model of this laboratory version of manual tracking illustrates how threaded cognition accounts for interference in a continuous task that lasts for seconds to minutes or more, as a complement to the one-shot task represented by the dual-choice paradigm.

Research Connections

Threaded cognition builds on a vast space of earlier theoretical and experimental work, all aimed at furthering our understanding the capabilities and limitations of human multitasking. In the psychology literature, some of this work has addressed multitasking in terms of "bottlenecks" on the human processing system, typically in the context of very simple tasks like the dual-choice paradigm discussed above. Some of the earliest work (Telford, 1931; Welford, 1952) described the bottleneck as a single channel through which all processing flowed; later work emphasized potential bottlenecks that may arise in particular stages of simple choice-task behavior, such as stimulus perception (Broadbent, 1958) or response selection (Pashler, 1994). Research has also framed these bottlenecks in terms of capacity-limited processes (Just & Carpenter, 1992; Navon & Gopher, 1979) that can also be limited by the amount of information available to the system (Norman & Bobrow, 1975). As illustrated in our account of dual-choice tasks and the psychological refractory period, this view of a cognitive bottleneck aligns very well with the basic tenets of threaded cognition. As discussed earlier, the capacity-limited view of cognition also meshes well with the theory, although threaded cognition draws a somewhat harder line in defining how the processing allocation is determined.

A related body of work has addressed how the cognitive system focuses on a particular task, as is critical for both concurrent and sequential tasks. Research on cognitive or executive control (Botvinick et al., 2001; Cohen, Dunbar, & McClelland, 1990; Cooper & Shallice, 2000; Logan, 1985; Norman & Shallice, 1986) has explored, typically at the level of neural processes, how cognition guides task performance and modulates its guidance according to task demands. At the same time, studies of automatic versus controlled processes (Schneider & Shiffrin, 1977; Shiffrin & Schneider, 1977), and their relationship to skill acquisition (Anderson, 1982), emerged to paint a richer picture of both single-task performance and dual-task interference. In this book, we describe threaded cognition at a level above the neural theories of cognitive control; nevertheless, the resources that form the basis of the theory as derived from ACT-R theory have been grounded in neural processes in a number of recent brain-imaging studies (Anderson, 2005, 2007; Anderson et al., 2004).

More closely related to threaded cognition are those efforts that have attempted to unify the broad spectrum of empirical phenomena with a single, integrated approach. Perhaps the most widely known of these theories is Wickens' multiple resource theory (Wickens, 1984, 2002, 2008), which has evolved over several decades and has been used to understand behavior in both laboratory and applied contexts. Multiple resource theory characterizes the potential interference between two tasks in terms of dimensions of stages (perceptual and cognitive vs. spatial), sensory modalities (visual vs. auditory), codes (visual vs. spatial), and visual channels (focal vs. ambient). The theory uses the values of these dimensions to quantify the interference between two tasks as a numeric value. Thus, multiple resource theory offers a higher-level abstraction of multitasking behavior than threaded cognition, which aims to account for the temporal sequence of observed events, along with quantitative measures of task performance.

The most closely related work to our own is that involving computational modeling of multitasking behavior. Kieras and Meyer (see Meyer & Kieras, 1997; Kieras et al., 2000; Kieras, 2007) have set the tone for this research in their efforts to integrate the cognitive, perceptual, and motor aspects of multitasking into the EPIC cognitive architecture (Meyer & Kieras, 1997). Their work has focused on exploring executive processes that govern how multiple tasks share processing resources, both general executives that operate for any sets of tasks and customized executives that apply to particular task pairings. These executive processes would, like normal task processes, be specified in terms of production rules and would operate alongside the individual task processes. Research efforts using the QN-MHP cognitive architecture (Liu, Feyen, & Tsimhoni, 2006; Wu & Liu, 2007, 2008) have also investigated computational multitasking models based on queuing networks that represent the brain's parallel network of processing resources. This work has also incorporated more complex representations of cognitive control to handle, for example, task prioritization and self-monitoring of performance. In contrast, threaded cognition posits that multitasking emerges naturally from a parsimonious architectural mechanism (threading) without the need for rule-based general and customized executives; although higher-order planning may arise from time to time, the common case in multi-tasking is this basic ability to thread multiple tasks and perform them together. This difference has strong implications, especially for the relationship between multitasking and learning. As we will see in Chapter 6, multitasking becomes more efficient with practice because the individual task processes themselves become more efficient, as declarative task knowledge is transformed into more automatic procedural skill.

The Big Picture

Threaded cognition allows us to take any two tasks and say something about the behavior that would result from doing the two tasks concurrently. Let's then revisit the questions we posed at the start of this chapter. First, what task combinations are more difficult for people to perform concurrently? It is perhaps not surprising that two tasks that utilize the same perceptual or motor resource—for example, two tasks that require vision, or two that require hand movements—will typically result in moderate to severe interference between tasks. As we pointed out earlier, certain resources have their own ability to perform concurrent tasks; for example, the visual system can track five independently moving objects (Pylyshyn & Storm, 1988), and the motor system can type with multiple fingers moving simultaneously. However, this type of within-resource multitasking is still in service of a single task goal (to track objects or type words, respectively). Two truly independent threads will generally have to time-share a resource that they both rely on, resulting in at least some amount of interference between tasks.

Then what task combinations are easier for people to perform concurrently? Clearly, the flip side to the above argument is that two tasks that do not overlap in terms of the usage of perceptual and motor resources will facilitate better multitasking. But perhaps more interestingly, no overlap in perceptual and motor resources does not mean that there will be no interference between tasks; all tasks make use of the procedural resource, and this resource is always a potential source of dual-task interference. (In a later chapter, we will explore two further cognitive resources—the problem state and declarative memory—that can become major sources of interference for particular tasks and task combinations.)

Are there task combinations for which we can achieve perfect time-sharing? We saw one example of exactly this phenomenon in the dual-choice domain. But where might perfect time-sharing occur for arbitrary task combinations? Assuming two tasks have no overlap in perceptual and motor resources, there is a single dominant factor that facilitates efficient, sometimes even perfect, time-sharing: the frequency and timing of procedural steps in a task. Intense tasks with frequent procedural steps (i.e., production firings) will make heavy use of the procedural resource, and thus any secondary task will need to interleave its own procedural steps and will likely cause some reduction in performance of the first task, as we saw in the tracking task. (Note that this reduction in performance may not be observable, however; for the tracking task, the secondary choice task had a significant effect but a very small one, amounting to only a few additional pixels of error in tracking performance.) Less intense tasks with only occasional procedural steps, such as tasks with long perceptual or motor processing in between steps, are much less susceptible to this kind of interference in the procedural resource. In situations where two procedurally less intense tasks are performed concurrently, and where the timing of procedural steps allows for efficient interleaving—as in the Schumacher et al. dual-choice task—people can indeed achieve perfect time-sharing.

That the procedural resource is central to our account of multitasking can be seen, in some sense, as both a strength and weakness of threaded cognition. When we have well-founded ideas of the procedural steps for a given task—as we do for many laboratory tasks, and many applied tasks, as well (e.g., solving math problems, Anderson, 2005; browsing a web page, Fu & Pirolli, 2007)—threaded cognition can tell us a great deal about multitasking behavior and potential interference. When we do not have such well-founded ideas for a task, we must rely on our best estimates of procedural usage, and threaded cognition's predictions may only be as good as these estimates allow. For example, what are the procedural steps for walking? changing a baby? shooting a basketball? Or, to pose the question differently, how much cognitive "thinking" is involved in doing these tasks, as opposed to work being done by other resources like perceptual and motor resources? We do not yet have clear answers for these questions, but when we do, threaded cognition should help to understand multitasking behavior for these tasks as well.

3

Driving and Driver Distraction

Of the many examples of concurrent multitasking, driving is one of the most common, most complex, and most fascinating examples today. Driving itself involves a host of interleaved subtasks, from simple steering control, to basic maneuvers (lane changing, merging on a highway), to higher-level planning and decision-making (destination planning, navigation). When combined with interactive in-vehicle devices such as phones, radios, navigation devices, etc., driving becomes an even more complex multitasking environment, in which secondary devices sometimes distract from the primary driving task. What skills are involved in the basic driving task? When the driver attempts to do secondary tasks while driving, what secondary tasks interfere with driving, and how much do they interfere? And what might this tell us about the design of in-vehicle devices specifically, and driver safety more generally? In this chapter, we apply our theory of threaded cognition to investigate these questions.

Multitasking while Driving

It is widely acknowledged that today's drivers do more than just drive. Whether the distraction arises from built-in "infotainment" systems or from portable electronic devices brought into the vehicle, drivers have a wide array of nondriving tasks available to them at any given time—calling a friend, finding a radio station, looking up restaurant information, programming a navigation destination, and so on. Meanwhile, drivers are spending more and more time in their vehicles; for example, American drivers average an astounding 87 minutes a day behind the wheel (ABC/ Time/Post, 2005). Not coincidentally, drivers have been increasingly engaging in secondary tasks while driving. A recent poll of 5,288 American drivers (GMAC, 2006) found that 40% of drivers talk on a cell phone while driving, and among younger drivers aged 18-24, 24% send text messages and 20% use a portable music player while driving. As a result, driver inattention (due to in-vehicle devices as well as other factors, such as child passengers or objects outside the vehicle) has been identified as an extremely critical, if not the foremost, factor in vehicle crashes (Dingus et al., 2006; Hendricks et al., 2001). This, in turn, has energized the search for ways to mitigate distraction and its effects on driving (Regan, Lee, & Young, 2008).

When we think of driver distraction and inattention, the most salient type of distraction arises in tasks that interfere with the visual and/or motor demands of driving. Dialing a cellular phone while driving is the most common example, and it is now well known that dialing a phone while driving can have negative effects on driver performance (Alm & Nilsson, 1994; Brookhuis, De Vries, & De Waard, 1991; Reed & Green, 1999; Salvucci & Macuga, 2002). Similarly, other studies have reported on the effects of perceptual-motor interference due to interaction with in-vehicle devices such as radios (Sodhi, Reimer, & Llamazares, 2002), email systems (Lee et al., 2001), navigation devices (Lee, Forlizzi, & Hudson, 2008; Tijerina et al., 2000; Tsimhoni, Smith, & Green, 2004), and portable music players (Salvucci, Markley, Zuber, & Brumby, 2007).

At the same time, eliminating visual or motor demands from an in-vehicle task does not necessarily eliminate the task's potentially negative effects on driving. A number of recent studies (Alm & Nilsson, 1995; Lee et al., 2001; Levy, Pashler, & Boer, 2006; Horrey & Wickens, 2004; Strayer & Johnston, 2001) have shown that primarily cognitive tasks can also result in negative effects on driver performance, although these effects are often smaller than those arising from perceptual and manual interaction. Through these studies, it has become clear that the cognitive aspects of in-vehicle tasks also play a critical role in driver distraction— that keeping drivers' minds on the road is just as important as keeping their eyes on the road, or their hands on the wheel.

Driver distraction is thus an excellent domain in which to explore the core ideas of threaded cognition. As we saw in the previous chapter, threaded cognition can account for perceptual–motor interference due to contention for these resources by multiple threads. In addition, the theory makes predictions about how cognitive tasks may affect driving, due to contention for the procedural resource. The remainder of this chapter expands on this theme, and demonstrates how threaded cognition provides a parsimonious account of various aspects of driver distraction within its unified framework.

The Basic Driving Task

Before examining driving in its various multitasking contexts, we must first examine how a driver controls the vehicle as a single task. Stripped down to essentials, the basic driving task involves steering to maintain a central lane position, and acceleration/braking to maintain proper speed and distance from a lead vehicle. These two aspects of driving can be thought of as *vehicle control tasks*—steering in service of lateral control (side-to-side), and acceleration/braking in service of longitudinal control (in the direction of the roadway). (One might also consider attention to external events to be yet another central driving task; we address this issue in later models.) Let us start by examining the lateral control task, and later integrate the resulting model with an analogous model for the longitudinal control task.

Steering a vehicle involves a continuous process of looking at the road and adjusting the angle of the steering wheel in response to the road. As a starting point for our formalization of the steering task, what visual information does the driver use to perform these steering actions? Several research efforts (e.g., Donges, 1978; Land & Horwood, 1995) have characterized drivers' vision of the road in terms of two separate regions of interest: the near region of the road closer to the driver, which provides information about the vehicle's location with respect to the road (i.e., how close the vehicle is to the lane center); and the far region of the road, which provides information about the direction and curvature of the upcoming roadway. Figure 3.1 illustrates these two regions on a view as seen by the driver through the front windshield.

While the use of near and far information seems intuitive enough, one experiment (Land & Horwood, 1995) explicitly tested this idea by having participants operate a driving simulator in which only particular segments of the road were visible. When only a near region was visible,

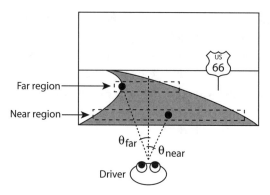

Figure 3.1. Near and far regions of the road as seen by the driver. The circles in the near and far regions represent the near point and far tangent point, respectively.

drivers stayed reasonably close to the lane center but produced "jerky," unstable driving—an indication of their inability to predict the upcoming roadway. However, when only a far region was visible, drivers produced smooth, stable driving but strayed much farther from the lane center. Additional tests examined how drivers performed with varying positions of the near and far region; overall, drivers performed best when the near and far regions were spaced farther apart, providing further evidence of the separate functions of the two regions.

How might this knowledge of drivers' use of the visual field help to formulate a model of steering? Salvucci and Gray (2004) developed a mathematical steering-control law founded on the use of two points within the two regions of driver attention: a near point, defined as the center of the road at a set small distance ahead of the vehicle; and a far point, defined as a distant road point such as the vanishing point on a straight roadway, or a tangent point on a curved roadway, as depicted in Figure 3.1. Let us define θ_{near} as the horizontal visual angle to the near point, and θ_{far} as the horizontal visual angle to the far point, both with respect to the driver's direction of travel. The control law says that the steering angle can be periodically changed based on how these two visual angles change over time. Specifically, after a short period of time Δt, the control law states that the steering angle φ can be changed by $\Delta\varphi$ as follows:

$$\Delta\varphi = k_{far}\Delta\theta_{far} + k_{near}\Delta\theta_{near} + k_{I}\theta_{near}\Delta t$$

The equation includes three terms (with corresponding scaling constants) that attempt to maintain a stable far point (such that $\Delta\theta_{far} \approx 0$), maintain a stable near point (such that $\Delta\theta_{near} \approx 0$), and maintain a centered near point (such that $\theta_{near} \approx 0$). Simply using these three criteria, the control law produces the steering behavior observed in the Land and Horwood (1995) study: "jerky" steering with only a near region visible, and smooth but uncentered driving with only a far region visible.

The control law, while useful in itself in understanding driver steering behavior, does not provide some of the necessary details we will need to understand driving while multitasking; for example, the equation says nothing about the cognitive demands of realizing such a control law, and does not specify how the relevant perceptual features (the two visual angles) should be acquired and used. To provide this understanding, Salvucci (2006) embedded the control law into a full-fledged ACT-R driver model. The driver model aims to implement the control law in as simple a cognitive model as possible. In this spirit, the driver model includes four procedural rules that perform the following actions:

- Determine the visual angle to the near point (θ_{near})
- Determine the visual angle to the far point (θ_{far})
- Update steering (φ) based on the control law
- Check vehicle stability and repeat

Figure 3.2 depicts this basic steering model as an iterating loop of these four procedural steps. The first two steps require visual processing, but this can be done very quickly by the architecture (as defined by its visual system) because only the visual locations of the two points are needed. The third step also requires visual processing to encode the far-point object, but this too is presumed to occur very quickly (approximately 5 ms in the model) due to the high saliency and low information content of the far point. The third step also involves motor actions needed to adjust the steering wheel and accelerator/brake pedals; the model assumes that these actions can be done in parallel with other actions. Finally, the last step uses the visual angles and changes in visual angles to determine whether the vehicle is stable, defined as a situation in which the velocity of both visual angles is below threshold, and the near visual angle is also below threshold; the thresholds were estimated during the process of fitting the model's behavior to that of human drivers. The execution of each rule takes 50 ms as dictated by the ACT-R architecture, and thus one iteration requires approximately 200 ms of processing time—in other words, the model can update steering roughly five times per second when driving is the only active task. (This assumes that the driver is driving

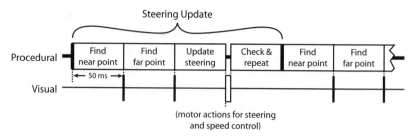

Figure 3.2. Process timeline for basic steering control.

intensely with no breaks; later we will discuss a modification to the model that lowers the frequency of steering updates when the vehicle and environment allow.)

The lateral control model for steering can be augmented in a straightforward way, with a model of longitudinal control that manages the vehicle's acceleration and deceleration. Specifically, we can devise a longitudinal control law that produces a change in accelerator (or brake) depression according to the time-headway to the far point, where time-headway is the time needed for the vehicle to reach the specified point's position on the road. The far point, in this case, would often be a lead vehicle in front of the driver's vehicle, but could also be a tangent point on a curve, or a vanishing point on a straight road. The model can adjust acceleration by considering a combination of the current time-headway, the change in time-headway, and the desired time-headway in a car-following situation (e.g., whether the driver wishes to follow the lead vehicle at 1 second behind, 2 seconds behind, etc.). In fact, the equation used to update the accelerator and brake pedals is directly analogous to that above for lateral steering control (see Salvucci, 2006). In addition, because time-headway information can be obtained from the far point, and pedal motor actions can be included with steering motor actions, acceleration control can be embedded into the same four procedural rules used for steering. Interested readers can refer to Salvucci (2006) for the precise formulation of the acceleration control equation; for now, however, it suffices for our analysis of multitasking to understand simply that acceleration and braking can be performed along with steering, within the iterative loop of four procedural rules.

This very simple model of basic steering, as we will see shortly, can be used along with threaded cognition to predict multitasking while driving in a surprisingly rich set of task domains. Before exploring the model's behavior in a multitasking context, however, it is important to establish confidence that the model indeed provides a reasonably accurate account of how people drive. For this, we can connect the model to driving simulation software and, through ACT-R perceptual-motor capabilities (extended with knowledge about the steering wheel and pedals), allow the model to drive the simulation (see Salvucci, 2001a, 2006). The simulation then records all driver behavior just as it would for a human driver, and by comparing the model's behavioral data to that of human drivers, we can test and validate particular aspects of the model. We now examine two aspects of basic driving—namely, corrective steering and curve negotiation—to see how the model accounts for each.

Corrective Steering

Hildreth et al. (2000) performed a driving-simulator study of corrective steering maneuvers: the necessary maneuvers when the vehicle is off its proper heading and needs to be brought back to center and aligned with the roadway. In the experiment, drivers navigated a straight road at a constant speed, but occasionally the simulator took control and turned the vehicle to a predetermined heading angle off the road centerline. At this point, the driver took control and performed a corrective maneuver to re-center the vehicle in the roadway. Note that two steering actions are required for the corrective maneuver: one to direct the vehicle toward the lane center, and another to straighten the vehicle upon reaching the center. This sequence of events is depicted in Figure 3.3. The study varied two factors: the initial heading angle and the initial speed, both of which were determined at the onset of the driver retaking control of the vehicle.

Figure 3.4 graphs the behavior of one driver that was representative of the general trends observed in the Hildreth et al. study. The top left graph depicts steering-wheel angle over time with varying initial heading angles

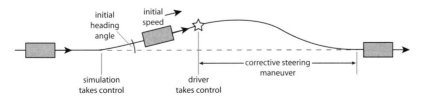

Figure 3.3. Sequence of events during a trial in Hildreth et al. (2000).

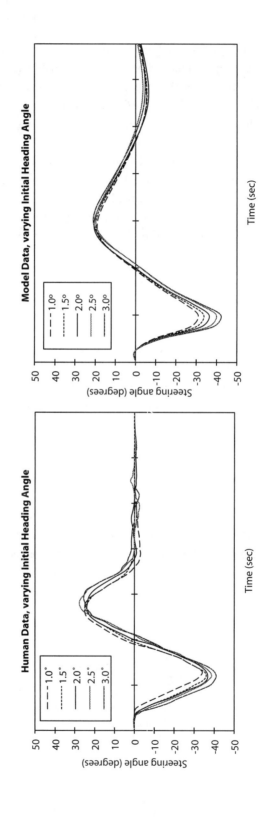

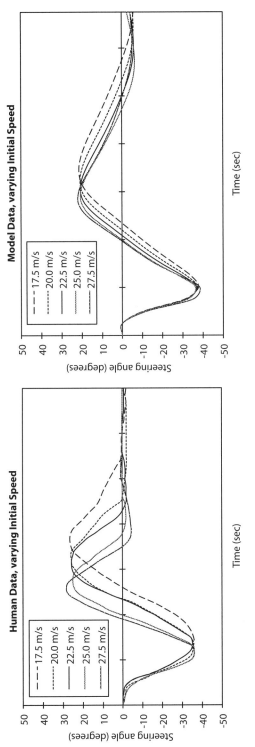

Figure 3.4. Steering profiles over time during corrective steering for human drivers (Hildreth et al., 2000) and the steering control law model. From Salvucci & Gray (2004), Copyright 2004 Pion Limited, London. Adapted with permission.

of 1.0–3.0°. As initial heading angle increased, this driver produced larger steering angles at the peaks of the curves—the downward curve denoting the initial steering movement toward the lane center, the upward curve denoting the correction of the vehicle to align it with the road. Perhaps surprisingly, regardless of initial heading angle, the timing of the steering profiles were largely unchanged; that is, the temporal position of the peaks of steering movement stayed the same across all initial heading angles. In contrast, the bottom left graph depicts steering angle for varying initial speeds of 17.5–27.5 m/s. Here, the driver generated the same magnitude of steering across all speeds, but the steering profiles were stretched temporally at smaller speeds.

Salvucci and Gray (2004) ran simulations of the model's steering control law in the same sets of conditions, and the (partial) results are included in Figure 3.4. First, it is important to note that the overall shape of the steering profiles for both graphs is very similar to that of the graphs for the human drivers; the model does a very good job reproducing the first larger, sharper steering curve and the second smaller, more gradual curve. The top right graph shows how, like human drivers, the model produces larger steering angles but the same temporal profiles for varying initial heading angles. This arises from the core components of the control law: θ_{near} and θ_{far} increase at larger heading angles, which produces a larger change in steering angle in response. The bottom right graph depicts how the model's steering profiles stretch out over time as initial speed decreases. Just like human drivers, the model changes the steering angle by the same magnitude regardless of velocity (since θ_{near} and θ_{far} are identical in all cases) and allows the vehicle to move and realign itself at whatever rate its current speed dictates.

There are aspects of the human data not captured as well by the model: the temporal stretching for varying initial speeds is more pronounced for human drivers, and the model's steering profiles for both graphs tails off more gradually than that for human drivers. Nevertheless, the model does account for the basic profile, as well as two subtle effects of corrective steering related to heading and velocity.

Curve Negotiation

A second important aspect of steering behavior is curve negotiation, or managing steering into, during, and out of a curved segment of road. Salvucci (2006) reported data on how drivers navigated curves in a

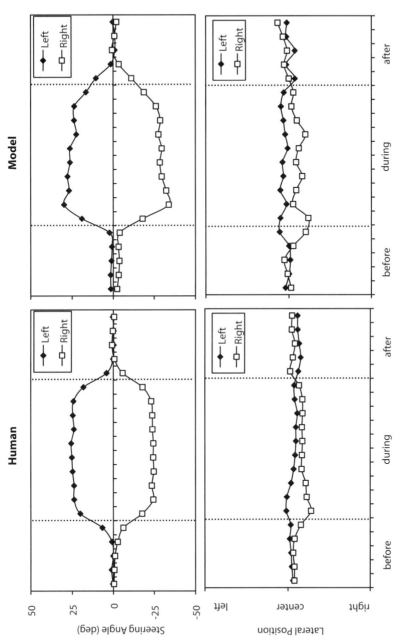

Figure 3.5. Steering and lateral-deviation profiles over time during curve negotiation for human drivers and the ACT-R driver model. From Salvucci (2006), Copyright 2006 Human Factors and Ergonomics Society. Reprinted with permission.

standard highway environment in a driving simulator. The left half of Figure 3.5 shows two aspects of the driver data over time—steering angle and lateral position in the lane. The graphs represent all curves normalized into 10 temporal segments within the curve, and 5 temporal segments before and after the curve; the dotted lines denote the vehicle's entry into and exit from the curve. In the top left graph, we see that drivers started steering into the curve slightly before the curve begins (the first dotted line), maintained a fairly constant steering angle through the curve, and returned the steering wheel to the center as the curve ends (the second dotted line). In the bottom left graph, we see that lateral position stays fairly close to center; however, particularly early on in the curve, there is a very slight bias toward the inside part of the curve (leftward in the lane for left-hand curves, rightward in the lane for right-hand curves).

Salvucci (2006) ran simulations of the ACT-R driver model navigating the same highway environment as the human drivers. The right half of Figure 3.5 shows the steering and lateral-deviation profiles for these model simulations. The basic pattern in the human steering profile is evident also in the model data: the gradual adjustment of steering angle early in the curve, constant steering through the curve, and adjustment back to center late in the curve. Again, there are limitations in the model's account, most notably the sharper peaks early in the steering profiles that do not appear in the human data. In the lateral-deviation data, we see two things: first, the model reproduces the overall pattern of maintaining a fairly central lane position throughout the curve, and second, the model also reproduces the slight bias toward the inside part of the curve. In fact, it even shows the subtle effect that the slight bias is larger on right-hand curves than left-hand curves. Interestingly, the bias arises as an emergent property of the model: the tangent point moves slightly in the direction of the curve as the curve approaches, pulling the model's steering inward as well, and the fact that the driver sits to the left of center in the vehicle causes a slightly larger effect for right-hand curves.

Beyond Steering and Vehicle Control

The studies described above, along with additional studies of the driver model (see Salvucci & Gray, 2004; Salvucci, 2006; Salvucci & Taatgen, 2008) provide evidence that our fairly simple driver model behaves like a human driver, at least in terms of the basic vehicle-control aspects of driving. Of course, the driving task involves much more than simply steering, accelerating, and braking. In one example at a slightly higher level, the driver model has been used to examine how drivers change lanes (Salvucci, 2006). For this work, the basic control model was augmented with a number of procedural rules to represent (still in a limited way) two higher-level processes: situation awareness in looking around its environment and noting the presence and position of other vehicles, and decision-making in examining the current situation and deciding whether or not to change lanes. The model was shown to fit not only the basic steering aspects of the lane-changing maneuver, but also the visual sampling patterns (as shown by eye movements) evident before and during a lane change.

At even higher levels, driving involves a host of higher-level reasoning processes, from spatial navigation (how do I get to the party?), to planning (what friend should I visit first?), to other considerations (is there too much snow to drive to the store safely?). Unfortunately, we do not currently have a sufficiently rigorous understanding of many of these processes to formalize them as cognitive models. Nevertheless, even our fairly simple driver model is sufficient for predicting some very interesting aspects of multitasking behavior while driving, with threaded cognition as the linchpin that integrates the driving task with other concurrent tasks. The next few sections describe several studies that illustrate how threaded cognition and the driver model help us to better understand driving in a multitasking context.

Driving and Phone Dialing

Of the many secondary tasks performed while driving, the use of cellular phones stands out as one of the most common, most discussed, and most relevant for current legislation. As mentioned earlier, phone use can be roughly classified in terms of two potential distractions: those that arise from the perceptual and motor interactions with the phone (e.g., reaching for the phone, dialing a number), and those that arise from the cognitive aspects of conversing on the phone. With respect to the former, the most commonly studied perceptual-motor interaction task is that of dialing a phone, and research studies (e.g., Alm & Nilsson, 1994; Brookhuis, De Vries, & De Waard, 1991; Reed & Green, 1999; Salvucci & Macuga, 2002) have examined how and why dialing behavior may affect driver performance. One particular aspect of this behavior is whether and how different perceptual and motor modalities for dialing may differentially affect performance. Perceptual modalities may include visual and/or auditory feedback while dialing, and motor modalities may include pressing of buttons and/or speech commands to operate the phone. Because the driving task itself makes resource demands, particularly the visual resource, threaded cognition should be able to account for some of these differential effects from various modalities.

In this section we focus on phone dialing as an excellent example of perceptual-motor distraction while driving. In the next section, we return to the idea of cognitive distraction and apply our theory to account for cognitive interference that sometimes arises from phone conversations and related cognitive tasks while driving.

Effects of Dialing Modality

Salvucci (2001a) performed a study of dialing while driving that examined several possible phone-dialing interfaces with different dialing modalities. First, the study included manual dialing, which involved pressing digits on a mounted hands-free phone, as well as voice dialing, which involved speaking into the phone. Second, the study included full dialing of all seven digits of a memorized seven-digit phone number (e.g., "867-5309"), and speed dialing of a single typed digit or spoken phrase that represented a particular number (e.g., the speed digit "2" and the phrase "Jenny" to represent Jenny's phone number). These two factors were combined to create four dialing task conditions: full-manual, speed-manual, full-voice, and speed-voice. Dialing for each task condition required the driver to press a power button to initiate the dialing sequence, and the manual-dialing conditions also required the driver to press a *send* button to initiate dialing (the voice-dialing conditions substituted a voice-recognition message in place of the *send* button, to mimic commonly used voice interfaces). The four conditions and associated examples are illustrated in Table 3.1.

How might we represent the four dialing tasks as cognitive models? The sequence of perceptual and motor actions required by the dialing tasks heavily constrains the models, in that the sequences dictate the order of these actions. The unconstrained aspect of the models, however, involves the cognitive steps that guide the sequence of actions, which center on the memory retrieval process in recalling the phone number.

Table 3.1. Dialing conditions and examples from Salvucci (2001).

Full-Manual	Speed-Manual
press *Power*	press *Power*
press 8675309	press 2
press *Send*	press *Send*
Full-Voice	**Speed-Voice**
press *Power*	press *Power*
say 867 5309	say "Jenny"
listen for 867 5309	listen for "Jenny"
listen for "Connecting…"	listen for "Connecting…"

Fortunately, there have been a number of ACT-R modeling efforts focused on recalling a list of items (e.g., Anderson & Matessa, 1997), and these efforts have developed a consensus representation for such lists: memory chunks organized into blocks of items where each block holds roughly 3 to 4 items. Since the North American convention for writing a phone number places a dash after the third digit (e.g., 867-5309), the representation for the phone number assumes the corresponding blocked structure. Figure 3.6 illustrates the memory representation for the full 7-digit number, as well as the single-digit speed dial number. Each block is headed by a block chunk (e.g., "block #1") that specifies its position within the entire phone number (first or second block), and each digit points back to the block with its corresponding position. Thus, the model can use the declarative resource to recall the particular block, and subsequently recall the particular digit within that block. Note that the start of each block requires two retrievals (of the block and digit chunks) instead of one (of the digit chunk), incurring additional time and additional opportunity for other tasks such as driving to be interleaved with the dialing task. Given this memory representation, the model of each dialing task is a straightforward interpretation of the sequence of actions required by the task.

We (Salvucci & Taatgen, 2008) took the model of each driving task and allowed threaded cognition to interleave dialing and driving to predict behavior on the combined task. A segment of the resulting process timeline for the full-manual dialing task is shown in Figure 3.7. The upper segment shows a period of time immediately after the model has pressed the power key and is preparing to dial the first digit. The dialing thread retrieves the next block chunk and the first digit of this block, while the driving thread continues its execution; the driving thread incurs a large cost in moving the eyes and encoding the far point (point A in the figure),

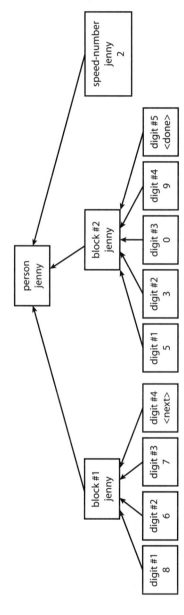

Figure 3.6. Memory representation for the full phone number and speed number.

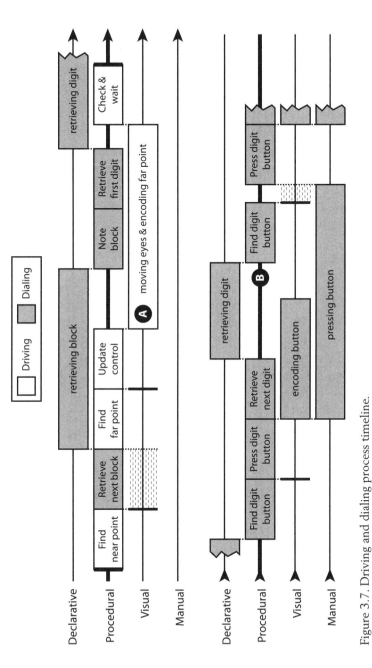

Figure 3.7. Driving and dialing process timeline.

because the eyes had been previously directed to the phone while the power key was pressed. The lower segment shows the continuation of this timeline in which, for each digit, the model retrieves the next digit, finds the button on the phone, and presses the button. Interestingly, the dialing thread itself here shows some amount of parallelism: while the manual resource moves the hand, with the visual resource guiding the movement, the dialing thread is able to retrieve the next digit in parallel with these actions. When the last digit of the block is retrieved (labeled "next" and "done" in Figure 3.6), the model notes this fact at point B and iterates by retrieving the next block (if any). While the model dials a block of digits, the visual resource is continually utilized, and thus the driving thread is not able to interleave execution until the visual resource becomes free (while the next block is being retrieved).

The model of driving for this experiment required one modification. The actual driving task in the experiment was rather simple: steering down a straight, single-lane road at a constant speed. Because of its simplicity, drivers did not need to allocate full attention to the driving—even a less frequent response to steering was sufficient to maintain a fairly central position on the roadway. Thus, the driver model was modified such that, in stable situations (as deemed by the "check & wait" procedural step), the model delayed the next control update for a specified period of time. An estimate of roughly 500 ms as the delay time was found to account best in two separate studies (Salvucci, 2005; Salvucci & Taatgen, 2008). In fact, we have also explored how appropriate delay times can be learned over time, and can adapt to changing scenarios (Salvucci, Taatgen, & Kushleyeva, 2006), but we assume a simple constant delay time for the current modeling study.

We ran simulations of dialing while driving for all four dialing-task conditions (Salvucci & Taatgen, 2008) and compared these to the human driver results (Salvucci, 2001a). Figure 3.8 graphs the total time needed to complete the dialing tasks for both dialing only as a solitary task, and dialing while driving. Not surprisingly, the two full-dialing conditions (full-manual and full-voice) resulted in larger dialing times than the two speed-dialing conditions; the full-voice condition had the largest dialing time and the speed-manual condition the smallest time. But, perhaps surprisingly, the concurrent driving task did not add a large amount of time to the total dialing time. Dialing while driving was, on average, 21% slower than dialing as a single task—a statistically significant difference, but not a large one. Thus, people were, to a large extent, able to efficiently

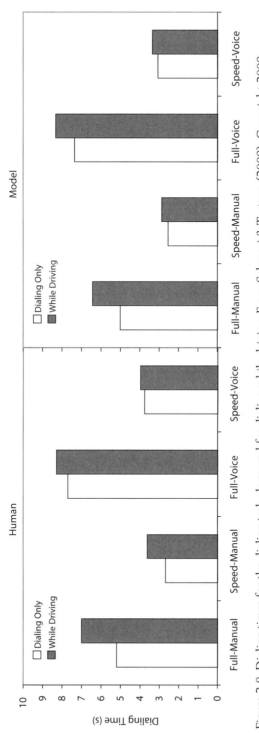

Figure 3.8. Dialing times for the dialing task alone and for dialing while driving. From Salvucci & Taatgen (2008), Copyright 2008 American Psychological Association. Reprinted with permission.

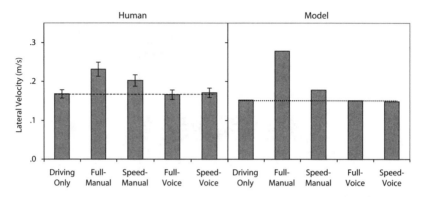

Figure 3.9. Lateral velocity for driving alone and for driving while dialing. From Salvucci & Taatgen (2008), Copyright 2008 American Psychological Association. Reprinted with permission.

interleave the dialing and driving tasks. The model results, shown in the figure, mirror this pattern of results, with a good fit to the overall times and a very similar prediction of slowdown due to the driving task (16%).

Figure 3.9 graphs the corresponding driver performance results for each of the conditions, where driver performance was measured as lateral velocity—the average absolute side-to-side velocity direction (as a measure of vehicle stability) for the entire period of the dialing task, plus five seconds of steering-correction time after task completion. Both the human drivers and the model drive imperfectly even while driving as a single task, and thus exhibit some baseline amount of lateral deviation. While performing a concurrent dialing task, the human drivers exhibited significantly larger deviations for the two manual-dialing tasks, with the full-manual task resulting in the largest deviations. The voice-dialing tasks, on the other hand, did not result in deviations significantly different from single-task driving. (The results for a related measure, lateral deviation as root-mean-squared error to the lane center, show the same pattern of performance.) The driver model also produced the largest effect of dialing for the full-manual task, a smaller but significant effect for the speed-manual task, and no significant effect for the voice-dialing tasks. For both the model and human drivers, the main source of distraction was the contention for the visual resource. The manual tasks required visual guidance for the motor movements, whereas the voice tasks allowed driving to be interleaved more efficiently without visual-resource interference.

The Time Course of Dialing

The above results illustrate how threaded cognition captures performance while dialing, aggregated across the span of the entire dialing task. Salvucci (2005) collected more detailed data on the time course of dialing by examining the time needed to enter each digit of a phone number. In the experiment, drivers drove a desktop simulator and occasionally dialed a 10-digit phone number followed by the *enter* key on a standard numeric keypad. The driving task included both steering and speed control while following a lead vehicle, which accelerated and decelerated in an abrupt random manner similar to what might be experienced in a highway construction zone. Thus, in contrast to the previous task involving steering alone, this task involved both steering and speed control in a more realistic environment.

Salvucci (2005) compared the experimental results obtained from human drivers to those derived from simulations of the driver model.[1] Again, we can examine the aggregate performance results, shown in Figure 3.10: dialing time, lateral deviation as the root-mean-squared error of the driver's vehicle from lane center, and speed deviation as the root-mean-squared error between the driver's speed and that of the lead vehicle. The dialing time and lateral deviation results closely resemble those in the study above, showing a slight increase of dialing time and a more significant increase in lateral deviation in the dual-task condition. The model's behavior reflects these results just as it did for the above study. Interestingly, the human drivers exhibited no statistically significant effect of dialing on speed deviation; apparently drivers were able to match speed with the lead vehicle while dialing, approximately as well as when driving alone. The model also did not exhibit an effect on speed deviation. Although there was slight visual and cognitive interference (producing the lateral-deviation effect), this slight interference was washed out by the slow-changing nature of speed deviation when filtered through the dynamics of the vehicle accelerating and decelerating.

To examine the detailed dialing process that produces these aggregate effects, we can analyze the time needed to enter each digit of the phone

---

1. The multitasking model in this case used a theoretical precursor to threaded cognition based on a general executive for interleaving multiple tasks; threaded cognition produces the same pattern of results as those discussed here.

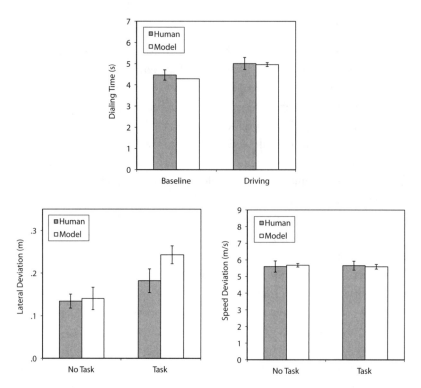

Figure 3.10. Results from Salvucci (2005) for dialing time, lateral deviation, and speed deviation. From Salvucci (2005), Copyright 2005 Cognitive Science Society. Reprinted with permission.

number, plus the final *enter* key. These key delays are graphed in Figure 3.11. The human data show an interesting pattern: At the block boundaries of the phone number—that is, where the dashes occur in the standard North American representation (123-456-7890), before the fourth and seventh positions—the key delays for dialing alone (the baseline condition) are almost double those in the other positions (ignoring the first position, which includes a large initial startup cost). When dialing while driving, these block-boundary positions show a significant increase in key delays, whereas the nonboundary positions show no significant differences. Thus, it seems that drivers utilize the block boundaries as switch points for interleaving driving actions with the dialing task. Threaded cognition, along with our models of driving and dialing, would predict the same pattern. The dialing thread uses the visual resource intensely within a block, and does not allow driving to intercede, but at the block

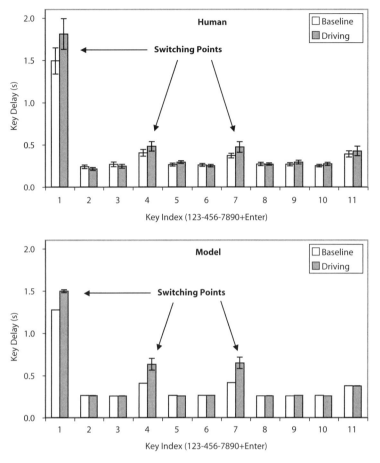

Figure 3.11. Key delay times for the individual digits of a 10-digit phone number. From Salvucci (2005), Copyright 2005 Cognitive Science Society. Reprinted with permission.

boundary, the dialing thread retrieves a new block chunk and allows the driving thread to resume execution.

Driving and Cognitive Tasks

The above results demonstrate that threaded cognition can account for a number of effects of perceptual-motor interference while dialing a phone. In some ways, this type of interference is the most apparent. Most people would readily agree that when drivers do not look at the road, their performance suffers as a consequence. Now, however, there is also an accumulating body of evidence that primarily cognitive tasks have the potential to diminish driver performance (Alm & Nilsson, 1995; Lee et al., 2001; Levy, Pashler, & Boer, 2006; Horrey & Wickens, 2004; Strayer & Johnston, 2001), although these effects are not always observed (as in the voice-dialing interaction discussed earlier). How can we quantify when the mind is "off the road," and how can we use this knowledge to predict effects on performance?

In this section, we use threaded cognition to examine three cognitive tasks and their effects on driver behavior. The first task involves a concurrent simple choice task—identical to that discussed in Chapter 2, but in this case combined with the driving task. The second task involves an intense cognitive task, the sentence-span task, intended to mimic the demands of natural conversation. The third task is a purely cognitive task, specifically a memory-rehearsal task, that is intended as a surrogate for everyday cognitive demands such as a person remembering directions to a friend's house, or what to buy at a store. There are many other possible cognitive tasks that we might examine, such as unconstrained conversation while driving (Strayer & Johnston, 2001); however, such unconstrained tasks are beyond our current ability to model behavior in a rigorous way (i.e., at the moment-to-moment level needed by our theory). Nevertheless, the tasks discussed in this section provide an interesting window into the effects of cognitive interference on driver performance, and demonstrate that threaded cognition can greatly facilitate our understanding of the sources and effects of cognitive distraction while driving.

Driving and a Simple Choice Task

In the previous chapter, we illustrated the workings of threaded cognition using a dual-choice task in which people perform two very simple choice tasks concurrently. As a first step in our analysis of cognitive distraction, it is useful to begin by looking at how driving can be combined with the same simple choice task used in the basic experiments outlined previously. In a sense, this is a natural stepping stone: we now have a model of driver behavior, as well as a model of behavior in a simple choice task, and thus threaded cognition should be able to tell us how people might perform both tasks concurrently, and what interference might arise in the process.

A recent experiment by Levy, Pashler, and Boer (2006) collected data on exactly this scenario. In the experiment, participants drove in a simulator behind a lead vehicle, while occasionally responding to a choice task. The choice task had four conditions analogous to those we discussed in the last chapter: a visual or auditory stimulus, combined with a manual or vocal response. The visual stimulus involves changing the color of the lead vehicle's rear window for 100 ms either one or two times, with 100 ms between the two changes for the double stimulus. The auditory stimulus used the same timing with a simple auditory tone instead of the visual color change. Manual responses comprised either one or two presses of a response button on the steering wheel, whereas vocal responses involved saying either "one" or "two" (corresponding to the number of stimuli presented).

At the same time, drivers not only had to steer down the simulated roadway, but also had to perform a brake-response task: the lead vehicle's brake lights would light up, and the driver would tap the brakes in response. This braking task was timed to occur at a specified time after the presentation of the choice-task stimulus. The stimulus onset asynchrony (SOA), first mentioned in Chapter 2 as a relevant feature of the dual-choice task, was used as the time interval between the onset of the choice-task stimulus and the onset of the brake-response stimulus (i.e., illumination of the brake lights).

Starting with the aforementioned models of behavior for driving and the choice task, we (Salvucci & Taatgen, 2008) began with these individual models and modified them to fit the structure of the Levy et al. experiment. For driving, the only difference between the experiment and normal driving was the behavior required for the brake-response task. Thus, the driver model needed only a slight modification, such that it tapped the brake pedal when the lead vehicle's brake lights illuminated (bypassing its normal speed control using the accelerator and brake pedals). The model for the choice task required slightly more modification because of the nature of the stimuli and responses—namely, that instead of a single visual or auditory stimulus representing each choice in the task (e.g., a left or right arrow, or high or low tone), the Levy et al. experiment used single and double stimuli to represent each choice (due to the constraining nature of the driving task). The choice model in Chapter 2, then, was modified to abide by this new structure simply by encoding either one or two stimuli, and then producing either one or two responses, respectively; to encode the stimuli, the model waits 100 ms after the first

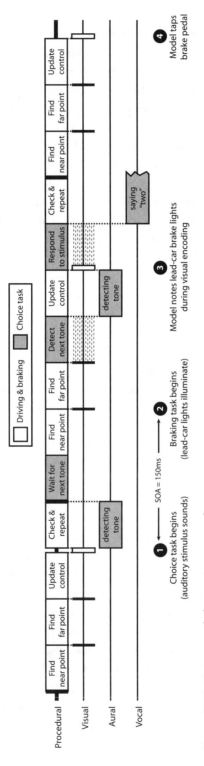

Figure 3.12. Driving and choice process timeline.

stimulus to check for the presence of the second (an interval that participants presumably learn in the practice session). We also estimated one
parameter to represent the delay in the voice recognition system used to
collect vocal responses (300 ms).

Threaded cognition allowed us to integrate these individual task models
together to predict concurrent behavior, as illustrated in Figure 3.12 for
an aural–vocal version of the choice task. While the model drives, the
choice task begins at point (1) with the onset of the auditory tone. The
thread handling the choice task then waits for a second tone, and upon
hearing it, generates the vocal response "two." The driving thread continues to perform its procedural steps, and when the lead vehicle's brake
lights illuminate (2), the model eventually notes the illumination during
visual encoding of the far point (3) and finally taps the brake at the next
opportunity for updating control (4). As is evident in the timeline, the
driving thread is for the most part able to interleave its steps effectively;
however, the three procedural steps of the choice-task thread produce
some interference with the driving thread, predicting a small but important slowdown in brake response time (100 ms in the figure example due
to two choice-task steps interleaved during the braking task).

Levy et al. analyzed their experimental results in several ways, in search
of this type of interference. Figure 3.13 shows the reaction time to the
choice task in the single-task condition (while driving but no braking),
the choice task in the dual-task condition (while driving and braking),
and the braking task in the dual-task condition. Times are broken down
into the four choice-task conditions (auditory–manual, auditory–vocal,
visual–manual, visual–vocal). Overall, the visual conditions required more
time than the auditory conditions because of contention for the visual
resource while driving. The vocal conditions also required slightly more
time because of the time needed to speak the responses and have the
voice recognition system interpret the response. Interestingly, Levy et al.
found no effect of the braking task on the choice task: the single-task
choice times were no different than the dual-task choice times. In addition, the choice-task condition (i.e., which modalities were used for stimulus perception and response) did not affect brake response times. The
model results show precisely the same patterns. The choice task experiences no interference from the braking task, because of threaded cognition's ability to effectively interleave the choice-task procedural steps
with the driving steps; at the same time, the modalities used in the choice
task do not affect the braking task, because the choice task involves the

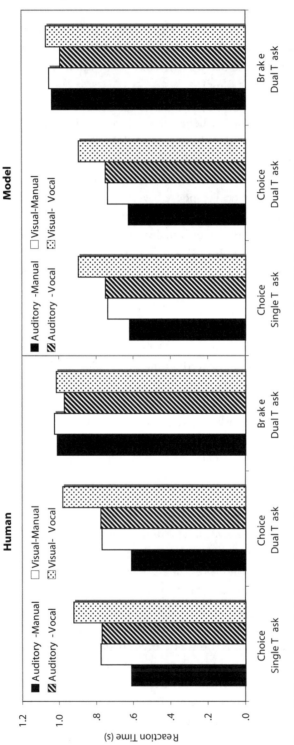

Figure 3.13. Driving and choice study, reaction time by choice condition, human and model. From Salvucci & Taatgen (2008), Copyright 2008 American Psychological Association. Reprinted with permission.

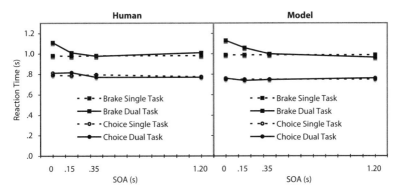

Figure 3.14. Driving and choice study, reaction time by SOA, human and model. From Salvucci & Taatgen (2008), Copyright 2008 American Psychological Association. Reprinted with permission.

same number of procedural steps (and thus the same interference) regardless of modality.

Figure 3.14 provides a different view of these data; specifically, a graph of reaction time as a function of SOA. Recall that the classic perceptual refractory period (PRP) effect involves no interference for the first task, but increased interference for the second task at short SOAs (see Figures 2.10, 2.11). Levy et al. found exactly this PRP effect for their driving and choice experiment. The choice task experienced no slowdown at any SOA, but the braking task experienced a slowdown of roughly 150 ms at an SOA of zero (simultaneous task onset), roughly 50 ms at an SOA of 150 ms, and no slowdown at larger SOAs. The model reproduces the classic PRP effect for this experiment because of the additional procedural steps for the choice task. Referring back to Figure 3.12, we see that the choice task involves three procedural steps. At an SOA of zero, all three procedural steps will likely interfere with the braking task, predicting a total slowdown of 150 ms (for three 50-ms procedural rule firings). At shorter SOAs, only one or two steps may interfere, resulting in a smaller slowdown, and at the longer SOAs, the choice-task steps terminate before the braking task begins, resulting in no interference or slowdown. The model's resulting PRP curves, as seen in the figure, closely match those of the human drivers.

The study of concurrent driving and choice tasks emphasizes two important aspects of multitasking. First, the experimental results demonstrate that cognitive interference can arise even in the performance of a well practiced, simple task, such as braking while driving. This suggests that braking, and driving more generally, are not as "automatic" as we sometimes believe—that is, cognition (specifically, the procedural resource) is actively engaged in even the basic underlying tasks of driving. Threaded cognition supports this notion in representing the skill of driving as an iterative loop of four procedural steps, which can experience interference just like any other procedural skill. Second, even when performing steering, braking, and choice tasks simultaneously, people are able to interleave the tasks very efficiently: The size of the effect of cognitive interference, roughly 150 ms in the zero-SOA condition, is still rather small compared to the overall reaction time of roughly one second. Threaded cognition also illustrates how people can achieve such efficiency; namely, by rapidly interleaving procedural steps and allowing the other resources (e.g., perception, motor movement) to run in parallel while another task's procedural steps are executed.

Driving and the Sentence-Span Task

In one early study of cognitive distraction, Alm and Nilsson (1995) asked experiment participants to drive in a car-following task in which the lead vehicle would brake suddenly, thus requiring the driver to brake in response. While driving, participants also occasionally performed a sentence-span task in which each trial was broken into two stages. In the first stage, drivers heard five sentences of the form, "X does Y"—for example, "The boy brushed his teeth" or "The train bought a newspaper"—and judged whether each sentence made sense, responding verbally to each sentence (e.g., "yes" and "no" for the two examples, respectively). At the same time, drivers had to memorize the final word in each sentence ("teeth" and "newspaper" in the two examples), and in the second stage the driver reported back the memorized list of five words. The sentence-span task is challenging even as a single task, and thus placed a substantial cognitive workload on drivers as they managed the driving task, along with the braking task in response to the lead vehicle.

We modeled the combined sentence-span and driving tasks (Salvucci & Taatgen, 2008) using our standard driver model, as well as a new model of the sentence-span task. In fact, the sentence-span model was itself developed as a combination of components from existing models. The representation of memorized items was based on the same block-and-item hierarchy discussed earlier for the phone-dialing task. The procedural process for rehearsing memorized items, and retrieving and reporting the items in order, was derived from a model by Lovett, Daily, and Reder (2000) of a closely related task. Finally, a very simple model of listening and responding to a sentence was included; the model simply encoded each word in sequence and generated a spoken response (without a detailed account of linguistic parsing and understanding, assuming that this would be done during sentence encoding).

A segment of the process timeline for the concurrent sentence-span and driving tasks is depicted in Figure 3.15. The sentence-span task thread itself performs two subtasks in parallel: rehearsal of a list item (i.e., one of the words being memorized) and encoding words of the sentence. For rehearsal, as can be seen from the long process block on the declarative resource, the retrieval process requires a time equivalent to many rule firings, and thus the thread launches a retrieval and then begins listening for a new word. At point (1) in the figure, the word is finally heard, and the model hears and encodes the word using the aural resource. It can then respond to the sentence just as the rehearsal retrieval completes execution. All the while, the driving thread interleaves its procedural steps with those of the sentence-span thread. It is clear in the figure how

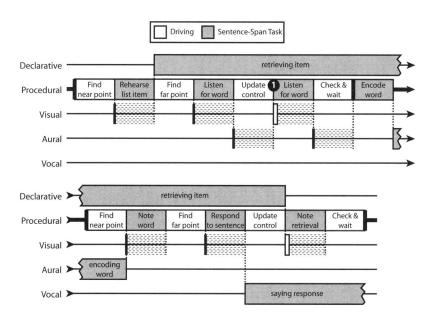

Figure 3.15. Sentence-span and driving task process timeline.

the cognitive workload of the sentence-span task produces significant interference between the tasks: the driving thread can only execute steps on every other production cycle, which results in a much longer interval (roughly twice as long as normal) between driving control updates.

The experimental results included two measures of driver performance: brake response time to the lead vehicle braking, and lateral deviation during the interval of the secondary task. Figure 3.16(a) graphs brake reaction time for the two conditions of driving only, and driving while performing the sentence-span task. Alm and Nilsson found that brake reaction time increased by 0.56 seconds while performing the secondary task. As is likely apparent in the process timeline in Figure 3.15, the model also experiences a slowdown in reaction time in the dual-task condition. The fact that control updates are much less frequent in this condition translates to a reduced ability to react to the changing driving environment. Although the model predicted faster overall brake response times than those exhibited by human drivers, the size of the effect predicted by the model is almost precisely the same as that found in the experiment, 0.54 seconds.

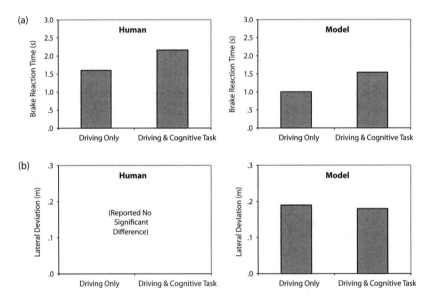

Figure 3.16. Sentence-span and driving task results for human drivers (Alm & Nilsson, 1995) and the model for (a) brake response time and (b) lateral deviation.

Figure 3.16(b) includes the results for lateral deviation. Although Alm and Nilsson did not report the specific values for lateral deviation, they did report that there was no statistically significant difference between the two conditions. The model also predicts effectively no difference (0.19 m for driving only versus 0.18 m for driving with the secondary task). The lack of effect for the model may seem surprising, given the strong effect for the other performance measure, brake response time. In fact, the measures relate to separate aspects of performance: brake response time is a very sensitive measure that can be affected by even small amounts of interference (as we have seen in the driving and choice task study), whereas lateral deviation is an aggregate measure over time that is filtered through the dynamics of the vehicle. Thus, although the driver model does not perform control updates as frequently in the presence of a secondary task, even less frequent but regular periodic updates suffice to maintain a reasonably central position on the roadway. The regularity of steering for the sentence-span task is more akin to the steady but small interference in voice dialing, which also did not significantly affect lateral deviation, as opposed to the lengthy and irregular interference in manual dialing, which produced large and significant effects.

Driving and Memory Rehearsal

While the sentence-span task is primarily a cognitive task, it still involves some amount of perceptual and motor interaction: listening to sentences and producing verbal responses. The effects of the integrated perceptual and motor behavior, whether they be large or small, become tangled with the cognitive effects of the task, and make it challenging to isolate the cognitive aspects in particular. To address this issue, Salvucci and Beltowska (2008) recently investigated the effects of memory rehearsal alone on driver performance. The experiment asked participants to study a list of numbers and then drive for a short time while mentally rehearsing the list. The experiment thus explored the driver-performance effects of a purely cognitive task, one that includes no perceptual or motor actions (during the driving segment). The task aims to simulate the many situations in which memory may be used repeatedly while driving—for instance, a driver trying to remember items needed at the grocery store, or directions along an unfamiliar route.

The structure of the experiment is depicted in Figure 3.17. Participants first memorized a list of 5 or 9 digits, presented one after another for

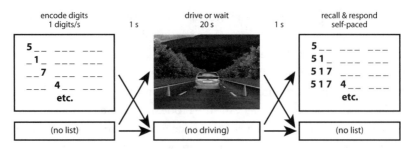

Figure 3.17. Structure of the memory rehearsal and driving experiment. From Salvucci & Beltowska (2008), Copyright 2008 Human Factors and Ergonomics Society. Reprinted with permission.

1 second each. They then drove for 20 seconds while rehearsing this list and, finally, after the driving segment concluded, they recalled and typed the digits in order. The driving task also incorporated a brake response task—braking when the lead vehicle's brake lights illuminated—thus providing two measures of driver performance, brake response time and lateral deviation (over the entire driving segment). The experiment included trials in which there was either no list or no driving, such that memory rehearsal and driving could be measured as a single task. Overall, the experiment included four conditions: Drive+Rehearse5 and Drive+Rehearse9, for driving while memorizing 5 or 9 digits (respectively); Drive-Only with no memorized list; and Recall9-Only with a 20-second waiting period replacing the driving task. There was no significant effect of driving on the participants' ability to recall (between the Drive+Rehearse9 and Recall9-Only conditions), and thus we focus below on the driving conditions, to evaluate how memory rehearsal affected driving performance.

Salvucci & Beltowska (2008) set out to model this combined task in terms of the three concurrent tasks of driving (steering), braking, and memory rehearsal. Figure 3.18(a) illustrates a segment of the process timeline in our initial attempt to represent the multitasking scenario. The rehearsal thread is interleaved with the driving thread, as we have seen in previous models. When the lead vehicle's brake lights illuminate at point (1), the braking thread detects the change and taps the brake. The total brake response time in this case is slowed down by the two procedural steps (one for rehearsal, one for driving) that interleave between the two steps of the braking thread.

The results for the human drivers and our initial model in terms of lateral deviation and brake response time are shown in Figure 3.19. For lateral deviation, the human drivers showed a statistically significant increase in deviation (albeit small in magnitude) when rehearsing both the 5- and 9-digit lists. The initial model (shown as X's in the figure) predicts the same effect due to the frequent cognitive interference brought about by the memory-rehearsal procedural steps. The initial model also correctly accounts for the fact that the 5- and 9-digit lists result in the same effect on lateral deviation, because the iterative rehearsal process occupies the same amount of cognitive processing regardless of list size (simply retrieving again and again). For brake response time, the picture is less clear. The human drivers exhibit a 44 ms slowdown in brake response time for 9-digit rehearsal, but no slowdown whatsoever for 5-digit rehearsal. The initial model correctly predicts the effect for 9-digit rehearsal but incorrectly predicts that 5-digit rehearsal leads to the same interference effect.

This one data point—the lack of brake response effect for the Drive+Rehearse5 condition—led us to rethink how drivers notice and respond to the illumination of the lead vehicle's brake lights. The task instructions for the experiment asked that drivers tap their brake as soon as possible after seeing the lit brake lights. Given these instructions, it seems likely that participants encoded these instructions into their behaviors for driving and rehearsal as well, delaying driving or rehearsal when the brake lights are illuminated. In ACT-R terms, a visual chunk representing the brake lights appears in the visual buffer upon illumination, and thus the driving and rehearsal threads can simply include the constraint that there be no brake-light chunk in the visual buffer. One other interesting aspect of the task might affect driver's behavior, namely the difficulty of memorizing the 9-digit list. Although not in the task instructions, drivers would quickly note that the 9-digit list takes significantly more effort than the 5-digit list, and thus might relax the above brake-light constraint to rehearse whenever possible in the 9-digit condition. We incorporated both of these ideas into a revised model and reran the above simulations. (Note that the revised model does not perform any metacognitive analysis of the difficulty of the two rehearsal conditions, but simply omits the braking constraint for the 9-digit rehearsal model.)

The revised model's process timelines in the 5-digit and 9-digit conditions are included in Figure 3.18. In the 5-digit condition, the model performs both braking steps immediately, because the driving and

(a) Initial Model

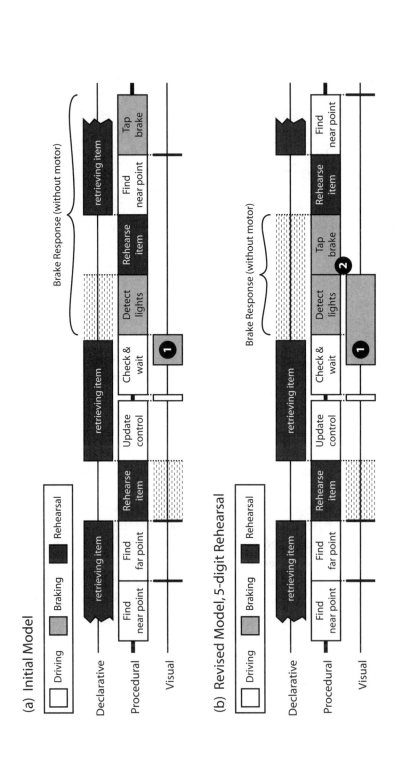

(b) Revised Model, 5-digit Rehearsal

(c) Revised Model, 9-digit Rehearsal

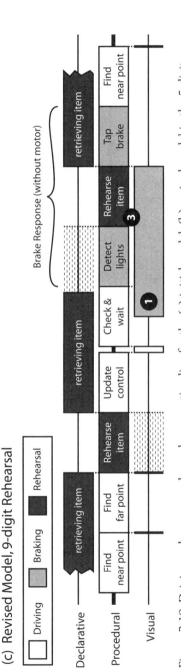

Figure 3.18. Driving and memory rehearsal process timeline for the (a) initial model, (b) revised model in the 5-digit rehearsal condition, and (c) revised model in the 9-digit rehearsal condition.

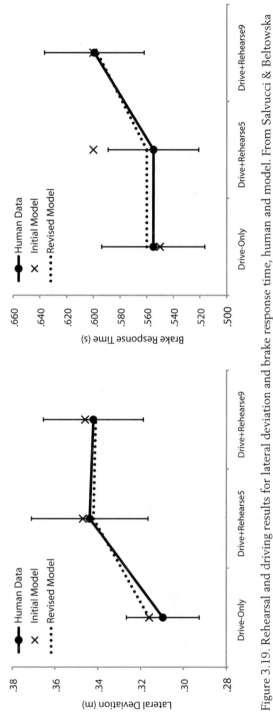

Figure 3.19. Rehearsal and driving results for lateral deviation and brake response time, human and model. From Salvucci & Beltowska (2008), Copyright 2008 Human Factors and Ergonomics Society. Reprinted with permission.

rehearsal threads note the illuminated brake lights in the visual buffer and delay execution until the visual buffer is cleared at point (2). In the 9-digit condition, the rehearsal thread ignores the brake-light constraint at point (3) in its attempt to run as fast as possible to ensure successful retrieval of the difficult list. Thus, one rehearsal step interleaves between the two braking steps, resulting in a 37 ms increase in brake response time. (The increase is less than the 50 ms production firing time because the rehearsal step may not fall between the braking steps on every trial.) The resulting quantitative results are included in Figure 3.19; the model maintains a close-fitting account of lateral deviation, and now also accounts for the brake response time results.

Even this revised account is only partially satisfying, given the need for different assumptions in the 5-digit and 9-digit conditions. Nevertheless, even with the exception of the one troublesome data point (5-digit rehearsal brake response effect), the model generated a very good fit to human performance—with an excellent prediction of the subtle but statistically significant interference with respect to lateral deviation and brake response time.

Research Connections

There has been a wide variety of research efforts related to our work here, first and foremost the body of experimental literature that forms the bedrock upon which theories of driver behavior are developed. From classic early studies of driver attention (Brown, Tickner, & Simmonds, 1969; Senders et al., 1967) to more recent studies focused on driver distraction (Alm & Nilsson, 1994, 1995; Brookhuis, De Vries, & De Waard, 1991; Drews, Pasupathi, & Strayer, 2008; Hancock, Lesch, & Simmons, 2003; Horrey & Lesch, 2009; Lee et al., 2002; Lee, Hoffmann, & Hayes, 2004; McKnight & McKnight, 1993; Reed & Green, 1999; Strayer & Drews, 2004), we now have an assortment of empirical phenomena with which to evaluate our theories of how people drive (see also Groeger, 2000), and how their attention can be divided between driving and in-vehicle secondary tasks (Horrey, Wickens, & Consalus, 2006).

The research efforts most closely related to our own are those that have aimed to derive mathematical, computational, or other types of formal models to describe and predict driver behavior and performance. Some research has focused on developing control-theoretic models of the driver–vehicle system (Brackstone & MacDonald, 1999; Donges, 1978; Godthelp, 1986; Hess & Modjtahedzadeh, 1990; McRuer et al., 1977). These approaches provide rigorous formulations of driver control problems, but ignore the fact that driving typically receives intermittent (not continuous) attention, and that such models must be centered on perceptual variables that are readily available to the driver (Boer, 1999). Other research has characterized driving in terms of basic perception and action (Fajen & Warren, 2003; Wilkie & Wann, 2003), which addresses the desire for more perceptually salient variables, but still formulates driving as continuous control, making it difficult to place in a multitasking context.

To address these concerns, several efforts have aimed to create integrated models of driver behavior that incorporate cognitive, perceptual, and motor capabilities and limitations into a single, formal model. Levison and Cramer (1995) developed the first such model, combining optimal control and cognitive information-processing in a single model. The original ACT-R driver model was developed soon after (Salvucci, Boer, & Liu, 2001), based on the same integrating principles but taking advantage of the ACT-R cognitive architecture as the unifying framework for development. This model sparked the evolution of the steering control law (Salvucci & Gray, 2004) and driver model (Salvucci, 2006) used throughout this chapter. Closely related work includes Aasman's (1995) model of intersection negotiation, developed in the Soar cognitive architecture, and Liu, Feyen, and Tsimhoni's (2006) integrated driver model, developed in the QN-MHP architecture. Ritter, Van Rooy, St. Amant, and Simpson (2006) also created a model of driving guided by perceptual mechanisms that operate directly on the screen's pixel representation of a driving simulation.

An integrated modeling approach (see Salvucci, 2001a; Gray, 2007) is useful not only for integrating the various skills of driving into a more complete driver model, but also for integrating the driver model itself with models of secondary-task behavior. We have emphasized this point throughout the chapter, drawing on our own work in this direction (Salvucci, 2001a; Salvucci & Macuga, 2002; Salvucci, 2005; Salvucci & Taatgen, 2008). Wu and Liu (2007) have similarly used the QN-MHP driver model for predicting driver distraction and workload. And, in a different modeling approach not dependent on computer simulations, recent work by Pettitt, Burnett, and Stevens (2007) extended the Keystroke Level Model (Card, Moran, & Newell, 1980, 1983) to provide preliminary predictions of driver attention-based measures.

Other approaches to accounting for driver multitasking behavior do not use cognitive models at all (at least in the same sense as we use them here), but rather attempt to quantify a secondary task's demands on perceptual, motor, and cognitive processes, and reconcile these demands with those of driving to predict potential task interference. The IVIS DEMAnD system (Hankey et al., 2000) provides a graphical user interface in which a user can specify the secondary task from a built-in library, or from its component resource demands; its library of tasks contains common tasks (e.g., tuning a radio, adjusting power windows), along with relevant parameters taken from the research literature. The resulting output shows expected measures of behavior (e.g., task completion time, single glance time) from which the user can better gauge its potential for interference with driving. As a more general methodology, Wickens' (2002a, 2008) multiple resource theory, given a specification of resource demands for two or more tasks, allows for computation of a conflict matrix that quantifies the level of interference between the tasks in a multitasking scenario.

The Big Picture

As we did in the previous chapter, let us revisit our initial questions and explore how threaded cognition might help to provide answers for these questions. What skills are involved in the basic driving task? This question relates not so much to threaded cognition, but to the driver model that underlies much of our work on driver multitasking. The driver model's ability to capture a number of aspects of driver performance (in single- and dual-task scenarios) offers support for the core concepts of the model—namely, that steering relies on both near and far regions of the roadway, and that a straightforward control law based on near and far points nicely meshes with a number of phenomena related to driving and control. One of the most unique aspects of our driver model is its account of cognitive processing; namely, that basic driving (steering and speed control) requires a rapidly executing loop of procedural steps that encode the visual environment and incrementally update steering and acceleration controls. Importantly, although driving often feels effortless to many of us, this model suggests that driving is not as automatic as one might think; in fact, it imposes a heavy procedural workload on cognition that, especially in difficult driving conditions, leaves little processing capacity available for other tasks.

Given this account of basic driving, what secondary tasks would interfere with the driving task? The heavy cognitive workload of driving suggests that any secondary task has the potential to affect driver behavior: Any concurrent task would necessarily involve procedural steps and thus, whether large or small, create additional cognitive workload. At the same time, not all secondary tasks are created equal, and we would expect some tasks to interfere with driving more than others. Not surprisingly, tasks involving significant visual demand have the greatest potential for negative effects on driver performance, as we saw for manual cell phone dialing (which assumed visual guidance of button presses). These effects seem to pervade a host of performance measures, including lateral deviation and velocity as well as brake response time to an external event. But even primarily cognitive tasks with little perceptual-motor interaction (like conversation) can result in performance effects, which extend, perhaps most surprisingly, to even "purely" cognitive tasks with no perceptual-motor interaction (like memory rehearsal). However, the effects of more cognitive tasks are much smaller in magnitude than effects of visual tasks, and may require more sensitive measures of performance (e.g., brake response time) to be observed (as opposed to, say, lateral deviation).

What might these results tell us about the design of in-vehicle devices and driver safety more generally? There are certainly interesting nuggets of guidance that we might extract from a more global view of threaded cognition, along with the driver model. For instance, the majority of legislative efforts to curb phone use while driving have focused on the issue of whether the driver is holding the phone in hand ("handheld" use) or has the phone mounted in a stationary place inside the vehicle ("hands-free" use). Unfortunately, such legislation seems to be misguided. Our theory agrees with recent findings (Strayer & Johnston, 2001; Horrey & Wickens, 2006) that there are no significant performance differences between handheld and hands-free phone use, since the visual and cognitive requirements are effectively identical. Our hope is that, in more cases such as this one, threaded cognition and the driver model can help to better understand potential sources of interference, and determine which particular aspects of the task might be most important with respect to negative effects on performance.

At the same time, we should be cautious in generalizing such research results to the amazingly complex realm of human driver behavior. Our work on driving in this chapter has focused on the basic vehicle-control aspects of driving, but has largely ignored the many more complex situations that drivers must deal with (e.g., intersections, highway merging, navigation, etc.). These situations often involve not only additional cognitive processing for decision making and problem solving, but also additional task-relevant problem representations that must be stored and retrieved as stepping stones for these higher-level cognitive processes (e.g., partial routes while planning a final route to a destination). The next two chapters will address how people represent such information, and how task interruptions may affect their ability to maintain and recall the information when suspending and resuming tasks.

It is also important to recognize that statistically significant effects are not necessarily significant in a practical sense. Is an additional lateral deviation of 6 inches when dialing a phone (Salvucci, 2001a) significant in everyday driving? What about a half-second increase in brake response time for a cognitive task (Alm & Nilsson, 1995)? What about a 50-millisecond increase in brake response time for memory rehearsal of a long list (Salvucci & Beltowska, 2008)? One might attempt a comprehensive analysis of such effects in a large-scale virtual simulation (e.g., Shinar, Rotenberg, & Cohen, 1997). A more simplistic answer, however, is that the implications of these effects depend on many complex factors. The important benefit of our approach, however, is that these computational models can make these types of quantitative predictions and allow transportation experts to determine whether they fall within acceptable safety boundaries.

Arguably the most significant limitation of our current models is the lack of metacognition—the ability to reason about one's own performance and adapt behavior accordingly. For instance, it has been noted (e.g., Greenberg et al., 2003) that, when faced with a distracting secondary task, drivers sometimes slow down and back away from a lead vehicle; presumably drivers are aware that their attention may be compromised during the task and compensate by giving themselves a larger margin for error. As another example, today's vehicles incorporate increasingly complex automation to assist the driver with basic tasks (e.g., antilock brakes, intelligent cruise control); drivers in turn must learn to understand this automation and adapt their driving behavior accordingly (Stanton & Young, 1998; see also Lee & Moray, 1994; Parasuraman, Sheridan, & Wickens, 2000; Sheridan, 1970, 1992). Cognitive models that account for metacognitive processes like these have been slow to develop, but are needed to better account for this type of adaptation to distracting situations. Under our theory, metacognitive processes would be represented by the same procedural steps as normal task processes, and thus would similarly contend for resources—in other words, metacognition while performing a task could be thought of as multitasking in itself, and would require threaded interleaving like all other task processes. As we better understand metacognitive processes in general, and those for driver behavior in particular, threaded cognition should help to understand how these processes might interact with the primary component tasks.

4

Sequential Multitasking, Problem State, and Task Suspension and Resumption

Threaded cognition, as formulated to this point, describes how people perform concurrent multitasking, rapidly interleaving task threads to achieve efficient, balanced execution of multiple tasks. On the other end of the multitasking continuum, however, sequential multitasking involves stopping one task and starting another, focusing on one particular task for seconds, minutes, or hours on end. How do people switch focus from one task to the next? Are people slower at tasks when switching from another task? How do people manage task interruptions from the outside world, and how do they manage their own self-imposed interruptions? And, ultimately, how does task switching during sequential multitasking relate back to the rapid interleaving of tasks described by threaded cognition for concurrent multitasking? This chapter explores some answers to these questions.

From Concurrent to Sequential Multitasking

Thus far in our study of multitasking, we have focused on the more concurrent end of the multitasking continuum; namely, tasks that involve switching tasks roughly every second, or even more frequently. One way to characterize points along this continuum is in terms of how much one task interferes with the others, because task interference is related to

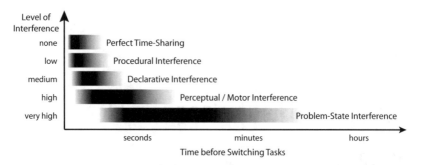

Figure 4.1. Levels of multitasking interference and approximate corresponding ranges along the multitasking continuum.

position along the continuum. In general, the more interference, the longer the time period between task switches. Figure 4.1 shows the range of where typical tasks might lie along the continuum as a function of the level of interference between tasks. At one extreme, perfect time-sharing, as we have seen for dual-choice tasks in Chapter 2, involves no interference between tasks, and thus would typically result in subsecond time between task switches. If there is interference on the procedural resource, as seen for driving combined with a choice or memory-rehearsal task in Chapter 3, the occasional procedural conflicts result in small delays of up to 50 ms in one or both tasks. These small delays can result in similarly small, but statistically significant, effects on task performance—for instance, the roughly 50 ms delay in brake response when memorizing a long list of numbers.

Moving rightward along the continuum in Figure 4.1, interference between major cognitive, perceptual, and motor resources can result in longer lags between task switches. When interference arises for perceptual and/or motor resources, the effects on performance are much larger than for procedural interference. For example, when driving while dialing, the visual resource could remain occupied by the dialing task for one second or more, reducing performance in the driving task. The declarative memory resource, mentioned briefly in Chapter 2, can also be a significant source of interference when two or more tasks are frequently accessing memory for information. In Chapters 6 and 7, we will look closely at declarative interference in the context of learning, because much of learning while multitasking can be attributed to the dropping-out of memory retrievals as skill knowledge transforms from memorized instructions to procedural steps.

As it turns out, there is a major class of resource interference that we have not yet addressed; namely, interference that arises due to *problem state*. In essence, problem state is the temporary information required during the execution of task. Problem state is especially important for understanding multitasking, because problem-state interference can often result in delays lasting several seconds to several minutes (or more). The next section will further explore this idea of problem state, and its effects on multitasking. In addition, there are times when interference becomes so great that a person suspends a task—that is, puts a task on hold and saves it for some later time. The end result is that multitasking becomes more sequential, with larger chunks of one task being interleaved among chunks of other tasks, while memory processing needed to rehearse task information invokes a level of concurrent multitasking in its own right (i.e., rehearsing suspended tasks while performing other active tasks). The following section will build on our understanding of problem state to examine this process of task suspension and resumption, and its relationship to sequential multitasking.

Problem State: An Additional Cognitive Resource

The mind's resources described to this point have all been processing resources that embody some cognitive, perceptual, or motor process, such as recalling a memorized fact, looking at an object, or moving a finger to a location. In fact, the mind also contains another type of resource: a problem state resource that keeps track of task-related information that is not readily available in the external environment. For example, consider a student solving a math problem presented as "3+4". The student visually encodes the first addend (3), then encodes the operator (+) while remembering the addend, and then encodes the second addend (4) while remembering the other two components. In this case, the problem state is the temporary information acquired during the encoding process, which is gradually filled in and allows the student finally to recall the correct answer to the problem.

Over the past decade, Anderson and colleagues (Anderson, 2007; Anderson et al., 2004; Qin et al., 2003) have used neuroimaging data to identify problem state as a distinct cognitive resource in the ACT-R theory. Using task domains based on solving algebra problems and variants thereof, they found that problem-state information was separate from information that directed the mind to the current goal—in other words, what a person is doing (the goal) and the information for doing it (the problem state) are maintained in distinct areas of the brain. This distinction has direct implications under our theory: cognition only allows multiple goals to be active, not multiple problem states, and thus only one task thread can utilize the problem state resource at a given time. Thus, the problem state itself emerges as another important source of cognitive interference.

Borst, Taatgen and van Rijn (2010) recently tested this idea directly in an experiment that manipulated problem state in a dual-task setting. The experiment included two tasks (subtraction and text entry), each of which was presented in one condition that required a problem state (e.g., requiring borrowing in the subtraction task) and one that did not. Borst et al. found that when both tasks required a problem state, participants exhibited significantly more interference between tasks than would be predicted based solely on task difficulty. Their results support the idea that only a single task thread can use the problem state resource, and that significant interference arises when more than one thread requires the resource. Later in the chapter, we will revisit the Borst et al. experiment and present a theoretical account of their results, based on the more general account of task suspension and resumption in the next section.

The problem state resource is thus an additional resource to utilize in our analysis of multitasking, and in fact is often a critical resource for sequential multitasking, as we describe shortly. We can also use the term *problem state* more generally to refer to the information associated with performing a task, and, in this sense, the complexity of the problem state can vary greatly among task domains. The simple addition example seen earlier has a simple problem state represented as a single declarative chunk, namely one that includes the two addends "3" and "4" and the operator "+". On the other extreme, problem state may include a very complex mental context—a linked structure of facts and concepts that would best be represented as a network of declarative knowledge relevant to the current "working sphere" (Mark, Gonzalez, & Harris, 2005; Gonzalez & Mark, 2004). For instance, consider a student working on a final term paper for a college course. The student, having studied a number of related readings and fleshed out the conceptual connections among the readings with respect to the paper topic, would need to maintain (probably with the help of notes, an outline, etc.) this complex structure throughout the writing of the term paper. In ACT-R terms, a complex problem state would exist as a network of chunks in declarative memory, and would be activated piecemeal during processing. A single chunk of information would be placed into the problem state resource buffer for processing, and, in time, would be substituted with a newly retrieved chunk associated with the next step in processing.

It is also worth noting that many tasks do not need to maintain any problem state at all. Some tasks (such as the basic tracking task described in Chapter 2) are entirely reactive: they entail simply encoding some aspect of the environment (e.g., the position of the moving target in tracking) and generating an action in response to this information (e.g., moving the mouse to the target). Other tasks may utilize the problem state resource, but not need to maintain the information therein. For example, when a dynamic task such as game playing or driving is suspended, problem-state information may not need to be maintained because it may become obsolete immediately, and needs to be regenerated when the task is resumed. Just as for the other resources, threaded cognition predicts that interference only arises when the problem state resource is needed by two or more tasks, and thus tasks that do not require problem-state information will not experience interference on the problem state resource.

Task Suspension and Resumption

The many possible sources of interference during multitasking—including procedural, declarative, perceptual, motor, problem state—all have the potential to slow down one or more active concurrent task threads. At times, this interference can reach the point at which one task cannot make adequate progress. The person can then suspend one or more threads by pausing its active processing until a later time, when it can resume and proceed with less interference. Consider a situation in which a computer user, busy filling in a spreadsheet, answers the phone and begins talking. The two tasks have no perceptual–motor conflicts (visual–motor resources for the spreadsheet task, aural–vocal for the phone conversation), and thus if neither the spreadsheet nor conversation task is mentally taxing, the user may continue with both tasks concurrently. For many situations, however, this would be difficult: Most spreadsheets and conversations would require less-than-trivial cognitive resources (declarative, procedural, problem state) and we might expect moderate to heavy contention for these resources. Thus, more often than not, the user would suspend the spreadsheet task while talking on the phone, and resume the task after the phone call.

The threaded cognition account of suspending and resuming a task centers on saving and restoring the task's problem state. When a task is suspended, the task's thread remains active to maintain awareness of the task. Critically, this awareness allows for background processing of the suspended task when needed or desired. For example, many of us have had the experience of coming up with an idea while doing an unrelated task—such as a college student who suddenly realizes the solution to a physics problem while walking to class. In this case, even when a suspended task cannot be actively performed (e.g., the college student cannot write on paper while walking), the mind can continue to process information related to the suspended task. In this section, we focus on one very important background process; namely, the rehearsal of problem-state information to enable and/or facilitate eventual resumption of a suspended task.

The precise nature of the suspension and resumption process depends on at least two factors: the duration of the task suspension, and the complexity of the problem state (both the problem state resource and declarative network). When task suspension lasts a short time, and/or the problem state has a low complexity, memory processes are sufficient for maintaining problem state. The person can memorize the problem state upon suspension, and then recall it upon resumption. When a task suspension lasts a longer time, and/or the problem state has a high complexity, memory may be too unreliable or it may be altogether infeasible to maintain the problem state. In this case, a person would likely have to reconstruct the suspended task—for example, looking at the spreadsheet after hanging up the phone, finding the cursor, checking the lines around the cursor, etc., all in an attempt to resume the spreadsheet task. Figure 4.2 represents this two-dimensional continuum with gray areas in the middle indicating that, between the extremes, some combinations of suspension duration and problem-state complexity may involve a combination of memory and reconstruction processes.

For our account of memory-based task suspension and resumption, we lean heavily on two bodies of research. First, the ACT-R theory (Anderson et al., 2004; Anderson, 2007), which serves as the core foundation for threaded cognition's multitasking resources and computational models, also provides a rigorous account of human memory that will be required

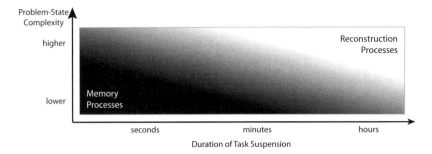

Figure 4.2. The relationship between problem-state complexity and dependence on memory or reconstruction processes for task resumption.

for quantitative predictions of suspension and resumption behaviors (such as timing and errors). Second, the recently developed Memory for Goals theory (Altmann & Trafton, 2002) embeds this general ACT-R theory into a more specific theory of the memory processes involved in task suspension and resumption. We place both these components in the context of our account of problem state, and derive a computational process model for task suspension and resumption that aims to specify the mechanisms by which people suspend and resume tasks to achieve sequential multitasking.

The remainder of this chapter lays out this account of memory-based task suspension and resumption, focusing on shorter task suspensions. In the next chapter, we will revisit the idea of reconstructing problem state in the context of more realistic tasks and longer task interruptions.

The ACT-R Theory of Memory

The ACT-R theory of memory (see Anderson, 2007) begins with a representation of memory as a linked network of declarative facts, as discussed in Chapter 2. Figure 4.3 illustrates an example of how the declarative chunks representing the numbers 3, 4, and 7 are linked to the chunk representing $3+4=7$. Given this representation, ACT-R defines a concept of activation that indicates how easily a particular chunk can be retrieved. Activation arises from two sources: base-level activation, a measure of a chunk's inherent likelihood of being recalled; and strengths of association, a measure of how the current environment context facilitates cueing of the particular chunk. Both sources of activation play an important

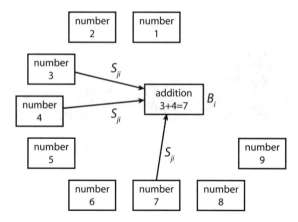

Figure 4.3. A sample network of ACT-R memory chunks showing associations for the information representing '3+4=7'.

role in memory for goals theory, and especially its relationship to task interruption.

A chunk's base-level activation (B_i) represents how easily or success-fully that chunk can be retrieved. Base-level activation changes with prac-tice, such that, for example, frequent uses of a chunk (e.g., repeatedly greeting a new friend by name) increase the chunk's activation and make it increasingly likely that the chunk can be recalled. Figure 4.4(a) shows a sample activation timeline for a newly learned chunk, as a simple ACT-R model rehearses the chunk (i.e., retrieves it from memory) every 3 sec-onds. Each peak of the activation timeline corresponds to a single rehearsal retrieval—the retrieval temporarily boosts activation for a short time, after which activation again begins to decay. However, after repeated rehearsals, two things happen: overall activation grows, and activation decays less quickly after a rehearsal. Figure 4.4(b) shows how retrieval time is related to activation: as activation grows, the chunk can be retrieved in a shorter amount of time. Similarly, the probability of successfully retrieving the chunk increases with increasing activation, as illustrated in Figure 4.4(c). The spacing of retrievals need not be regular as in this example; the theory also accounts for various spacing effects that can arise in laboratory and applied domains (Pavlik & Anderson, 2005).

A chunk's strengths of association represent how the current context may cue the chunk, and potentially boost its activation and speed up retrieval. The "current context" can mean any information in the current cognitive and perceptual environment that may cue this information; in ACT-R terms, the context is defined as the contents of the various buffers,

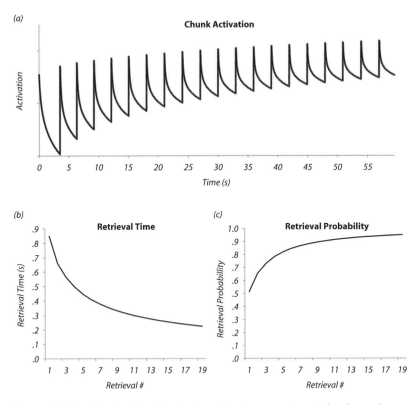

Figure 4.4. Graphs showing (a) chunk activation over time with rehearsals every 3 seconds, and (b) retrieval time and (c) retrieval probability for each rehearsal retrieval.

including cognitive (especially problem state) and perceptual (visual and aural). For example, in Figure 4.3, the number chunks 3, 4, and 7 each have a strength of association (S_{ji}) to the linked chunk 3+4=7. If the person has just encoded the 3 and the 4, these numbers would appear in the problem-state buffer and would boost activation of the 3+4=7 chunk, helping the memory system retrieve this chunk (and speeding up the retrieval time). The presence of 3 and/or 4 in the visual buffer would similarly boost activation. This type of cueing has been found to account well for how people recall information in the presence of both correct and incorrect cues. For example, the chunks 3 and 4 would not boost the chunk 1+5=6, but would provide a small boost for 3+5=8 (because of the 3); indeed, children learning addition facts incorrectly retrieve such related addition facts more often than they retrieve addition facts with no common numbers (Siegler & Shrager, 1984).

Table 4.1.   Primary ACT-R memory equations

Name	Equation
Activation equation	$A_i = B_i + \sum\limits_{j \in C} W_j S_{ji}$
Base-level learning equation	$B_i = \ln\left(\sum\limits_k t_k^{-d}\right)$
Retrieval time equation	$Time = Fe^{-A_i}$
Retrieval probability equation	$Prob = 1/\left(1 + e^{-(A_i - \tau)/s}\right)$

(Anderson, 2007)

While the high-level description above may suffice as an introduction to memory for goals theory, it is important to note that the ACT-R computational framework includes a set of equations that govern the above phenomena; thus, any model developed in the framework generates specific predictions of memory learning and retrieval—as will be critical for our upcoming models of task suspension and resumption. The three primary equations that embody ACT-R memory theory are shown in Table 4.1. The activation equation shows how activation is a sum of the base-level component and the strengths of association, where each strength is weighted by a factor (W_j) related to the number of chunks in the context (C). The base-level learning equation shows how individual retrievals that occur at a time before the current time (t_k) decay by a negative exponential factor (–d) and are summed to produce the current base-level activation (B_i). The retrieval time equation shows how the time needed to retrieve a chunk can be computed by the exponential of the negated activation (where F=1 in general). Finally, the retrieval probability equation shows the probability of recalling a particular chunk based on a given threshold (τ) and noise value (s). Further details can be found in Anderson (2007).

Memory and Problem State

Given the ACT-R formulation of human memory, Altmann and Trafton (2002) developed a theory that describes how memory processes are critical to suspending and resuming tasks. Their theory, called *memory for goals*, posits that task suspension and resumption can be broken down into the core processes of rehearsal (or strengthening) and recall. First, when a task is suspended, its context is stored in memory and rehearsed to provide a boost in the context's activation in memory. Second, when a task is resumed, the old context is recalled from memory and restored, such that the suspended task can continue from the point where it left off. The recall process may also be facilitated by environmental cues that relate to the suspended task and help to activate its associated context.

The threaded cognition interpretation of this theory is that the task context is, in fact, the problem state, and that these memory processes act in service of saving the problem state (task suspension) and restoring it (task resumption). Consider our earlier example of the computer user performing a spreadsheet task, who is interrupted by the ringing phone. When the user suspends the spreadsheet task, she takes the current problem state, stores it into memory, and then strengthens it by means of rehearsal. The phone conversation would then involve its own problem state, thus utilizing the problem state resource for its own purposes. When the phone conversation ends, the user must recall the spreadsheet-task problem state and restore it in the problem state resource, with environmental cues (the open spreadsheet application, related papers on the desk, etc.) potentially facilitating recall.

Combining Altmann and Trafton's theory with the detailed predictions of ACT-R memory theory, we can better understand the mechanisms of the rehearsal and recall processes as part of suspension and resumption. Rehearsal is represented simply as repeated retrievals of the problem-state chunk, and each individual retrieval provides a small boost in activation as dictated by base-level learning equation in Table 4.1. Figure 4.5 shows two sample base-level activation timelines representing (a) two rehearsal retrievals and (b) six rehearsal retrievals. The peaks of the timelines represent the boosts in activation from individual retrievals, and the baseline of the graph (where activation is zero) indicates the approximate threshold below which the memory can no longer be retrieved. For two retrievals, activation remains above threshold for approximately 10 seconds, whereas for six retrievals, activation remains above threshold for 45 seconds (beyond the time range shown). In the latter case, the six retrievals can be performed (assuming no other interference) in only 1.4 seconds; thus, a memory can be maintained for a great deal more time with only a small additional cost in rehearsal time.

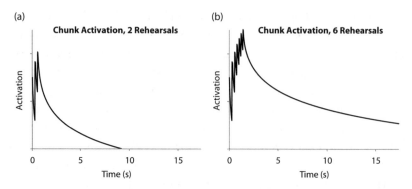

Figure 4.5. Activation timelines for (a) two rehearsals and (b) six rehearsals. The spikes in the graphs correspond to boosts of activation that come from a rehearsal retrieval; the declines in the graphs correspond to decay over time.

The recall process—more specifically, the success and timing of recall—is largely a function of the problem state's activation at that time. As detailed in the activation equation in Table 4.1, the total activation is the sum of two quantities: the base-level activation (illustrated in Figure 4.5), and the spreading activation from related information that may be present in the ACT-R resource buffers (e.g., a visual cue in the visual buffer). The total activation can then be used to compute the retrieval probability and time (see Table 4.1): the higher the activation, the more likely the retrieval will successfully recall the correct problem-state information, and the lower the total retrieval time. Thus, more rehearsal and/or helpful cueing of the problem state will generally lead to faster task resumption, whereas less rehearsal and/or longer task suspension periods will lead to slower (or even unsuccessful) task resumption.

A Threaded Account of Task Suspension and Resumption

Considering the above relationship among task suspension, memory, and problem state, we have the beginnings of a working computational model of suspension and resumption. However, we are still missing a precise process model—a step-by-step account of behavior throughout the suspension and resumption process. Altmann and Trafton (2002) put forth an initial ACT-R model as a proof-of-concept process model. Below, we develop our own process model account using threaded cognition, which

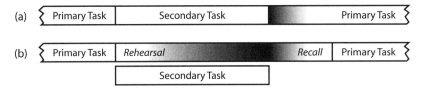

Figure 4.6. A depiction of task stages over time in (a) a standard interpretation of task suspension and resumption, and (b) a threaded interpretation in which rehearsal of primary-task problem state occurs in parallel with the secondary task.

offers a new conceptualization of memory for goals, using task threads, and provides new predictions about the interference between goal-rehearsal processes and concurrent tasks.

A standard depiction of task suspension and resumption is shown in Figure 4.6(a), where a person suspends a primary task, performs a secondary task, then resumes the primary task. The final resumption typically involves a resumption lag in which the person cannot immediately resume the task, but rather spends some time (shown as a gradient) to recover the previous place in the task execution. A different interpretation based on threaded cognition and Altmann and Trafton's (2002) work is shown in Figure 4.6(b). When the primary task is suspended, the primary-task thread begins to rehearse this task's problem state, while the secondary task begins as a separate thread. The primary task rehearsal may continue or, when rehearsal is no longer needed, pause processing until resumption is possible. After the secondary task is finished, the primary-task thread initiates recall of the problem state and then resumes execution of the primary task. An important aspect of this threaded interpretation is that, for at least some time, rehearsal and the secondary task are active at the same time, and thus may experience some of the same types of interference we have analyzed in other concurrent tasks.

The process timelines for problem-state rehearsal and recall are shown in Figure 4.7. Rehearsal of the problem state is very straightforward; namely, a simple repetition of memory retrievals. Recall of the problem state is similarly straightforward, with a single retrieval to recall the state information, and an additional step of 200 ms (Anderson, 2007) to restore the problem state (placing the retrieved problem state into the problem state resource buffer). This recall step could be triggered by the completion of the interruption itself—after completion, the person asks herself,

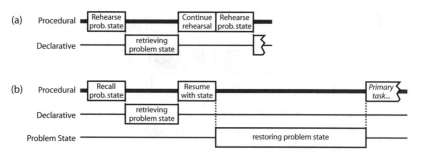

Figure 4.7. Process timelines for (a) problem-state rehearsal and (b) problem-state recall.

"What was I doing?" and initiates the retrieval. (The same process would be invoked for subgoals related to the primary task, as discussed by Altmann & Trafton, 2002.) The retrieval could also be triggered by environmental cues, such as the reappearance of the primary task after interruption (e.g., the reappearance of a primary-task computer application after dismissal of a chat window).

Two important predictions arise from this threaded account of task suspension and resumption, both concerning the interaction between the secondary task and the concurrent primary-task thread that is performing problem-state rehearsal. First, the rehearsal task (like any task) requires occasional procedural steps to initiate retrievals. Thus, it is possible that these procedural steps will produce interference with the secondary task; as we have noted earlier, procedural interference is often not large, but it can indeed produce significant effects on behavior for certain secondary tasks (as it did for driving in Chapter 3). Second, the rehearsal task is a memory-intensive task, with repeated use of the declarative memory resource. As a consequence, when the concurrent secondary task also requires declarative memory, we would expect both tasks to experience interference and likely a decrement in performance.

Illustrative Models

The above account provides a process model of task suspension and resumption, including an account of problem-state rehearsal and recall, and an overarching representation using threads for these processes as well as the primary and secondary tasks. We now apply this process model to two illustrative task domains, to demonstrate how the model accounts for several aspects of sequential multitasking behavior. At the same time, these modeling studies help us to explore some open issues with the above account. The first study focuses on how contention for the problem state resource can result in interference between two tasks that require a problem state. The second study focuses on when exactly rehearsal takes place, while also testing the prediction that memory rehearsal of the problem state can itself create observable effects on performance of the secondary task.

Problem-State Interference in Rapid Sequential Multitasking

As outlined earlier, Borst, Taatgen and van Rijn (2010) performed an experiment to better understand the relationship between problem state and multitasking. The experiment was aimed at testing two assumptions that can be derived from threaded cognition, but are not supported by more general working memory accounts: that different threads cannot share the problem state resource, and that interference will occur when two or more threads require maintenance of a problem state. The neuroimaging evidence for a problem state (Anderson, 2007; Anderson et al., 2004) suggests that this resource can be well represented as a separate cognitive resource, and threaded cognition's resource seriality would imply that the problem state can only be used by a single thread at a given time. In turn, when two or more threads each require a distinct problem state, threaded cognition predicts that interference will arise, and that usage of the problem state resource needs to be shared between task threads.

In the experiment, participants had to alternate between two tasks. The two tasks are a multicolumn subtraction task and a text-typing task, illustrated in Figure 4.8. In the subtraction task, participants had to enter numbers on the keyboard to solve the 10-column subtraction problem from right to left. In the typing task, a 10-letter word or string of letters had to be entered by clicking on the letter keys with the mouse. Participants had to alternate between the tasks, doing one column in the subtraction task, then one letter in the typing task, and so on until all 10 columns and letters were done.

Each task had two variants: a hard version that required maintenance of a problem state, and an easy version that did not. For the subtraction task, the easy version never required borrowing, whereas the hard version included six out of ten columns that required borrowing. If borrowing was not necessary, no problem state had to be maintained, because

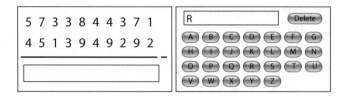

Figure 4.8. Display from the Borst et al. (2010) experiment. This example shows the hard subtraction task that requires a problem state (for borrowing) and the typing task that does not (with the letter to be typed shown in the text box).

reading the numbers in the column was sufficient to determine the answer; however, if there was a possibility of borrowing, the borrowing status had to be maintained between columns. For the typing task, the easy version simply showed the next letter to be typed, whereas the hard version showed a 10-letter word only at the beginning of each trial, forcing participants to keep track of the word and the position within the word. Experiment participants each performed the hard and easy subtraction tasks combined with the hard and easy typing tasks, thus experiencing four conditions overall, representing the four combinations of these tasks (easy/easy, easy/hard, hard/easy, hard/hard).

The threaded cognition prediction, as mentioned earlier, is that the condition for which both tasks require a problem state will produce more interference than the other conditions. The experimental results are shown in Figure 4.9 for both response time and accuracy in each task. There was, not surprisingly, an overall effect that the easy versions of both tasks required less time and resulted in fewer errors than the hard versions of the tasks. More importantly, there was a significant over-additive effect in the hard–hard condition. Response time for an easy task was affected very little by the difficulty of the other task, whereas response time for a hard task drastically increased when the other task was hard. Similarly, accuracy for an easy task was not affected by the other task, whereas accuracy for a hard task significantly decreased when the other task was hard. In particular, for the subtraction task, participants made more errors when they had to borrow, but the error rate increased even more when hard subtraction was combined with hard typing.

A straightforward theoretical account of behavior in this task can be represented as a model with each task as its own thread (Borst, Taatgen, & van Rijn, 2008, 2010). In the hard typing task, the model uses the problem

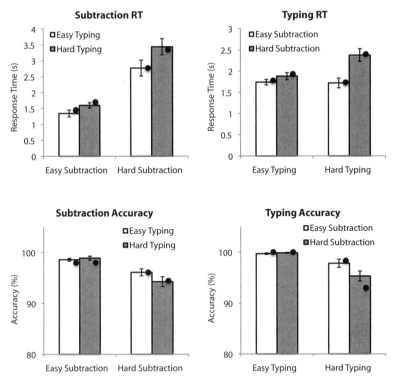

Figure 4.9. Results from the Borst et al. (2010) study. Column bars represent human data; black dots represent model results.

state to store the word, and the position in the word being typed. The hard subtraction thread uses the problem state to keep track of borrowing. The easy versions of both tasks do not use the problem state. As a consequence, if only one of the threads uses the problem state, that thread can use the resource exclusively. However, if both threads need the problem state, a thread clears its own problem state when its task display disappears (i.e., when the thread is interrupted by the task alternation in the experiment), so that the other thread can utilize the resource—thus following the "politeness" criteria for threaded cognition described in Chapter 2. When the problem state is cleared, the representation is stored in declarative memory and can be retrieved when that thread's task reappears in the display, as specified in the process model account in the previous section. This retrieval and subsequent reinstatement of the problem state buffer takes time, explaining the increased response times.

Given that the alternation between the two threads is reasonably fast (a few seconds per task at most before switching), the model does not rehearse the problem state that is currently inactive. The model's excellent fit to the data, included as the black dots in Figure 4.9, suggests that this is an accurate depiction of participants' behavior in the task. In particular, the retrieval of the problem state is the critical process for predicting errors in the task—as response times increase for the harder tasks, the longer times lead to greater decay of the declarative problem-state representation, thus leading to a higher likelihood of a retrieval failure (or retrieval of an incorrect problem state) and increased error rate. The model's success at capturing both the response time and error data, then, is strong support for the memory-based account of behavior in the task.

At the same time, one might raise the question of whether there might be alternative explanations for the data. A general finding in many tasks is that increased working memory load increases response times on a variety of tasks (e.g., Logan, 1979; Woodman, Vogel, & Luck, 2001). An alternative account for the results can, therefore, be that the additional slowdown in the hard/hard condition is due to a nonlinear impact of working memory load on reaction times. A possible model of working memory load is that information assumed to be maintained in the problem state must be stored in the phonological loop (Baddeley, Thomson, & Buchanan, 1975). If the phonological loop contains more items, it will take longer to retrieve and update items in that loop.

To rule out this alternative explanation, Borst, Taatgen, and van Rijn (2010) repeated the experiment with one modification: participants now had to switch tasks after two responses in each task, making it possible to examine the response times and error rates both with and without task switches. According to the threaded cognition model, the hard/hard condition should not be any slower than the corresponding easy/hard or hard/easy condition, because it is not necessary to swap out control states when the task remains the same. According to the working memory load account, on the other hand, the interaction effect in the hard/hard condition would remain, because the working memory demands are not dependent on whether or not there is a switch. Figure 4.10 shows that the threaded cognition model made the right prediction. After a task switch, the results showed the same interaction as the original experiment, but when the task was repeated ("non-switch"), there was no impact at all on performance of the other task.

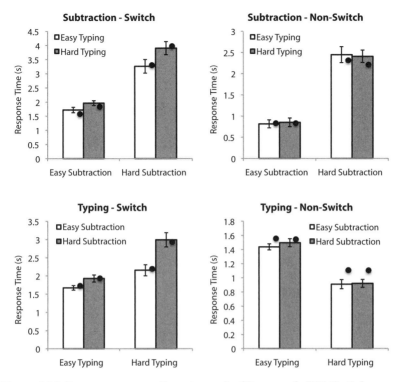

Figure 4.10. Response times in Experiment 2 of Borst et al. (2010). Column bars represent human data; black dots represent model results.

The two Borst et al. experiments show that as long as no more than a single thread needs a problem state, that thread can claim the problem state resource, and suffers from no interference from other tasks. When multiple threads need a problem state, they have to share the resource, requiring a mechanism that swaps out the problem state whenever another thread needs access to it. In a more applied version of this setup, Borst and Taatgen (2007) let participants alternate between a typing task (like that above) and a very simplistic driving task; the driving task had hard and easy versions, depending on whether participants needed to remember a sequence of turns to be made. Switching between the two tasks was voluntary, but the participants could not suspend the driving task for too long, or the car would drive off the road. The result was an interaction in response time when both tasks were hard, as seen in the experiments discussed here.

Problem-State Rehearsal Timing and Effects
in Sequential Multitasking

The rapid switching in the Borst et al. task obviated the need for participants to rehearse one task's problem state during execution of the other
task. There are clearly limits to such a strategy, however, and one indication of these limits can be inferred from prior research—for example,
people can rehearse approximately two seconds' worth of information in
a phonological loop (Baddeley, Thomson, & Buchanan, 1975), and the
"half-life" of an item in working memory can be estimated at roughly
seven seconds (Card, Moran, & Newell, 1983). Thus, the limitations of
memory for an unrehearsed item seems to be roughly on the order of a
few seconds. For longer task suspensions, rehearsal is needed to maintain
the problem state at a level at which it can be successfully retrieved
during task resumption.

Monk, Trafton, and Boehm-Davis (2008) recently conducted an experiment that nicely elucidates when problem-state rehearsal occurs, and for
how long it occurs. In the experiment, people performed a complex primary task (VCR programming) and occasionally were interrupted with a
secondary task. They looked in particular at the effects of interruption
duration and interruption task demand on people's ability to resume the
primary task after interruption. Monk et al.'s Experiment 3 used three
different secondary tasks: manual tracking, the N-back task, and a no-task
condition. The manual tracking task involved moving a mouse to keep
a cursor over a moving target, just like the tracking task described in
Chapter 2. The N-back task involved seeing a sequence of letters presented one after another every 1.6 seconds, and for each letter, the participant judged whether the current letter was "higher" (closer to Z) or "lower"
(closer to A) than the previous letter (which was no longer visible). The
no-task condition involved simply waiting for the duration of the interruption. In all cases, the primary task disappeared at the start of the interruption and reappeared immediately after the interruption. Interruptions
were varied to last 3, 8, or 13 seconds for each interrupting task.

We accounted for this task by combining a number of the theoretical
components we have developed thus far (extending the results of Salvucci,
Monk, & Trafton, 2009). The models of the secondary tasks were adapted
from previous work. The tracking model was taken from the earlier study
of concurrent multitasking (see Chapter 2), with only a modification to
the task specifics to align it with the current tracking task. The N-back

model was derived from a recent model by Juvina and Taatgen (2007) and was simplified to account only for the 1-back condition present in the experiment; this model required, for each response, a memory retrieval to recall the previous stimulus for comparison with the current stimulus. The no-task model trivially waited for the end of the interruption. A detailed model of the primary task was, in fact, not needed; it sufficed to have a single chunk representing the problem state for this task, that could be rehearsed and retrieved as dictated for memory for goals. Finally, the overall process model for rehearsal and recall were identical to those described in the previous section.

Because we did not have an exact specification for the timing of problem-state rehearsal, we examined five possible candidate strategies for when to rehearse:

- S1: rehearse during the entire interruption
- S2: from the start of the interruption, rehearse for n seconds
- S3: from the start of the interruption, rehearse until a retrieval takes no more than n milliseconds
- S4: rehearse for n seconds prior to interruption
- S5: rehearse n times prior to interruption

S1 is fairly straightforward, and maximizes the time spent rehearsing. S2 represents the fact that rehearsing for an entire interruption may be overkill; rehearsing for only a short period of time is often sufficient to remember the goal information. S3 allows for the timing of the retrieval itself to be the deciding factor: repeated retrievals result in shorter retrieval times, and S3 puts a threshold on how much to reduce retrieval time. S4 and S5 both assume that the interruption occurs at a predictable time (as in Monk et al.'s Experiment 3) and thus a person may actually stop and rehearse the problem state before the interruption. For S5, n was set to 3 to mimic the behavior of the Altmann and Trafton (2002) model. All timing was done with the recent ACT-R extension for prospective time estimation (Taatgen, van Rijn, & Anderson, 2007), which itself accounts for various phenomena related specifically to time estimation.

For the strategies incorporating concurrent execution of rehearsal and the secondary task, it is instructive to analyze traces of the model's behavior. Figure 4.11(a) shows how the tracking task interleaves with rehearsal. The tracking task experiences slight procedural interference from the rehearsal task, causing slight delays in the execution of the "move cursor" and "repeat iteration" procedural steps (delays shown as hashed areas in

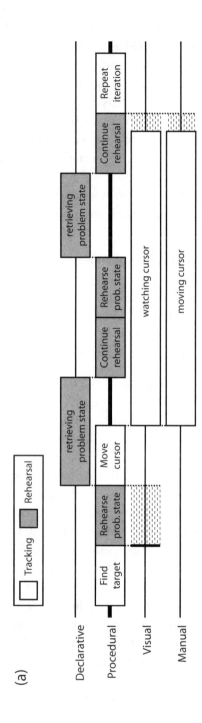

(a)

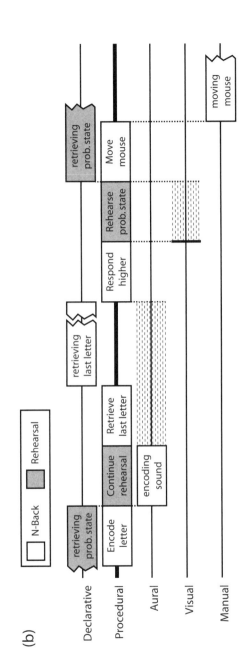

(b)

N-Back ☐   **Rehearsal** ▨ (gray)

Declarative
retrieving prob. state (gray) | retrieving last letter | retrieving prob. state (gray)

Procedural
Encode letter | Continue rehearsal (gray) | Retrieve last letter | Respond higher | Rehearse prob. state (gray) | Move mouse

Aural
encoding sound

Visual

Manual
moving mouse

Figure 4.11. Process timelines for (a) tracking task and (b) N-back task interleaved with problem-state rehearsal.

the figure). Thus, the model predicts slightly decreased tracking performance while rehearsal is taking place. The rehearsal task continues for the most part unabated in its ability to execute its rehearsal iterations. In contrast, rehearsal experiences heavy interference when performed concurrently with the N-back task, shown in Figure 4.11(b). The retrieval component of the N-back task—retrieving the previous stimulus for comparison—frequently blocks problem-state rehearsal. The model's prediction, then, is that the declarative component of the N-back task will lead to significant interference with problem-state rehearsal, and thus longer resumption times after interruption.

Figure 4.12 shows the experimental results of Monk et al. (2008) as measured by resumption lag—the elapsed time between the end of the interruption and the first observable action in the primary task (i.e., keystroke or mouse click). In all conditions (including, somewhat surprisingly, the no-task condition), resumption lag increased as a function of interruption duration. Resumption lag in the tracking condition was significantly higher than that in the no-task condition because of two factors: residual actions for the tracking task (e.g., completion of a ballistic mouse movement), and the necessary eye movements from the tracking task back to the primary task. Resumption lag for the N-back task increased even more, resulting in a steeper effect of interruption duration than in the other two conditions.

We ran simulations of the model with the five possible rehearsal strategies, estimating best values for n for each strategy, as well as a global parameter—the time between task resumption and the first observable action, common to all strategies. The model results are included in Figure 4.12. Rehearsal strategy S1 did not account well for the human data at all: rehearsing during the entire interruption effectively caused retrieval time to asymptote to very similar values, eliminating any effect of interruption duration. The two strategies representing rehearsal before the interruption, S4 and S5, produced no interaction effect between the N-back task and the other tasks. S3 exhibited a surprising dip in resumption lag for the N-back task at a duration of 8 seconds—the model was only able to achieve the retrieval-time threshold after approximately this much time, and thus retrieved the goal information quicker for this duration than for the others.

Strategy S2, rehearsing for 2.5 seconds from the start of interruption, produced the behavior most like those of the human participants. The model generates the same resumption-lag increase as a function of

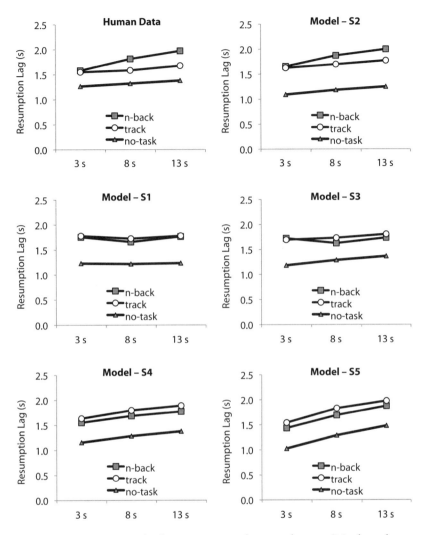

Figure 4.12. Resumption lag by interruption duration, human (Monk et al., 2008) and model (Salvucci, Monk, & Trafton, 2009). Strategy S2 exhibited the closest match to the human data.

interruption duration due to decay after the 2.5-second rehearsal period. Importantly, the model exhibits the interaction effect for the N-back task due to declarative interference. Because the N-back task competes with rehearsal for use of declarative memory, the model fits in fewer rehearsal retrievals during this 2.5-second period, and thus the problem state decays faster and is retrieved more slowly for longer interruptions.

As further evidence for the S2 rehearsal strategy, Monk et al. (2008) collected tracking-error data for the tracking interruption task across three experiments, as shown in Figure 4.13. They found a slightly higher error in the 3-second interruption condition than the other conditions, even when eliminating the first second of data due to possible adjustment to the task. (Caveat: this difference was statistically significant only for Experiment 1.) The model with strategy S2 exhibited the same behavior; the rehearsal process in the first 2.5 seconds of the interruption created just enough procedural interference to result in a slightly higher tracking error (see Figure 4.13). While S3 also produced this behavior, the other strategies did not (because rehearsal either wholly overlapped the interruption, as in S1, or did not overlap the interruption at all, as in S4 and S5).

Thus, for task suspensions longer than a few seconds, it seems that problem-state rehearsal starts at the onset of the secondary task, and continues for a short time afterwards, executing concurrently with the secondary task. We can then revisit our process model for task suspension and resumption, and fill in an important gap in that model. When the primary task is suspended, it stops actively processing the actual task, instead initiating the rehearsal of its problem state. This process runs for a short time and then puts itself on hold until resumption is possible. Later, when the secondary task is completed, the primary task thread recalls its saved problem state, and immediately resumes the task. The model of Monk et al. (2008) provides us with an estimate of 2.5 seconds for the duration of rehearsal. We might expect that this rehearsal period

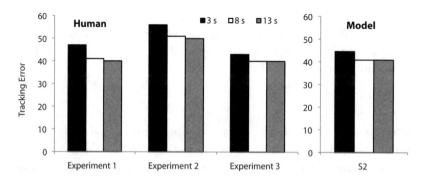

Figure 4.13. Tracking error by interruption duration for three experiments (Monk et al., 2008) and simulations of the S2 model (Salvucci, Monk, & Trafton, 2009).

would vary with the duration of task suspension. At the same time, Hodgetts and Jones (2006a) found that prior knowledge of the suspension duration did not affect rehearsal; specifically, they found that participants performed the same amount of rehearsal regardless of whether or not they knew the duration of an imminent suspension. Rather than a predictive mechanism, it may be more likely that rehearsal is an adaptive process, such that people adapt to perform more or less rehearsal based on their success or failure in resuming the task after suspension.

Research Connections

Research related to sequential multitasking has spanned both applied and basic research areas. In terms of basic psychological research, one popular paradigm is the task-switching paradigm (see Monsell, 2003) in which a person receives a simple stimulus and performs one of two possible tasks on the stimulus, alternating between tasks. For example, a common version of the task involves a single-digit stimulus with two possible tasks: judging whether the digit is even or odd, or judging whether the digit is greater than, or less than, five. In this paradigm, the primary measure of interest is the switch cost; namely, the additional time needed to switch tasks for trials that involve a different task than the previous trial. Task switching has been attractive as a basic research paradigm because of its simplicity and its potential for seemingly endless variations. However, the task-switching paradigm is severely limited in its generalizability to sequential multitasking more broadly. It involves forced rapid switching between tasks (unlike the self-driven concurrent multitasking we have seen in previous chapters), and uses an identical stimulus for two separate tasks (unlike the vast majority of tasks that would involve different perceptual stimuli and environments).

Nevertheless, task switching has enabled some detailed exploration of the functional aspects of cognitive control during sequential multitasking. Most importantly for our purposes, the work of Altmann, Trafton, and colleagues has been instrumental in supporting a memory-based functional account of task switching. This work has evolved alongside the formulation of memory for goals theory (Altmann & Trafton, 2002), which offers a similar account focusing on the (closely interrelated) issues regarding task suspension and resumption. A number of empirical studies have provided support for, and extended the core ideas in, this work

(Altmann, 2004; Altmann & Trafton, 2007; Hodgetts & Jones, 2006a, 2006b; Li et al., 2006; Monk, Boehm-Davis, & Trafton, 2004; Monk, Trafton, & Boehm-Davis, 2008; Trafton et al., 2003). The computational models embodying the theories (especially Altmann & Trafton, 2002, and Altmann & Gray, 2008) have also demonstrated how integration with ACT-R memory theory (Anderson, 2007) allows for more rigorous predictions of behavior in both task switching and related tasks.

We should also note that suspension and resumption of task goals applies not only to sequential multitasking but to sequential behavior more generally. Theories of cognitive or executive control (Baddeley & Della Sala, 1996; Cohen, Dunbar, & McClelland, 1990) have implications for both sequential and concurrent behavior, as mentioned in Chapter 2. Some of these theories, most notably Norman and Shallice (1986), have attempted to provide a unified account of both single-task routine behavior and dual-task behavior; both single- and dual-task performance are viewed in terms of the modulation of attention to multiple tasks, or even subtasks within the same task. More recent computational modeling work has focused more specifically on routine sequential behavior in specific everyday tasks, such as making tea or coffee (Botvinick et al., 2001; Cooper & Shallice, 2000). Our theoretical account has not yet been bridged to these types of routine action. However, the fact that the underlying memory for goals theory (Altmann & Trafton, 2002) was developed originally for behavior in a goal driven, single-task domain (Tower of Hanoi) offers promise that our theory will generalize in a straightforward way to routine sequential behavior.

Our account of sequential multitasking could be viewed as reinterpreting earlier theories, especially memory for goals, to center on problem state—that is, in positing that problem state is the representation that must be remembered and recalled during task suspension and resumption. While the specific concept of problem state is relatively unique to the ACT-R theory, it is closely related to the notion of working memory (Baddeley, 2003). In ACT-R, working memory is not a singular concept. Instead, the function of working memory is carried out by several other resources. Remembering and recalling lists of items (e.g., phone numbers) would be modeled by declarative memory (Anderson, Bothell, Lebiere, & Matessa, 1998; Anderson & Matessa, 1997). Each of the items in the list is stored as a chunk in declarative memory, and recall involves retrieving these chunks one at a time. Verbal rehearsal of several items is normally associated with a phonological loop (Baddeley, Thomson, & Buchanan, 1975), and is modeled using the aural and vocal resources. Finally, representations that directly impact the choice of the next action have to be maintained in the problem state, because only the current contents of buffers influence which production can fire.

More applied studies of sequential multitasking have often focused on switch costs in terms of the particular task, such as studies in the areas of aviation (Dismukes & Nowinksi, 2007; Wickens, Dixon, & Ambinder, 2006) and emergency room care (Chisholm et al., 2001). The next chapter extends our theory to the applied setting of human–computer interaction, a field in which interruption and resumption of computer-based tasks has been under heavy investigation for the past decade. This exploration of an applied setting also allows us to revisit an important aspect of sequential multitasking—namely, reconstruction-based processes of suspension and resumption. Because reconstruction of problem state is intimately tied to the chosen domain, the analysis of human–computer interaction in particular facilitates a more detailed look at how computer users reconstruct problem state from a visual user interface, especially when dealing with task interruptions at longer time intervals.

The Big Picture

Looking back now on our expanded account of multitasking, how do people switch focus from one task to the next, especially at time intervals longer than those for concurrent multitasking? Our account suggests that two key aspects of the cognitive system govern task switching at this level. First, many tasks involve the creation and maintenance of problem state—the temporary information necessary for task execution. The problem state resource that maintains this information can be a source of interference in its own right: When two or more tasks (or often subtasks of larger tasks) require problem state, each task may experience delays in waiting for the other to finish using this resource. Because some tasks may use the same problem state for several seconds or more, this potentially creates longer delays than those that typically arise from perceptual, motor, or procedural interference.

Second, when a person switches away from a task, and that task has a problem state, the cognitive system can maintain this state through a process of rehearsal and recall. Specifically, a suspended primary task can rehearse the problem state briefly—according to our simulations, a few seconds—to prepare it for later recall; without rehearsal, the problem state would decay too quickly for it to be successfully recalled. Then, when the task resumes, it can retrieve the previous problem state and restart the task. Thus, the critical time cost for task switching is the time needed to retrieve and restore the problem state—typically on the order of a half-second to a second of switch cost.

Our account also speaks more generally to common issues associated with task suspension, most importantly the relationship between remembering a goal but forgetting its problem state. Consider a situation in which a person is buying items on a web site and needs her wallet to complete an order. She may walk into another room to get it, except that when she arrives at the room, she forgets why she is there—a common phenomenon that most of us have experienced. Often, that person would still be aware that she was trying to accomplish some task, and our theory suggests that this awareness comes from the still-active task thread. However, this thread is unable to recall the problem state associated with the thread goal, namely the wallet being fetched, and thus the person may stand confused for a few seconds while trying to recall this information. (By finding external cues for memory retrieval, say by retracing her steps in the process, a person would typically be able to recall the problem state and continue on.)

Memory-based processes nicely describe the types of task suspension, and resumption phenomena, for suspensions that last several seconds to several minutes of time. However, as mentioned earlier, longer task suspensions most likely incorporate additional reconstruction-based processes—that is, processes by which a person recreates problem-state information from the external environment. However, while memory-based processes can be characterized more easily in the general case, reconstruction is highly dependent on particular task domains because of its dependence on the task environment. The next chapter extends our analysis to include a combination of memory- and reconstruction-based processes grounded in an applied domain, namely human–computer interaction. In particular, the next chapter focuses on a class of suspension–resumption behaviors—namely, task interruptions—and allows us to extend our treatment of sequential multitasking further along the multitasking continuum.

5

Task Interruption in Human–Computer Interaction

The previous chapter began our exploration of sequential multitasking, describing our theoretical account of how people suspend and resume tasks. In the study of human–computer interaction (HCI), researchers have been vigorously investigating an important class of sequential multitasking behavior; namely, how people manage and mitigate task interruptions. How do interruptions disrupt a computer user's work and performance? What types of interruptions are disruptive, and when are they most disruptive? How do people handle and alleviate the negative effects of interruption? This chapter discusses the empirical literature addressing these questions, and how threaded cognition helps us to better understand task interruptions in the context of a unified theoretical account.

Computing and Interruption

When computing technology entered the mainstream in the 1970s and 1980s, interaction with a computer was largely a one-task-at-a-time endeavor. A user opened an application, worked in that application for some time, then closed the application before moving on to the next task. These early computers discouraged multitasking, explicitly and implicitly, in a number of ways. Hardware limitations constrained the amount of

available memory and processing speed, while software limitations constrained the ability to run multiple applications simultaneously. (For
example, the Apple Macintosh "Finder"—the operating system's core
interface for file management and application launching—only acquired
the ability to run concurrent applications in 1987.) The limited selection
of applications also ensured that there were only so many tasks that could
be performed on these computers. Perhaps most significantly, most personal computers in this era had very limited network connectivity to the
outside world, thus acting as standalone computing devices for which the
user alone dictated activity.

As computer hardware, software, and networking changed dramatically in the 1990s through the present, computers have increasingly
enabled and facilitated multitasking and interruptions. Modern software
and hardware can easily handle numerous active applications simultaneously (often spreading computation across multiple processors). The
proliferation of high-speed network connections has also opened up a
multitude of potential interruption sources in the form of email, instant
messages, news feeds, and so on. Just as significantly, computers are no
longer bound to user desktops. Laptop computers are frequent compan-
ions on business and pleasure trips, and digital devices such as personal
digital assistants, smart phones, portable music players, and related
devices offer rival functionality in an extremely portable package.
Computing technology now travels with us everywhere, and interruptions follow.

This evolution of computing has been accompanied by an evolution of
the study of human–computer interaction, particularly with respect to
considerations of multitasking and interruption. As one example, Card,
Moran, and Newell's pioneering 1983 book, *The Psychology of Human–
Computer Interaction*, is very much focused on single-task behavior—
a reflection of the fact that user behavior at that time was indeed largely
single-task in nature. In the decade that followed, however, multitasking
began to emerge as an important area of study, including both empirical
(Czerwinski, Chrisman, & Schumacher, 1991; Holden & O'Neal, 1992;
McFarlane, 1997; Miyata & Norman, 1986) and modeling (Gray, John, &
Atwood, 1993; John, 1990; Meyer & Kieras, 1997) research. Work in
this area has increased dramatically since that time: At least 75 research
papers related to multitasking and interruption have been presented at
Association for Computing Machinery (ACM) HCI-related conferences

in 2004–2009 alone,[1] not to mention work published in journals and other conference proceedings. Beyond the research community, the news media, recognizing the public's burgeoning interest in multitasking behavior, has written increasingly about the proliferation of interruptions during computer use (e.g., Rosen, 2008; Thompson, 2005). Thus, task interruptions in the context of human–computer interaction offer an excellent domain in which to apply and validate threaded cognition and its account of sequential multitasking.

External Interruptions

About half of all interruptions (Gonzalez & Mark, 2004) are external interruptions—interruptions initiated by some external event, such from the computer itself (e.g., an error message), from another person (e.g., an email or visit), or from other extraneous sources (e.g., a power outage). An external interruption can be characterized in terms of four critical events (Trafton et al., 2003), as shown in Figure 5.1. The first two events correspond to the onset of the interruption. Before the actual start of the secondary (interrupting) task, there is sometimes an alert that warns of an imminent interruption—for example, a phone ringing, or a person's greeting that leads to an interrupting conversation. The period of time between the alert and the start of the secondary task is called the *interruption lag*. The person then performs the secondary task, and when this task is completed, switches to and resumes the primary task. The period of time between completion of the secondary task and the first observed action related to the primary task is called the *resumption lag*, which includes the time cost of switching tasks in addition to some additional cost to perform the first observable action. The resumption lag is an important indicator of the effects of interruption, in that it represents the time needed to recover from the interruption and successfully resume the primary task.

To better understand a computer user's behavior throughout this interruption timeline, we now review a number of empirical phenomena related to external interruptions, and discuss how threaded cognition can

---

1. Results obtained from a search of the ACM Guide to Computing Literature (10/30/09) for HCI conference papers with keywords *multitasking, interruption*, or *distraction*.

Figure 5.1. The external interruption timeline (based on Trafton et al., 2003).

account for them. This exposition, based on an analysis first presented in Salvucci, Taatgen, and Borst (2009), emphasizes breadth of coverage over a range of reported results, using a combination of qualitative theoretical accounts and quantitative modeling analyses. In later sections of this chapter, we examine two other types of interruptions—*deferrable interruptions* and *self-interruptions*—in which users exert more control over the timing and nature of the interruption process.

Effects of Interruption Timing

One of the most studied aspects of task interruption relates to the effects of the timing of an interruption with respect to the primary task. Many studies have reported that interruptions at points of higher mental workload are more disruptive than at points of lower mental workload (Adamczyk & Bailey, 2004; Bailey & Iqbal, 2008; Czerwinski, Cutrell, & Horvitz, 2000; Iqbal et al., 2005; Iqbal & Bailey, 2005; Monk, Boehm-Davis, & Trafton, 2004). In the previous chapter, we discussed how task resumption can be associated with a combination of two processes: memory retrieval for shorter interruptions, and problem state reconstruction for longer interruptions. We now look in detail at two empirical studies, one exemplifying memory-based resumption and the other exemplifying reconstruction-based resumption.

Monk, Boehm-Davis, and Trafton (2004) performed a series of experiments examining the effects of interruption timing using interruptions of short durations (5 seconds). The primary and secondary tasks were the same as those used in their other study (Monk, Trafton, & Boehm-Davis, 2008) described in the last chapter: a VCR-programming primary task, and secondary tasks involving either a no-task or manual-tracking secondary task. They analyzed the resumption lag as a function of whether the interruption occurred within a subtask or between subtasks, shown in Figure 5.2. The resumption lag after a tracking interruption was longer

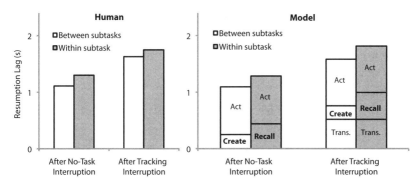

Figure 5.2. Effects of interruption timing for shorter interruptions, human (Monk et al. 2004) and model.

than after a no-task interruption, because of the shifts of visual attention from one portion of the screen to the other. More importantly, for both tasks, an interruption within a subtask led to a significantly greater resumption lag than an interruption between subtasks.

According to our theory, the central difference between the conditions involves the maintenance of problem state. Typically, within a subtask the cognitive system must maintain problem state that includes the temporary information related to the subtask; for example, a person might have some relevant information (e.g., a show's start time in the VCR task) that needs to be stored and acted upon (e.g., entered into the VCR interface). In contrast, between subtasks, there is typically no problem-state information to be maintained. The cognitive system can simply create a new problem state associated with the next subtask, and move on to performing it (e.g., acquiring and entering the show's end time).

Figure 5.2 illustrates a model analysis of this task, based on our model of the Monk et al. (2008) task in the previous chapter. When an interruption occurs between subtasks, the model simply creates a new problem state (labeled *Create* in the figure) without attempting to retrieve the previous state (because the old state did not need to be maintained). The timing for problem-state creation is set according to ACT-R theory, which posits that creation of a problem-state buffer chunk requires 250 ms (50 ms for the associated rule firing and 200 ms for setting the buffer; see Anderson, 2007). Predicted recall time (labeled *Recall*) is also derived from ACT-R theory; namely, the time needed to recall the problem-state chunk after the 5-second interruption used in Monk et al. (2004).

The difference of roughly 200 ms between problem state creation and recall accounts for the effect of interrupting between subtasks or within a subtask. The transition time between the tracking task and the primary task (labeled *Trans.*) is derived from the ACT-R model of eye movements (Salvucci, 2001b), as well as the model itself—specifically, as the time needed to shift the eyes from the tracking-task screen region to the primary task region. The presence of transition time accounts for the difference between the no-task and tracking interruption conditions. Finally, the time needed for a subsequent primary task action (*Act*) is assumed to be constant across all conditions, and is estimated as a single value to provide a best fit to the human data. Thus, the model, combined with ACT-R theory, nicely explains the important effects in the Monk et al. (2004) data—interrupting between subtasks or within subtask, and having a tracking or no-task interruption.

Longer interruptions make problem state retrieval difficult or impractical, and thus people rely instead on reconstructing the problem state—that is, searching the available environment and piecing together (perhaps in conjunction with remembered facts) the problem state at the point of interruption. Iqbal and Bailey (2005) investigated how interruption timing affects resumption for longer interruptions that arise from more realistic tasks. Specifically, they studied two user-interface primary tasks: a route-planning task, for which users computed distance and fare information for two routes and selected the shortest and cheapest routes; and a document-editing task, for which users looked over requested changes to a document and edited it accordingly. (A third task involving object manipulation is not analyzed here.) The secondary task was also a complex realistic task involving reading a news article and selecting an appropriate title for the article.

Like Monk et al. (2004), Iqbal and Bailey analyzed user behavior with respect to resumption lag at the "best" and "worst" possible points of interruption. These points were determined with respect to a formal GOMS (Goals, Operators, Methods, and Selection rules) analysis (Card, Moran, & Newell, 1983) of the primary tasks. In essence, their classifications of best and worst are directly related to the between-subtasks versus within-subtask distinction (respectively) used by Monk et al. (2004). Their empirical results, in Figure 5.3, paint a similar picture: interruptions that occur within a subtask are more disruptive than those occurring between subtasks, as measured by resumption lag. Iqbal and Bailey found similar effects with respect to self-reported ratings of annoyance and frustration.

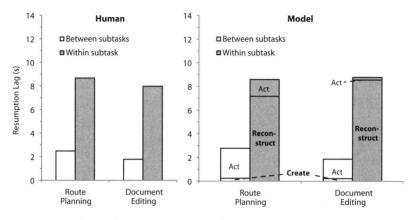

Figure 5.3. Effects of interruption timing for longer interruptions, human (Iqbal & Bailey, 2005) and model. From Salvucci (2010), Copyright 2010 Association for Computing Machinery. Adapted with permission.

Although the Iqbal and Bailey (2005) results correspond well to those of Monk et al. (2004), there is a critical difference. The longer and more mentally taxing secondary task in the Iqbal and Bailey experiment (analyzing a news article) made problem-state rehearsal and retrieval much more difficult. The effect size of roughly 6 seconds is also much larger than that in the Monk et al. study, and almost certainly outside the realm of a memory-based effect. Thus, the better interpretation of these results is that, after a within-subtask interruption, users had to reconstruct the problem state by visually scanning the user interface and reencoding the information necessary for the next step in the task. Table 5.1 details the reconstruction and subsequent action steps needed for each task and point of interruption.

Salvucci (2010) created models of these reconstruction steps and integrated them with implementations of the interfaces for the two primary tasks (see Iqbal, Adamczyk, Zheng, & Bailey, 2005, for screen shots of the interfaces). The models were run in simulation using default parameter settings for ACT-R as well as the EMMA model of eye movements (Salvucci, 2001b). After a between-subtasks interruption, the model creates a new problem state and performs the actions associated with the next subtask. After a within-subtask interruption, the model reconstructs the problem state as detailed in Table 5.1. The model results are included in Figure 5.3 and show a good correspondence to the human data. Thinking more generally, this type of reconstruction is clearly

Table 5.1.   Interruption timing and reconstruction action steps needed for
              tasks used by Iqbal and Bailey (2005)

Task	Interruption Timing	Reconstruction & Action Steps
Route Planning	*Best*: between completing the second route and selecting the shorter route	*Reconstruction*: None (create new problem state) *Action*: Read the distances of the two routes, compare them, and move the mouse to select the shorter path.
Route Planning	*Worst*: between finding information about the next trip and entering it into a table	*Reconstruction*: Find the next unfilled position in the table, read the associated cities, find these cities on the map *Action*: Move the mouse
Document Editing	*Best*: between completion of the last edit and saving the document	*Reconstruction*: None (create new problem state) *Action*: Find the File menu for saving, move the mouse
Document Editing	*Worst*: between placing cursor at editing point and typing	*Reconstruction*: Read the editing comment, read the sentence up to the cursor position *Action*: Type a character

From Salvucci (2010), Copyright 2010 Association for Computing Machinery. Reproduced with permission.

domain-specific; it would be difficult to provide a general account of reconstruction-based resumption similar to that of memory-based reconstruction provided in Chapter 4, because visual scanning or related reconstruction processes are very much tied to the external task environment. Nevertheless, given specifics about the task at hand, it is possible to represent these reconstruction processes explicitly in these models, and thus make similar quantitative predictions of resumption times.

The common element between the two studies above is that interruption timing is intimately related to the maintenance of problem state. When an interruption occurs within a subtask, the subtask's problem state must be maintained, thus forcing either memory- or reconstruction-based resumption after the interruption is over. When an interruption occurs between subtasks, there is typically no problem state to be maintained. The previous subtask's state is no longer needed, and the next subtask's state can be created fresh when the subtask starts.

Effects of Alerts and Interruption Lag

Besides the timing of the interruption, the presence or absence of an alert that warns of an imminent interruption—that is, an interruption lag—can have an impact on how easily the primary task is resumed. Trafton et al. (2003) tested this directly by comparing the behavior of users in a "warning" condition, who received an alert 8 seconds before an interruption, and those in an "immediate" condition who received no such alert (i.e., were immediately placed into the secondary task). The tasks used were both complex tasks based on real applications: a primary task involving resource allocation of military equipment to required missions, and a secondary task involving tactical assessment of incoming aircraft. During the interruption, the primary task was replaced with the secondary task, and the user performed the secondary task for 30 seconds before being returned to the primary task. In addition to their interest in interruption lag effects, Trafton et al. ran participants for three sessions (20 minutes each) to examine how task learning may change these effects over time.

Trafton et al.'s results for resumption lag in the first and last experimental sessions are shown in Figure 5.4. Participants exhibited a large effect of interruption lag in the first session: those in the warning condition were much faster (about 4 seconds faster) to resume the primary task than those in the immediate condition. However, by the third and last session, this effect had almost disappeared. Both sets of participants exhibited slight overall learning in the primary task, as measured by the inter-click lag—the time between task actions—which accounted for the slight decrease in resumption time in the warning condition with practice. The immediate condition, however, showed a very large drop, with learning such that the resumption lag in both conditions was almost equal.

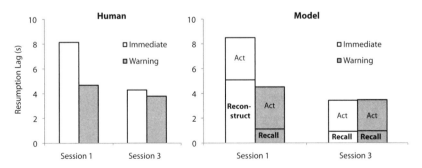

Figure 5.4. Effects of interruption lag, human (Trafton et al., 2003) and model. The Warning condition included an 8-second interruption lag; the Immediate condition did not include an interruption lag.

To understand these results in the context of threaded cognition, we need to preview our theory of learning described in the next chapter. When participants are introduced to the tasks, their knowledge of task procedures is in declarative form, and this knowledge is retrieved step by step from declarative memory; in other words, they memorize instructions, then retrieve each step of the instructions from declarative memory and execute the actions associated with that step. Eventually, with practice, these declarative instructions transform into procedural rules, and then people can perform the task more easily without reliance on declarative instructions. Chapter 6 details this learning theory and expounds on its implications for multitasking. For current purposes, the critical component of the theory is that early stages of learning require usage of the declarative resource, whereas later stages of learning do not. Because our account of task suspension and resumption centers on rehearsal of problem state using the declarative resource, threaded cognition predicts that novice performance of a secondary task will interfere with problem-state rehearsal and vice versa, whereas intermediate-to-expert performance will not.

Returning to the Trafton et al. results, this account then explains the large decrease in resumption lag for the immediate condition, and the lack of (interruption related) decrease in the warning condition. The immediate condition leads to concurrent rehearsal and secondary-task threads as shown in Figure 5.5(a). (Trafton et al. found direct evidence of concurrent rehearsal in their analysis of participants' verbal utterances.) In the first session of the experiment, the secondary task requires retrieval of declarative instructions, and the rehearsal thread experiences severe interference. Because of this interference, rehearsal does not sufficiently boost the activation of the old problem state, and then the thread fails to successfully recall the problem state upon resumption. By the last session, the secondary-task thread has transformed to rely on procedural knowledge, eliminating the declarative interference and the interference with rehearsal, thus allowing recall and resumption to occur normally. In contrast, the warning condition allows rehearsal to start and end prior to the secondary task onset, shown in Figure 5.5(b), and thus the two threads never interfere with each other.

We developed and simulated a minimal model of this account to demonstrate the effects of early- versus late-stage learning on rehearsal. As for the Monk et al. (2008) model in the previous chapter, a full model of the primary task was not needed to account for the basic effect; all that was needed was a problem-state representation to be saved and recalled.

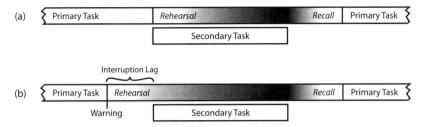

Figure 5.5. Task stages in Trafton et al.'s (2003) conditions for (a) immediate interruptions and (b) interruptions with a prior warning. Note that in the latter, rehearsal need not overlap secondary-task execution.

For the secondary task, the early-stage learning model for the first session repeatedly retrieved a declarative instruction and executed an action (a mouse click). (The retrieval was assumed to take 500 ms; the predictions below are fairly robust to different assumptions.) The model thus ignored the details of the real secondary task, and simply focused on the declarative aspects; namely, the fact that declarative memory was needed for instruction retrieval for each action. The late-stage learning model for the last session simply performed the action without the associated instruction retrieval. Finally, the overall model of suspension and resumption of the primary task was taken from the model of Monk et al. (2008) in the previous chapter, including the rehearsal period of 2.5 seconds beginning at the onset of interruption.

The model's ability to rehearse the problem state as a function of the number of rehearsal retrievals is illustrated in Figure 5.6. The model for the warning condition, where rehearsal does not overlap the secondary task, manages approximately 13 retrievals in the 2.5-second rehearsal period. The early-stage learning model for the immediate condition (Session 1) manages less than 4 retrievals on average during the same period—an indication of heavy interference from the secondary task's usage of declarative instructions. The late-stage learning model for the immediate condition (Session 3) is able to efficiently interleave rehearsal with secondary-task performance. Although it experiences slight procedural interference, and thus manages slightly fewer retrievals than the warning condition, its efficient rehearsal brings the resulting memory retrieval time to a level almost equal to that in the warning condition.

The model predictions for recall time, as well as other components of the resumption lag, are included in Figure 5.4. In the Session 1 immediate

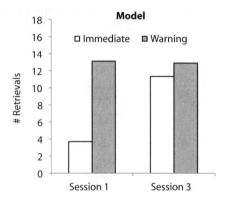

Figure 5.6. Number of rehearsal
retrievals for the model by session and
condition.

condition, the model is unable to recall the original problem state because
of insufficient rehearsal (see Figure 5.6). Thus, after the retrieval failure,
the model must reconstruct the problem state. In the other cases, the
model successfully recalls the problem state, and reconstruction is not
needed. The time needed to complete the first observable primary task
action is assumed to be the inter-click lag reported by Trafton et al.—that
is, the average time to perform an action during normal performance of
the primary task. Reconstruction is also assumed to take this amount of
time plus the time for failed memory retrieval (1 second in ACT-R), reasoning that the user fails to recall the state, then reconstructs the state by
following the path of behavior that led to the previous action. These
straightforward assumptions lead to a reasonably good fit to the human
data. Although our minimal model here does not attempt to predict the
actual reconstruction or inter-click behavior, the predictions demonstrate
that threaded cognition can account for the core aspects of interruption
lag, as well as the interacting effects of learning on performance.

Effects of Interruption Task Type

Once an interruption has begun, the type of task performed during the
interruption can itself affect a person's ability to resume the primary task.
In fact, we have already discussed two examples of this effect in the previous chapter. The work of Borst and colleagues (Borst & Taatgen, 2007;

Borst, Taatgen, & van Rijn, 2010) addresses differences with respect to whether the secondary task requires maintenance of a problem state. If the interruption does not require a problem state, and the interruption lasts only a short time (a few seconds), the primary-task problem state can remain in the problem state resource buffer and need not be replaced or rehearsed. Thus, a purely reactive task with no state—such as the simple typing task in the Borst et al. study, for which a person simply looked at a letter and pressed the associated button—would avoid problem-state interference, and facilitate faster primary task resumption. In contrast, if the secondary task requires a problem state—as in the typing of a memorized word—the primary-task problem state needs to be removed during interruption, and rehearsed for longer interruption periods.

The second example in the previous chapter was the work of Monk, Trafton, and Boehm-Davis (2008), and our theoretical account of these effects. In their experiment, people performed a tracking task, N-back task, or no task during the interruption. When no task was present during the interruption (i.e., the person just waited out the interruption period), resumption was fastest; resumption was slower when performing the tracking task; and resumption was slowest when performing the N-back task, due to this task's reliance on declarative memory and the resulting interference with problem-state rehearsal (see Chapter 4). Thus, two major factors that can interfere with resumption of the primary task are whether the interrupting task requires a problem state, and whether it requires declarative memory.

A third effect of task type involves the relevance of the interruption to the primary task. Cutrell, Czerwinski, and Horvitz (2000; see also Czerwinski, Cutrell, & Horvitz, 2000) found that instant-message interruptions related to the primary task (an information search task) led to speedups in both processing the interruption and resuming the primary task, graphed in Figure 5.7. They also found that participants exhibited a "tendency to delay switching to another task until completion of a subtask." By switching only at subtask boundaries, our theory would suggest that people were eliminating the need to maintain problem state across the interruption. Thus, the differences between conditions are not due to retrieval of problem state (as in the Borst and Monk tasks above); rather, they arise from the need to create a new problem state for irrelevant interruptions.

When an interruption is relevant to the current task, the current problem state is also relevant and does not need to be changed, either during

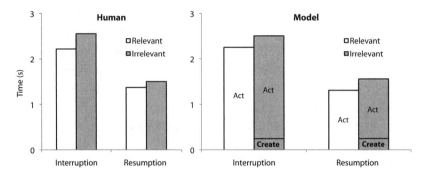

Figure 5.7. Time spent on instant-message interruptions and resumptions as a function of a message's relevance to the primary task, human (Cutrell, Czerwinski, & Horvitz, 2000) and model.

or after the interruption. When an interruption is irrelevant, the problem state must be replaced with a new problem state to handle the interruption, and then replaced again with a new problem state for the primary task. (Again, creation of a fresh state is sufficient, because the old problem state did not need to be maintained.) As mentioned earlier, creation of a new problem-state buffer chunk requires 250 ms in ACT-R theory (Anderson, 2007). Figure 5.7 includes a model analysis that estimates an overall action time (Act) for interruption processing and resumption, and includes additional time for problem-state creation (Create) for irrelevant interruptions. This very simple analysis illustrates how relevance can affect both the total time spent on the interruption and the total time spent resuming the task.

In all the domains above, the problem state is relatively simple—information that can roughly fit into a single chunk of memory. When problem states are complex, an interruption's relevance to the primary task is mostly a matter of the overlap in their declarative representations. Consider an office administrator working on an annual report, a task that would involve a large mental problem state (such as the associations among workers, tasks, deliverables, etc.). If the administrator experienced an interruption related to the annual report—perhaps a colleague responding to a request for report information—she would continue to access the same memory representations during the interruption. ACT-R theory would thus imply that these continued accesses help to keep these memories readily available. Thus, the effects would be similar to the Cutrell et al. results above: the interruption would be processed quickly, because those same representations are active, and resumption would be fast because the representations remain active. If the administrator experienced an unrelated interruption, the primary task representations would decay, and make resumption more difficult. There is some evidence that people can compensate for the additional resumption costs by working faster on the primary task, though at the cost of increased stress and frustration (Mark, Gudith, & Klocke, 2008). Nevertheless, whether the problem state is simple or complex, our theory suggests that both interruption processing and primary task resumption are affected by relevance of the interrupting task.

Effects on Secondary-Task Performance

The discussion to this point has focused on the effects of interruption on the primary task. In some situations, we may also be interested in potential effects on the interrupting task itself—in other words, whether a task used as a secondary (interrupting) task may experience different performance than the same task used as a primary (solitary) task. Our theory states that a primary task may mentally rehearse its problem state early on during the interruption, and that this rehearsal happens concurrently with the secondary task. Thus, the theory suggests two potential sources of interference. First, because rehearsal (like all threads) uses the procedural resource, the secondary task may experience procedural interference that hinders the execution of its procedural steps. Second, because rehearsal uses declarative memory, any secondary task that also uses declarative memory would experience interference effects on performance.

If a secondary task does not use declarative memory, the only interference would be procedural in nature. Can memory rehearsal generate enough interference that it would produce observable effects on secondary task performance? In fact, we have already seen an example of such effects in our Chapter 3 analysis of memory rehearsal while driving. Recall that in that experiment (Salvucci & Beltowska, 2008), people rehearsed a list of memorized numbers while driving down a straight road. The results showed a small but significant effect of rehearsal on two measures of driver performance (lateral steering accuracy and brake reaction time), as compared to a condition while driving only without rehearsal. Our model of this experiment demonstrated that threaded cognition accounts for similar effects, in that the occasional procedural steps for rehearsal interfere with the rapid steps for driving, and the slightly less frequent driving-related actions result in slightly worse driving performance.

The study of Monk et al. (2008) in Chapter 4 also provides an example of procedural interference. During the tracking task interruptions, participants in all three reported experiments exhibited a higher tracking error in the shortest interruption (3 seconds) compared to the others (8 and 13 seconds). Our account of behavior in the task posited that rehearsal of problem state early in the interruption produced procedural interference, and caused the increased tracking error in the shortest interruption; model simulations confirmed that the procedural interference was enough to produce almost identical (slight, but significant) effects in tracking error.

In the same study, however, Monk et al. found no effect of interruption duration on performance of the N-back task, in which participants recalled the previously seen letter and compared it to the currently visible letter. This result may seem surprising: given that the N-back task requires declarative memory, we might expect more interference, not less, than in the tracking task. In fact, a close understanding of threaded cognition's account helps to clarify this apparent discrepancy. The rehearsal thread issues repeated requests for memory retrievals, and assuming there are no other requests for this resource, these retrievals progress unimpeded. The N-back task thread, on the other hand, issues only occasional requests for a memory retrieval in the midst of several other behavioral steps (e.g., visually encoding the current letter, generating the motor response). During these other steps, the rehearsal thread can complete one or more retrievals, and thus the N-back thread is always the more urgent thread (i.e., the least recently used) when both threads attempt to start a retrieval. The N-back thread, then, acquires the memory resource whenever it needs it, whereas the rehearsal thread must occasionally wait for the N-back retrieval to complete. In addition, there is very little procedural interference with the N-back thread, because its procedural steps are fairly infrequent due to the much longer duration of the visual and motor processes between them. Overall, then, threaded cognition nicely explains the absence of observable performance effect for the N-back task.

Similarly, Monk et al. (2008) reported that the presence or absence of an interruption lag (i.e., warning) did not affect performance in the secondary task, a tactical-assessment task on a radar-screen-like display. Threaded cognition's account of their task would be similar to that of the Monk et al. (2008) task. We saw in Figure 5.5 that an interruption lag (their warning condition) allows the primary task to rehearse before the secondary task, clearly having no effect on secondary task performance. Without an interruption (their immediate condition), rehearsal is concurrent with the secondary task. However, concurrent rehearsal does not interfere with the secondary task. In the earlier stages of learning, instruction retrievals are broken up by task actions (perceptual and motor); interleaved rehearsal retrievals make sure that the secondary task remains the most urgent task (as in the Monk et al. task above) and that the secondary task experiences minimal memory interference. In the later stages of learning, the instruction retrievals have dropped out, and eliminated this potential for interference.

It should also be noted that the memory and procedural interference that may arise from primary-task problem state rehearsal only lasts a few seconds (as suggested by our analysis in Chapter 4). Thus, while we may observe effects on secondary task performance for short interruptions of a similar duration, the effects may disappear for longer interruptions. Measures aggregated over the course of a longer interruption may obscure these effects, or people themselves may, as they do for a primary task, compensate by working faster on the task (Mark, Gudith, & Klocke, 2008). To summarize, then, rehearsal of primary task problem state can indeed affect secondary task performance, but in general these effects are difficult to observe and pinpoint, even in controlled experimental studies. The effects seem to be most prominent for shorter interruptions, and for intensive tasks that make rigorous use of cognitive (memory and procedural) resources.

Deferrable Interruptions

The empirical results discussed in the previous section were derived using forced interruptions in which the system removes the primary task and replaces it with the interrupting task at a specified time. However, many interruptions are, in fact, deferrable (see Dismukes & Nowinski, 2007; Fogarty et al., 2005; McFarlane & Latorella, 2002): after perceiving the external alert for an interruption, the user can choose to switch to the interrupting task immediately, or at any time in the near future. For example, when a user receives an email as well as the typical audio alert, that user may choose to read the email immediately, or to defer reading and responding until a later (presumably more convenient) time. (There may also be time pressures associated with the interruption, such as needing to pick up a ringing phone within a few seconds, or perhaps respond to an important text message within a few minutes.)

Deferrable interruptions lead us to ask slightly different questions in terms of the nature of behavior. For forced interruptions, we discussed earlier how interruptions at points of higher workload are more disruptive than at points of lower workload. For deferrable interruptions, we can ask a complementary question: If users experience a deferrable interruption at points of higher workload, would they tend to delay the interrupting task until points of lower workload? A few recent studies have suggested that they would (Czerwinski, Cutrell, & Horvitz, 2000; Iqbal & Horvitz, 2007; Wiberg & Whittaker, 2005).

Salvucci and Bogunovich (2010) tested this idea explicitly in an experiment that carefully controlled mental workload by forcing users to maintain a single item of information in memory at different points in a task. The experiment involved a customer-support mail task with occasional deferrable interruptions in the form of chat messages, illustrated in Figure 5.8. In the (primary) mail task, the user read an email asking for the price of a fictitious product (e.g., "Samsung T-16"). The user then looked up the price in a browser window, which required the user to remember the product manufacturer and model number while clicking on two links in the browser. After finding the price, the user remembered this information while creating and typing a response email. Finally, the user filed the mail message away in an archival folder. This common sequence of events is diagrammed in Figure 5.9, along with two alternate paths (A1 and A2). Of note, the gray events in the figure are higher-workload events, after which problem-state information (product or price) must be maintained, while the white events do not require maintenance of problem state and thus represent lower workload.

As users performed this task, they were occasionally interrupted with a chat message. When a new chat message arrived, an audio alert was generated, and the background of the visible chat window was highlighted in yellow. Each chat message was a question about a recent movie and could be answered with a simple yes or no. Because the chat window was partially obscured by the mail task, users had to switch to the chat window to read the message, thus indicating exactly when they processed the pending interruption.

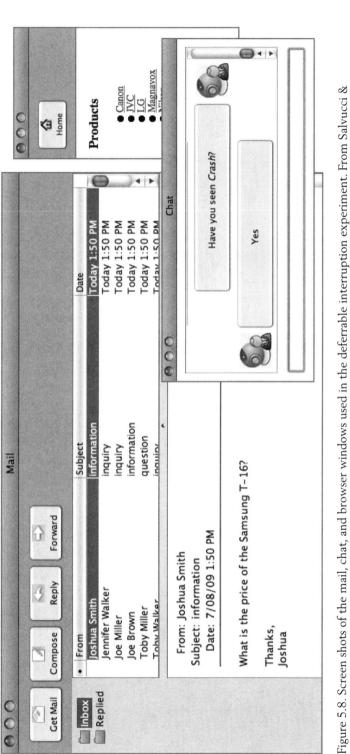

Figure 5.8. Screen shots of the mail, chat, and browser windows used in the deferrable interruption experiment. From Salvucci & Bogunovich (2010), Copyright 2010 Association for Computing Machinery. Reprinted with permission.

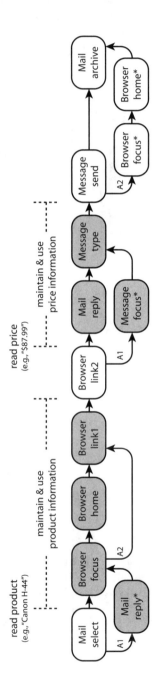

Figure 5.9. Steps taken in the mail task, the most common sequence (upper row) and alternate sequences (A1 and A2). From Salvucci & Bogunovich (2010), Copyright 2010 Association for Computing Machinery. Reprinted with permission.

Threaded cognition, combined with the notion of a problem state, makes a clear prediction for behavior in this task: When a deferrable interruption occurs while problem state is being maintained, users should delay processing of the interruption until problem-state information is not needed. The experimental results are shown in Figure 5.10—specifically, the total number of task switches occurring after each event in Figure 5.9. Although arrivals of chat messages were distributed roughly evenly (52% vs. 48%) across the higher- and lower-workload events, the vast majority of actual switches to the chat task—94% in all—occurred at points of lower workload (corresponding to the white events in the figure). The results strongly supported our theory: users showed a clear tendency to defer interruptions when maintaining problem state information, waiting until points of minimal problem state to actually process a pending interruption. These results also replicate and build on earlier, related studies (Czerwinski, Cutrell, & Horvitz, 2000; Iqbal & Horvitz, 2007; Wiberg & Whittaker, 2005) by carefully controlling mental workload and demonstrating that even maintaining a single piece of critical information can lead to deferral of interruption processing.

Self-Interruptions

The above phenomena deal primarily with interruptions (forced or deferrable) that are initiated by external sources, human or otherwise, which, as mentioned, comprise roughly half of all interruptions (Gonzalez & Mark, 2004). The other half of interruptions for everyday users are internal, self-initiated interruptions in which the person interrupts herself or himself and breaks from the current task to focus on a different task. This so-called self-interruption can occur across the multitasking continuum at very different spans of time. A person may self-interrupt for short periods of time, say, writing a quick email to a friend before returning to a online chat discussion, or switching among tasks while web browsing (Spink, Park, Jansen, & Pederson, 2006). A person may also self-interrupt for long periods of time; for example, a student remembering tomorrow's paper deadline and dropping everything to work on the paper.

Self-interruption closely resembles external interruptions in terms of many of the basic cognitive processes involved. When a person self-interrupts, any problem state that must be maintained should be rehearsed in memory to be made available for later resumption. Resumption after

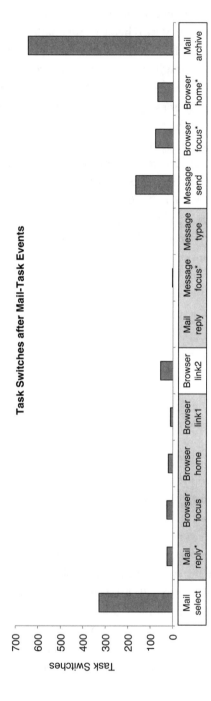

Figure 5.10. Number of task switches after each mail-task event. From Salvucci & Bogunovich (2010), Copyright 2010 Association for Computing Machinery. Reprinted with permission.

self-interruption can be memory based, in retrieving the original task's problem state, or it can be reconstruction based, in recreating the problem state from environmental information. The effects of interruption timing (especially whether or not a problem state is maintained), warnings (where the alert may be external but the exact switch time is self-controlled), and task type (e.g., relevance to the current task) all apply to self-interruptions as well as external interruptions.

At the same time, one aspect of self-interruptions is very different from external interruptions, and that is why the person is switching tasks. For external interruptions, the reason for switching is clear, because the environment forces or urges the person to start the secondary task. For self-interruptions, the reasons for switching are many and varied—they may be driven by time constraints, interest or motivation, the state of the primary task, and even by external cues. Jin and Dabbish (2009) identified seven categories of self-interruption related to computer activities in particular: changing the environment (*adjustment*) or seeking information (*inquiry*) to facilitate the primary task; temporarily switching to alleviate fatigue or frustration (*break*); remembering an unrelated task (*recollection*) or perceiving a cue to a related task (*trigger*); performing a task out of habit (*routine*); or filling idle time (*wait*). Of these categories, three (break, recollection, routine) arise primarily from a user's internal cognitive state, whereas the other four arise primarily from aspects of the current situation or environment.

Currently, threaded cognition's account of self-interruption is limited, but we can at least draw some implications out of the theory. At the shortest time intervals—up to roughly one minute—the ACT-R-based theory of prospective time estimation (Taatgen, van Rijn, & Anderson, 2007) can account for how a user may switch tasks at a desired future time. For example, if a user wants to spend just one minute checking Facebook, he or she can check this internal clock until the time has elapsed. Longer time intervals, from a few minutes to tens of minutes, are beyond the scope of the time estimation theory. We suspect that often in this time range, external triggers are indirectly related to task switching; for example, Jin and Dabbish's categories of Adjustment, Inquiry, and Recollection may all be, to some extent, triggered by environmental cues (e.g., seeing a document icon may remind a user of an imminent deadline). At even longer time intervals, from a half hour to several hours, self-interruption may often occur as part of explicit scheduling on the user's part, such as sitting down in the morning and listing out the day's meetings and tasks. In this case, a clock, hunger, fatigue, or other longer-term indicators of the passage of time may be used. Threaded cognition does not provide for a specification of these types of behaviors. However, the underlying ACT-R theory provides a framework for representing these behaviors as a cognitive model, and threaded cognition would predict how they might interfere with other tasks—for instance, how environment cues trigger new goals, or how continually checking a clock can interfere with progress on a primary task.

Research Connections

Throughout this chapter we have noted connections to a range of empirical phenomena associated with task interruption and human–computer interaction. Out of this work, we can identify a few larger themes connected in some way to threaded cognition. First, much of the empirical research has leveraged the structure of user tasks in studying how task interruption relates to mental workload. Mental workload can be a difficult concept to define rigorously, and indeed it can be associated with several aspects of cognition and perceptual–motor activity (see Wickens, 2008), as well as different observable measures of behavior (e.g., pupil dilation; see Bailey & Iqbal, 2008). Our theory suggests that one component of overall mental workload—namely, problem state and the maintenance of problem-state information—can be a bottleneck for multitasking behavior (Borst & Taatgen, 2007; Borst, Taatgen, & van Rijn, 2010; Borst et al., 2009) and is an extremely critical factor for task interruption.

The notion of problem state also offers new insight into how interruption timing affects behavior. Recent studies have illustrated how the task–subtask hierarchy can serve as a predictor of disruption (Adamczyk & Bailey, 2004; Iqbal et al., 2005), suggesting that interruptions during lower-level subtasks are more disruptive than between higher-level tasks. Under our theory, lower-level subtasks correspond to larger and/or more complex problem states, thus making interruptions during subtasks more disruptive because of the need to save and restore problem state. A problem state analysis is more general, as well, since it can be applied to "flatter" task–subtask hierarchies (i.e., those with fewer levels) like that of the customer-service mail task discussed in the context of deferrable interruptions.

A second theme of our analysis is the importance of both memory-based and reconstruction-based resumption processes. Basic psychological research on interruption (e.g., Hodgetts & Jones, 2006a; Monk, Boehm-Davis, & Trafton, 2004; Monk, Trafton, & Boehm-Davis, 2008; Trafton et al., 2003) have tended to utilize tasks with fairly short resumption times of less than one second or perhaps a few seconds. On the other hand, in many applied settings, resumption times can last seconds to minutes or even longer—beyond the typical range for rehearsing and recalling problem-state information, certainly for complex problem states, and likely even for simpler problem states. Thus, for any theory of interruption and resumption to span the multitasking continuum across these ranges, it needs to account for both memory- and reconstruction-based processes. Our theory developed in the last chapter focused on memory-based processes as grounded in the ACT-R memory theory. In this chapter, we have demonstrated several examples in which the theory can be extended to problem-state reconstruction. Nevertheless, reconstruction can often be, as mentioned earlier, a domain-specific process, and thus the further grounding of threaded cognition in a cognitive architecture such as ACT-R enables the framework to account for domain-specific reconstruction when needed or desired.

A third theme, which we have not yet discussed but that is also critically important, involves the relationship between our theory and the engineering of interruption-aware systems. There have been several efforts to date exploring real-time algorithms that detect and manage user interruptions (e.g., Horvitz, Apacible, & Subramani, 2005; Hudson et al., 2003), and evaluation methods for such approaches (e.g., McCrickard, Chewar, Somervell, & Ndiwalana, 2003). Typically, systems incorporating these algorithms aim to analyze and adapt such that incoming interruptions are timed with the least disruptive points of task execution. We hope that our theory, with its notions of problem state and the threaded execution of memory for goals, can validate or facilitate the refinement of these systems. It is also possible that the computational models can themselves be incorporated into such a system, using so-called model-tracing techniques that have been embedded into intelligent tutoring systems (e.g., Anderson, Corbett, Koedinger, & Pelletier, 1995). At the same time, our empirical results on deferrable interruptions indicate that users are often capable of deferring interruption processing and finding their own best points of interruption—which suggests that simply providing deferrable (rather than forced) interruptions, and allowing users to defer as desired, may be the best strategy for situations that are most challenging for automated systems.

The Big Picture

Recent HCI research has shed light on the many ways in which users experience and are affected by task interruptions. The body of empirical literature discussed in this chapter suggests that interruptions are often disruptive in terms of the extra time needed to return to the original task, as well as other measures of usability (such as annoyance with, or respect for, the system interface). These disruptions can be alleviated or eliminated when the interruption occurs at "good" times in the original task—namely, at times when there is minimal task context (i.e., minimal problem state). Warnings of imminent interruptions, and expertise in the individual tasks, also help to minimize disruptions.

Our theory has several implications in the context of this empirical literature. Threaded cognition and memory for goals theory emphasizes memory as a central process in task suspension and resumption; thus, interrupting tasks with more significant memory usage should, in general, cause more disruption. These tasks interfere with the primary task's ability to rehearse its own task context. Highly procedural interrupting tasks, such as fast reactive tasks (like our tracking example earlier), may also be disruptive because of procedural interference with rehearsal. As for primary tasks, those with more significant task context, especially information that has not been well learned, are more susceptible to disruption. In this case, the problem state needs to be rehearsed to prevent decaying, and any interference in rehearsal compounds the problem and makes it that much more difficult to recall the task context. When reconstruction is needed for resumption, primary tasks that display as much problem-state information as possible (e.g., a visual indicator of the last step taken) should alleviate the negative effects of interruption.

More generally, these phenomena seem to indicate that users sometimes experience a kind of "cognitive tunneling" (Thomas & Wickens, 2001) when performing computer-based tasks. They become so focused on the current task that most forced interruptions will lead to decreased overall performance on the task. Such focusing of cognitive attention is often a desirable trait, allowing us to concentrate on difficult tasks at hand; however, it leads to less flexibility as far as multitasking performance is concerned. Interestingly, the described study of deferrable interruptions illustrates how people can self-regulate their concentration by monotasking—focusing on a single task—until better switch points arise (specifically those with minimal problem state). In Chapter 7, we will return to this idea of monotasking and explore how, in many ways, our theory suggests that monotasking can be as challenging as multitasking when we are confronted with multiple concurrent tasks.

6

Multitasking and Learning

In the past chapters, we have seen many examples of how well people combine multiple tasks. But how do they learn to do it? Everyone who has learned to drive a car likely remembers that during the early stages of learning, it was almost impossible to do anything in parallel with the driving task itself. Indeed, controlling the car and planning upcoming maneuvers can already overtax the novice's brain; even simple additional tasks, like switching on the windshield wipers, may present a challenge, and fiddling with the radio might be completely out of the question. Clearly, the effortless multitasking we have seen in earlier examples is not applicable to novices, which suggests that multitasking is something we have to learn. However, according to the threaded cognition theory, multitasking is something that happens automatically, such that we can take two tasks and simply do them together. Why, then, is it so hard to do two new tasks at the same time? And is it a good idea to multitask in a learning situation, or is it better to stick to one task while learning something new?

To understand this, we have to examine how people learn new skills, and the nature of skilled behavior itself. In this chapter, we examine the basic mechanisms of skill acquisition, and how multitasking performance improves with practice even though multitasking itself does not have to be learned. In the next chapter, we will focus on learning larger complex tasks, and describe how a theory of multitasking can help to construct accurate accounts of behavior in these complex tasks.

Learning New Skills

The study of learning new skills has a long history, from which we can take Paul Fitts as a starting point. According to Fitts (1964), learning a new skill goes through three stages. In the initial, cognitive stage, behavior is slow and effortful with many errors. The new task demands full attention, and it is often difficult or impossible to do anything else in parallel. In other words, our novice driver in the above example is definitely in the cognitive stage. As practice accumulates, behavior becomes more fluent, and passes through an intermediate, associative stage: extensive deliberation or problem solving is no longer necessary to determine task actions, but behavior is still slow, uncalibrated, and demanding of attention. Learning eventually brings us to the autonomous stage, in which the learned behavior needs almost no attention, is fast, almost error-free, and can be performed in parallel with other tasks. Distinctions among these stages are not absolute: For example, though it may be virtually impossible for novice drivers to operate a cell phone, they are generally capable of listening to instructions from the driving instructor. At the same time, even highly practiced drivers have to suspend conversation when approaching a complex intersection.

Anderson (1982) proposed a theory of skill acquisition in which he assumed that knowledge for a new task is first represented in declarative memory. Declarative knowledge can be acquired easily through instruction or experience. To perform the new task, instructions are retrieved from declarative memory and interpreted by production rules. This process is similar to cooking from a cookbook. The cookbook assumes that the cook has basic cooking skills—like boiling water, cleaning vegetables, measuring quantities, setting timers, etc.—and the recipe prescribes how these basic skills should be combined to make the desired dish. According to Anderson's theory, learning a skill involves a gradual transition of declarative knowledge into procedural knowledge, through a process of *production compilation.* This idea was formalized in ACT-R by Taatgen and Anderson (2002; Taatgen & Lee, 2003). To learn a task-specific rule, the declarative instruction is combined with the productions that interpret it. Once learning is complete, the task can be carried out by the new production rules alone, and the declarative instructions are no longer needed. Continuing the cooking example, a cook that has memorized a recipe at first recalls each of the instructions, one at a time, and carries them out by performing the skills specified in the instructions. Eventually, when the cook has mastered the dish, s/he no longer needs the memorized recipe—the cook simply executes the (now well known) production rules specific for that dish.

The key distinction, then, between novices and experts is that novices need declarative memory to execute a task, and experts do not. Because experts do not rely on memory retrieval, they are faster at deciding on the next step, and make fewer errors. More importantly for multitasking, the experts' reduced reliance on declarative memory makes it easier for them to do tasks in parallel. Imagine doing two new tasks, and trying to retrieve what to do for both tasks at the same time! This would be akin to preparing two new recipes from a single cookbook at the same time, something no cook would relish. Instead of the smooth interleaving that we have seen in previous chapters, one task would be stuck waiting for the other's instruction retrievals, and might even get confused by declarative instructions actually intended for a different task.

The transition from declarative to procedural knowledge can explain learning within a thread. But is there also a learning process that discovers how threads can be optimally interleaved? According to threaded cognition, there is no such learning process: all learning is within threads. This proves to be sufficient to model learning in several tasks discussed in this chapter and in the next.

Production Compilation

Production compilation is a surprisingly simple mechanism that can account for a large set of different learning phenomena. Taatgen and Anderson (2002) used it to model how children acquire the English past tense, and Taatgen and Lee (2003) modeled how participants in a simplified air traffic control task gradually become faster and more accurate. The mechanism has also been used to explain how children gradually transition through various knowledge stages in a balance scale task (van Rijn, van Someren, & van de Maas 2003), and how both children and adults acquire algebraic skills (Anderson, 2005; 2007).

An important assumption of the theory of production compilation is that people have a collection of general strategies that they use to deal with new problems—for instance, retrieving past experiences, interpreting verbal instructions, using analogical reasoning, or searching for actions through means–ends analysis. If a general strategy is used repeatedly for the same problem, it is specialized into task-specific rules. An example of learning rules is the case of a child learning the English past tense. Production compilation accounts for past-tense learning through a combination of retrieving past examples, and using analogy on these examples to generate a past tense. For instance, to create the past tense of work, the child tries to retrieve an example from declarative memory: the past tense of work, or something similar. If the past-tense chunk of "work-worked" is retrieved from memory (possibly because the child has heard it from parents or older siblings), this chunk immediately supplies the answer. However, if a different verb is retrieved, such as "walk-walked," a pattern matching step has to be made to find a solution; namely, copying the first part of the verb and adding -ed. Production compilation then produces new rules on the basis of these activities: it learns a rule specifying that the past tense of *walk* is *walked*, and a more general rule that the past tense of a verb consists of the verb plus -ed. Once such rules are learned, they compete with each other, because they can both apply to a new verb. For example, the *walk-walked* rule is highly specific, but the rule that adds -ed is more costly because it lengthens all verbs, even the ones that have a more economical, irregular past tense. The dynamics of learning these rules and the competition between them creates the so-called "U-shaped" learning characteristic of the past tense (where the bottom of the "U" signifies the intermediate stage of incorrect generalizations of the -ed past tense rule).

Production compilation is often used to model skill acquisition through learning from instructions. Instructions are typically acquired through perception (e.g., hearing or reading) and stored initially in declarative memory. These declarative instructions are then interpreted by production rules, producing slow and potentially error-prone performance. Interpreting productions are, characteristically, independent of a particular task. Given an appropriate set of these interpreting productions, any task can in fact be specified in terms of the declarative knowledge. We will discuss the details of this mechanism later in this chapter.

Learning Perfect Time-Sharing

To examine a detailed laboratory example of learning multitasking, we now return to the perfect time-sharing example of Chapter 2. In that chapter, we showed how two choice tasks with no perceptual–motor interference—namely, a visual–manual task and an aural–vocal task—can be performed in parallel without any interference. In the experiments of both Schumacher et al. (2001) and Hazeltine et al. (2002), participants required multiple days of training before they achieved perfect time-sharing. Before that, they were not only slow at the individual tasks, but also exhibited considerable dual-task interference. In Schumacher's Experiment 3, participants went through six sessions of the task, one session per day. The particular challenge of this version of the experiment was that the perceptual–motor mappings were incompatible, so that a rightmost visual stimulus required a leftmost manual response, and vice versa. On Day 1, only single-task trials were trained, but on Days 2–6, single-task and dual-task trials were mixed.

A novice model for the dual-choice task—that is, a model in the very early stages of learning—can assume that every action needs to be retrieved from declarative memory (Taatgen, 2005). Figure 6.1 illustrates novice behavior in the dual-task scenario. At the start, both the visual stimulus and the tone are encoded, with the visual encoding finishing first. Once the stimulus is encoded, a production retrieves the declarative instruction to find a mapping between the visual pattern and a finger. A subsequent production retrieves the mapping, which is from a right circle to the index finger. Meanwhile, encoding of the tone has long since finished; the aural–vocal thread would like to retrieve its instruction from declarative memory, but must wait until the visual–manual thread has determined that the index finger is the appropriate finger. Once the aural–vocal thread has claimed declarative memory, the visual–manual thread must then wait to retrieve its final instruction to press the index finger. The trace demonstrates why multitasking new tasks is so difficult: there is a high demand for declarative memory, and, therefore, behavior tends to boil down to two tasks taking turns in consulting declarative memory. The situation becomes even worse for more complex tasks, because these tasks often retrieve multiple possible actions from declarative memory to decide which is most appropriate.

Production compilation produces learning by gradually removing these declarative retrievals. In the novice model, each step consists of a back-and-forth between declarative and procedural memory. Procedural memory asks declarative memory for the next action, declarative memory produces this step and, finally, procedural memory initiates or carries out the action. In the expert model, after production compilation, these steps

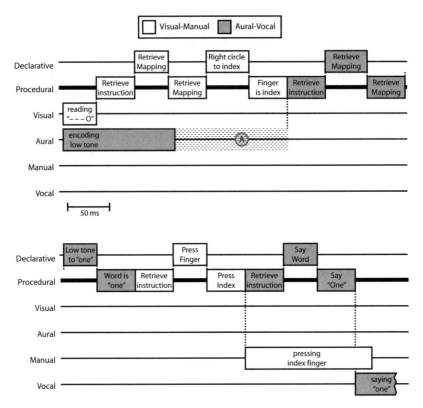

Figure 6.1. Illustration of novice stage of the combined visual-manual and aural-vocal task. The time diagram is split into two halves. The productions that initiate visual and aural perception have been omitted for space considerations.

are carried out by a single production rule. For example, Figure 6.2 illustrates the transition from the novice to the expert model. In the novice model, the model has to retrieve a set of instructions about which action to perform in response to the visual stimulus, which takes approximately 150 ms. In the expert model, these steps are replaced by a learned production rule that immediately retrieves the appropriate mapping as soon as it perceives a visual stimulus, reducing the total time cost to 50 ms and, just as importantly, eliminating the use of declarative memory.

As we noted earlier, the participants in Schumacher et al.'s (2001) study exhibited considerable interference, at first, in the dual-task scenario, but this interference gradually disappeared with practice. Figure 6.3 shows the results of the experiment, and the fit of the model to these results.

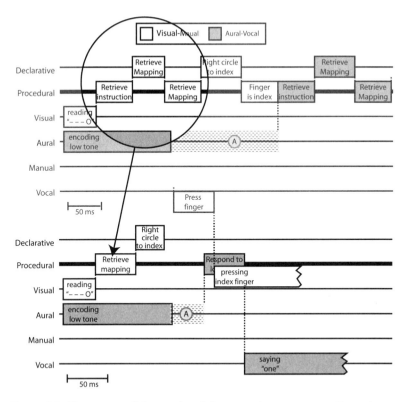

Figure 6.2. Illustration of the results of the compilation process. Compilation strongly reduces interference at point A.

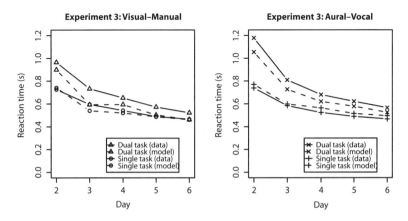

Figure 6.3. Results of Schumacher et al.'s (2001) experiment 3 (solid lines), and the model (dashed lines). From Salvucci & Taatgen (2008), Copyright 2008 American Psychological Association. Reprinted with permission.

On the second day of the experiment (Day 1 was only the single-task scenario), the interference was on the order of 200–400 ms per task. In contrast, on the last day, interference was strongly reduced, albeit not completely absent. The model also predicts some residual interference on the last day, though not as much as was present in the data. As discussed in Chapter 2, two-thirds of participants showed behavior consistent with the model, but the remainder showed considerably more interference. A possible explanation for the participants with high interference is that they employed an explicit control strategy that sequenced the two tasks, similar to what happens in the standard PRP task (see Chapter 2), and in sequencing target detection and memory consolidation in an attentional blink task (see Chapter 7). As with the attentional blink task, such a control strategy may often be counterproductive, and in fact lead to greater dual-task interference.

The Details of Production Compilation

Figure 6.4 illustrates some of the production rules from the novice model, as well as the rules learned by production compilation. The rule in Figure 6.4(a) is a generic rule that retrieves an instruction from declarative memory for the current goal. The rule itself does not care what the particular goal is, but simply retrieves instructions that match the goal-type of the current goal. Suppose that a retrieved instruction specifies that the system should say a word in the current problem state, which is one of the instructions in the aural–vocal task. In that case, we need another production that carries out this action. Figure 6.4(b) depicts this rule: given an instruction to say a word in the retrieval buffer, and the actual word in the problem state, the rule will initiate a vocal action to say that word. Note that this production also does not care what the particular goal is; it may also be part of a task in which onscreen words are read aloud, or a task in which participants are instructed to say the names of all the animals they can think of.

Once these two rules are carried out in sequence in the context of the aural–vocal task, the two rules and the instruction are combined into a single rule. Characteristic of this transformation is that elements from the instruction are substituted into the new rule. In this example, the current goal becomes part of the new rule (Figure 6.4(c)). The new rule will immediately say the word that is in the problem state without having to consult declarative memory, but will only do this if the current goal is to perform the aural–vocal choice task. The new rule is, therefore, more specialized than the old rules, but also more efficient. Furthermore, the new rule no longer needs the declarative resource, making this resource available to other threads. Once instructions in a new task are compiled into rules under this process, it is also possible to combine these learned instructions into even more efficient and even more specialized rules. Figure 6.4(d) shows how the rule that says the word is eventually combined with a rule that maps the low-pitched tone to the word "One." This final rule can immediately initiate the vocal "One" response once a low-pitched tone is perceived.

Production compilation can thus produce many possible productions applicable to a given situation, from very specific to very general. How does a person choose among these rules, and how do these choices affect learning? Production compilation makes use of an important aspect of ACT-R theory that assigns a utility to each production rule, which represents an estimate of the benefit of using that rule (Anderson, 2007). These utility values are then used to resolve conflicts between rules. If two (or more) rules are applicable at the same time, the rule with the highest utility value is chosen. Normally, the utility of a rule is determined on the basis of its success: each time a rule leads to a successful completion of a goal, its utility is increased, and each time it does not lead to success its utility is decreased. More precisely, the utility of the rule is equal to the expected future reward of the rule, minus the time to get that reward. Utility therefore favors big and quick rewards. If the model receives an actual reward at some point (which is something the modeler must set, for example on successful completion of a trial), all the productions that contributed to that reward are rewarded in turn by the value of the reward, minus the time between that rule's firing and the time at which the reward was given. A production uses this reward to adjust its utility according to the following equation:

$$U_{new} = U_{old} + \alpha(R - U_{old})$$

In this equation, R is the reward, U_{old} is the previous utility of the rule, U_{new} is the new utility of the rule, and α is the learning rate (typically in the range of .05–.20). Some readers may recognize this equation as deriving from standard formulations of reinforcement learning (Sutton & Barto, 1998).

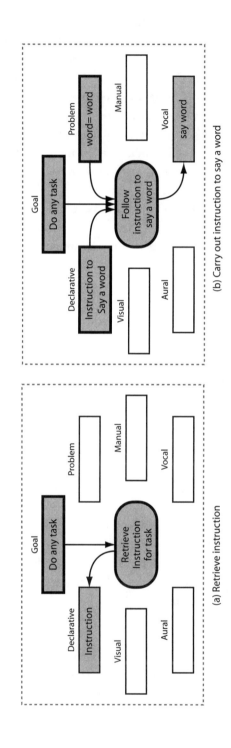

(a) Retrieve instruction

(b) Carry out instruction to say a word

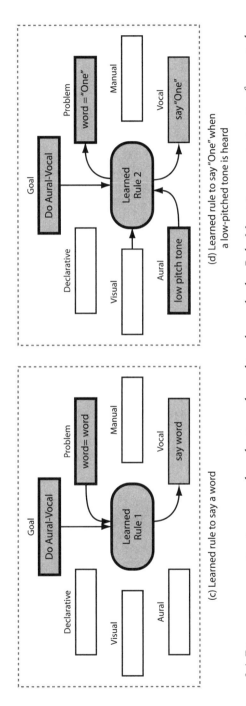

Figure 6.4. Diagrams representing two general production rules and two learned rules. Rule (a) retrieves any instruction for any task, rule (b) carries out an instruction to say a word, rule (c) says a word in the problem state when the goal is to do the aural-vocal task, and rule (d) says "One" when a low-pitched tone is perceived in the aural-vocal task.

The utility learning equation is also used to gradually introduce newly compiled rules. When a production rule is compiled for the first time, this new rule receives a utility value of zero. At the same time, the original production from which the new production was learned is still part of the system, so the new rule has to compete with that original rule—what we can call its "parent rule." Presumably, the parent has a positive utility value, and therefore the new child production will, at first, have a very low probability of winning the competition.

To have a chance to compete, every time production compilation reapplies, and the child is recreated, its utility is increased using the utility learning equation, with the parent rule's utility as a reward. This means that each time a child is recreated, its utility approaches the utility of the parent. Because of noise in the system, the child will sometimes be selected and given its own opportunity to gather experience, especially when its utility starts approaching that of the parent. Figure 6.5 gives an example of this process. Suppose the utility of the parent in Figure 6.4(a) (the parent) is 5—depicted by the thin horizontal line at the utility of 5 in Figure 6.5—and we have just learned the child production depicted in Figure 6.4(c). Initially, the child rule has a utility of 0 (represented by the thick line that starts at zero utility), which means it has no chance of winning against the parent (the probability of being selected is close to zero, represented by the crosses). Thus, the parent will win the competition, but the child will be recreated, adjusting its utility upwards by 0.5

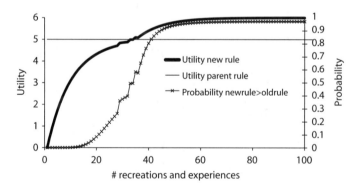

Figure 6.5. Illustration of the utility learning process for a new rule. Each point on the x axis is either a real experience (if the child wins the competition) or a case of relearning (if the parent wins).

(assuming an α of 0.1, using the utility equation: $0.5 = 0 + 0.1(5 - 0)$). After approximately 15 recreations, the probability of the child winning against the parent becomes significantly greater than zero (again, due to noise in the system), and in this particular example, after 28 recreations the child wins the competition with the parent. In this example, we set the parameters so that the child receives a reward of 6 if it wins the competition, As a consequence, it receives a large increase in utility when it receives true reward of 6, allowing it to surpass the utility of the parent (which is only 5) at around Trial 35.

One useful aspect of this slow introduction of new rules—apart from being consistent with research that shows that procedural learning is slow (Anderson & Fincham, 1994)—is that only rules that are recreated often, and thus based on frequent combinations of productions and declarative knowledge, are actually learned in the sense that they become part of active procedural knowledge. Other factors can play a role as well: learning will be faster if the new rule consistently leads to higher rewards, or if the initial utility of the parent is relatively low.

Perfect Time-Sharing in a (Slightly) More Realistic Task

In the dual-choice paradigm, people become so fast that it puts strong constraints on the model, and therefore serves as an excellent test of the core theoretical principles. At the same time, the task is highly artificial and raises the question of whether it generalizes to applied tasks. Spelke, Hirst and Neisser (1976) performed a classic experiment involving a more realistic scenario in which participants read text and took dictation simultaneously. In the experiment, two participants endured an 85-day experiment in which they simultaneously read stories for comprehension and wrote down dictated words. The study is especially interesting because it took two tasks at which participants are already skilled, and combined them in a dual-task scenario over a fairly long period of learning and practice.

On each daily session of the Spelke et al. experiment, participants read three stories, which varied in length between 700 and 5000 words and were selected from American, English, and translated European writers. While the participants were reading, the experimenter read one word after another (drawing from Kucera and Francis, 1967), and participants wrote down the words without looking at their handwriting. Once participants finished reading a story, they were tested for either comprehension of the story (10 times/week), or recognition of the dictated words (4 times/week). In addition, once per week participants received a control trial, in which they only did the reading task. Accuracy on both story comprehension and recognition did not change greatly with practice, nor did the writing speed, which remained fairly constant at roughly 10 words/minute. The primary change in performance was reading speed, as analyzed for the study's two participants, John and Diane. John, whose normal reading speed was 480 words/minute, slowed down to 314 words/minute in Week 1, but improved to 451 words/minute by Week 6. Diane's reading speed was normally 358 words/minute, which dropped to 254 words/minute in Week 1 but improved to 333 words/minute in Week 6.

To model the reading aspect of the task, we used an existing ACT-R model of reading developed by Lewis and Vasishth (2005). Lewis' model builds a syntactic parse tree of a sentence by attaching new words onto this tree as they are read. It has a fairly straightforward pattern of behavior—the model visually encodes each word, retrieves its lexical entry from declarative memory, retrieves a syntactical node in the parse tree from declarative memory, to which the word is attached, creates a new syntactical node with the word just read, and attaches it to the retrieved syntactical node. Because the visual system can read the next word while the current word is being processed, reading and parsing a word takes slightly over 200 ms using Lewis' parameter settings. Figure 6.6(a) illustrates how the model reads the first two words in a sentence. The model heavily uses both the procedural and the declarative resources, but there are gaps during which other tasks can use them. The result is that the model's single-task reading performance is 298 words/minute. Although not unreasonable, this estimate is slightly slower than the two participants (480 words/minute and 358 words/minute). Part of this discrepancy may be attributed to the fact that the model explicitly reads every word in the text, whereas studies have shown that people frequently skip words, especially determiners, auxiliary verbs, and prepositions (see Rayner & Pollatsek, 1989).

The model we constructed for taking dictation is straightforward. The model aurally encodes the spoken word, retrieves the spelling of the word from declarative memory, then writes the word one letter at a time. Although writing is a highly trained skill, writing without visual guidance is not particularly easy (try it!). The model therefore assumes that we only have compiled productions for writing with visual guidance, and that writing without looking requires a declarative retrieval for each letter. The retrieval is assumed to contain the movement pattern necessary to write down the letter. With practice, production compilation learns rules that produce the movement pattern for each letter right away. The only estimated parameter in the dictation model was the manual time to write a letter, which was set such that writing speed averaged 10 words/minute. Figure 6.6(b) gives an example of the expert dictation model. The novice model only differs in that the "Initiate movement" production is replaced by a production that retrieves the movement from declarative memory, the memory retrieval itself, and a production that executes the retrieved movement. Given that writing a word typically takes longer than what fits on the figure's time axis, Figure 6.6(b) only shows the first steps in writing "paper." Characteristic of the dictation model is that the manual resource and (to a lesser extent) the aural resource are used most heavily. At the beginning of a new word, there is some procedural/declarative activity, but after that, the occasional production keeps the process going forward. The novice model puts even more strain on declarative memory because it has to retrieve a movement pattern for each letter.

Figure 6.6(c) shows how the two tasks interleave once the dictation model has reached the expert stage. The time axis has been shrunk to show how the dictation model hears a word and writes the first two letters. In the meantime, the reading model has already read 8 words. The hashed areas indicate that there is some interference each time a new word is dictated, but once the word is being written out (which takes, on average, 6 seconds) there is little interference. The novice model, however, needs two production rules and a declarative retrieval for every written letter in the dictation task (instead of the "initiate-movement" production), creating substantially more interference.

In the simulation, the model's maximum reading speed of 298 words/minute slows down to 229 words/minute in Week 1 in the dual-task situation, but then speeds up to 270 words/minute by Week 6. Figure 6.7 shows a comparison between the model and the two participants for each of the first six weeks of the experiment, with performance scaled to maximum reading speed. Because of some residual interference, the model never reaches the single-task reading speed, but this is appears to be true for the two participants as well. Threaded cognition nicely captures the adaptation over time in the course of the reading and dictation study.

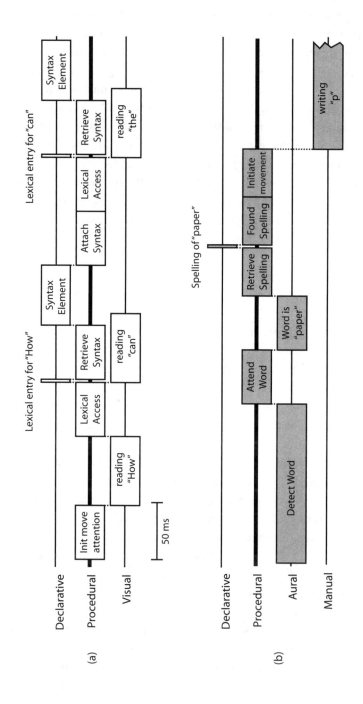

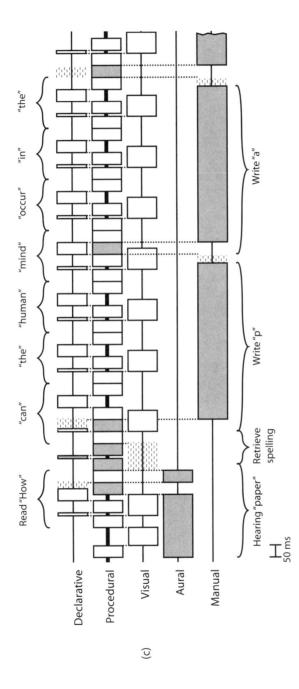

Figure 6.6. Illustration of the (a) reading model, (b) dictation model, and (c) combination of the two. The combination trace consists of compressed continuations of the reading and dictation model: the reading model reads eight words, while the dictation model hears a word and writes down the first two letters of the word.

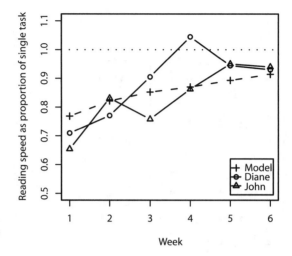

Figure 6.7. Results of Spelke et al.'s two participants in the first six weeks of the experiment, and the results of the model. The graph shows the reading speed in the dual-task situation as a proportion of the single-task reading speed. From Salvucci & Taatgen (2008), Copyright 2008 American Psychological Association. Reprinted with permission.

There are at least two interesting aspects to highlight in this model of reading and dictation. First, although our treatment here oversimplifies the many important aspects of language understanding, it does produce a plausible scheme in which mental resources are used in language situations, and can therefore be used in other multitasking situations where the effect of language understanding is one of the tasks. Second, the reading half of the model is a good example of reuse of previous work, and shows how threaded cognition can facilitate importation of other models into combined multitasking models.

Multitasking in the Game of Set®

As we have seen in earlier chapters, the multitasking perspective can also be useful to obtain a better understanding of what is normally considered single-tasking. In the following example, we describe behavior in a game that uses two threads, one for search and one for control. Initially, the two threads strongly interfere in their use of declarative memory. Learning through production compilation eliminates the need for the search thread to use declarative memory, and thereby eliminates almost all interference. The interesting aspect of this example is that it leads to qualitatively different behavior at the expert level.

We can illustrate this phenomenon in a card game called Set® (Set Enterprises, Inc.). Set is played with a deck of 81 cards and as many players as can sit around the table. Cards in Set show pictures composed of symbols. The pictures can be described by four attributes: color, shape, filling, and number of symbols. Each of the four attributes can have three possible values: blue, green, and red for colors; rectangle, circle, or wiggle for shape; solid, open, or speckled for filling; and 1, 2, or 3 for number. For example, one card has 2 solid red circles, and another has 3 blue speckled wiggles. Several more examples are depicted in Figure 6.8. There is one copy of each possible combination of attributes and values in the deck; hence, there are 3x3x3x3=81 cards. In the game, 12 cards are dealt face-up on the table, and each player's goal is to be the first to find a set—a combination of three cards that satisfies the following rule:

For each attribute, the three values that the cards have on this attribute are either all the same or all different.

For instance, cards with one solid red circle, two solid red circles, and three solid red circles comprise a set—all cards are red, have circles, and have solid symbols, but have numbers that are all different. As another example, cards with one solid red circle, two open blue wiggles, and three speckled green rectangles comprise a set for which all attributes have different values. Three cards with one solid red circle, two solid red circles, and three solid blue circles would not comprise a set because two cards are red, and the third is blue. Figure 6.8 shows an example of the game with twelve cards, including the sample set of cards with one, two and three red solid circles. The reader may try to find at least five more sets to get a sense of the game.

When we started our research project on Set, experienced players participating in the project made a number of observations about the game (Taatgen, van Oploo, Braaksma & Niemantsverdriet, 2003). The first observation, which is relatively obvious, is that sets differ in difficulty. It is much easier to find sets with many equal-value attributes than sets with many different-value attributes; the set with one, two and three solid red circles is much easier to find than the set with one green speckled rectangle, two open blue circles and three solid red wiggles. In fact, we can distinguish four levels of difficulty, defined by whether they have

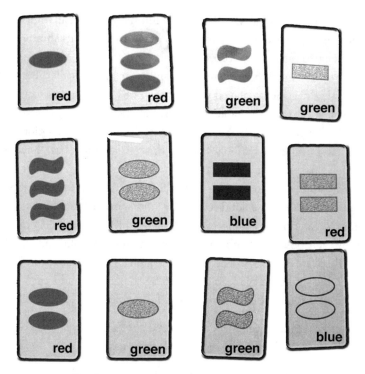

Figure 6.8. Example of 12 cards in the Set game. Color names are not on the actual cards, but are used here to identify the color of the symbols.

one, two, three or four attributes on which all values are different (zero difference is impossible in the real game, since it would require three identical cards). A second observation of experienced players is that they were likely much better than novice players in finding difficult sets, but about equal when it came to finding easy sets.

An experiment showed that these intuitions were correct. To test the impact of difficulty, we constructed Set problems consisting of twelve cards in which we made sure that there was only a single set of a given difficulty. We then presented these problems to novice and experienced players, and recorded their solution times. Figure 6.9 shows the results of the experiment. In agreement with the above observations, the results showed that solution times were longer for more difficult sets, and that experts were faster than novices at finding harder sets, but no faster at finding easier sets.

It may seem at first glance that playing Set is not a multitasking skill. However, playing the game in fact requires two independent threads

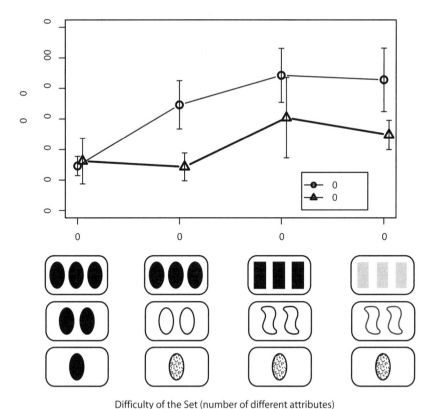

Difficulty of the Set (number of different attributes)

Figure 6.9. Average solution times for Set problems over four difficulty levels for novices and experts.

of thought: a search thread that tries to find sets, and a control thread that organizes and systematizes this search process. The search thread follows this sequence of steps:

1. Attend a random card and put its representation in the problem state.
2. Attend a second card that is as visually similar as possible to the first. If there are no unattended cards left, return to Step 1. The attended card stays in the visual buffer. So, by the end of Step 2, a first card is in the problem-state buffer, and a second card is in the visual buffer.
3. Make a prediction for the third card for each of the four attributes, based on the contents of the problem state and the visual buffer. If the attribute value in both buffers is the same,

the predicted value is that same value. For example, if the colors in the problem state and in the visual buffer are both red, the third card also has to be red. If both attribute values are different, then a third attribute value different from the first two has to be found. For example, if the color in the problem-state buffer is red, and in the visual buffer is blue, the color of the third card has to be green. In the latter case, the novice model needs a retrieval from declarative memory to determine the third value. Once a predicted value is determined, it is copied back into the problem-state buffer. Once all four attributes have been determined, the problem-state buffer will hold a representation of what the third card should be.

4. Scan the cards to see whether the predicted third card is actually present. If it is, announce that a set has been found; otherwise return to Step 1.

This search thread can explain why difficult sets take more time to find: In Step 3, a declarative retrieval is needed if the attribute values are different, but not when they are the same.

The search process above is fairly unsystematic, with no guarantee that all combinations of cards are examined. To produce a more systematic search, a control thread is needed to monitor the search process and make sure no duplications occur. There are many ways in which search can be controlled, so we chose a very simple strategy that checks if a current prediction in progress has been attempted before:

1. If there is a representation of a card in the problem-state buffer and one in the visual buffer, try to retrieve an earlier experience of predicting the third card.

2. If an earlier experience is retrieved, remove the current card from the visual buffer and restore the card in the problem-state buffer to the original card.

The result of Step 2 is that if the control thread detects a search pair that has been already checked, it resets the search thread to its Step 2, and forces the search thread to select a different second card. (Of course, not everyone would use this particular strategy to control their search, but, most importantly for our purposes, it is likely that almost any control strategy must rely on declarative memory to check previous actions. The use of declarative memory produces potential interference with Step 3 in the search strategy, in which the third card has to be predicted from the second, so other control strategies would produce comparable results.)

Figure 6.10(a) illustrates a segment of the process time. The interference starts after the model has attended a card with two open red squares (in the problem state buffer), and a second card with three solid red circles (in the visual buffer). The control thread will now check whether this combination has been tried before, and initiates a declarative retrieval to find an earlier experience with these two cards. Meanwhile, the search thread will predict the third card by going through the four attributes. The first attribute, the color, is red for both cards, so the third card should also be red. The search thread then wants to predict the shape, and needs to find the shape that is different from circle and square. For this, it needs to retrieve that value from declarative memory, and has to wait until the control thread is done with its retrieval (in the example, the retrieval leads to a failure because this particular combination has not been tried before). If more attributes had the same value, the prediction process could proceed further, because same-value attributes do not need retrieval.

With practice, production compilation learns rules that generate the third attribute value without declarative retrieval. For instance, a learned rule immediately sets the predicted shape to wiggle if the two other shapes are circle and rectangle. As a consequence, the contention for declarative memory between the two threads disappears, producing an efficiency improvement (Figure 6.10(b)) that is much larger than what is gained by simply skipping retrievals. The interference between the two threads is proportional to the number of attributes with different values, and therefore also to the difficulty of the set. This explains why novices and experts hardly differ on the easier sets, but considerably on the harder sets. Figure 6.11 shows the model's solution-time results alongside those of the human novices and experts.

Research Connections

The idea that skill learning involves a gradual transition from general but inefficient knowledge, to specialized and efficient knowledge, has been put forward by many researchers and incorporated into many theoretical models (e.g., Anderson, 1987; Crossman, 1959; Fitts, 1964; Fitts & Posner, 1967). It is not just a prevalent idea in psychological theory, but also in

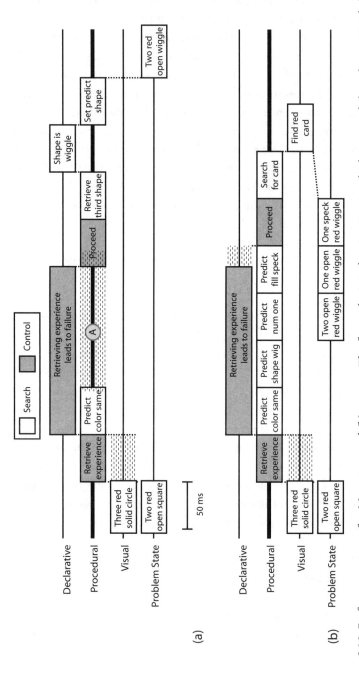

Figure 6.10. Performance in set for (a) novices and (b) experts. The figure depicts the situation in which two cards have have been attended, one in the visual and one in the problem state buffer, and the model predicts what the third card should be. Novices suffer from considerable interference (point A) between the search and control processes.

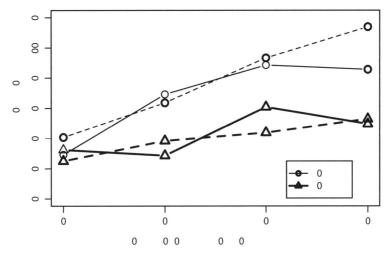

Figure 6.11. Average solution times of Set problems over four difficulty levels, human data (solid lines) and model (dashed lines).

machine learning and other branches of artificial intelligence. Explanation-based learning is a technique that specializes general domain knowledge on the basis of sample episodes of problem solving (Dejong & Mooney, 1986). The goal of the algorithm is similar to production compilation: to specialize general strategies, using actual experiences with those strategies. Anderson's original ACT∗ architecture (Anderson, 1983) specified several rule-learning strategies, among which were two components of production compilation (specialization and composition), but also others, such as generalization of rules by replacing constants with variables. Unfortunately, this set was never fully implemented, and probably would have been too diverse and unwieldy to function properly.

The Soar architecture (Laird, Newell & Rosenbloom, 1987) was the first cognitive architecture to incorporate an implemented rule-learning mechanism called *chunking* (Newell & Rosenbloom, 1981). Chunking also operated on the basis of the idea that acquiring a skill involves specialization of general problem-solving strategies. An aspect of Soar's general strategies is to set subgoals as a means to fill in particular knowledge gaps. For example, if Soar needs to choose between two actions, and it has no knowledge to guide the decision, it creates a subgoal to reason out the choice, possibly by trying to predict the outcome of each of the actions. Once the subgoal has been resolved, Soar will learn a new production rule that can choose between the two actions when they come up again in the future. For example, if we have to choose between cereal and bacon for breakfast, a subgoal might try to recall previous experiences with cereal and bacon, and evaluate the options on that basis. In the subgoal, we may recall that bacon gave us indigestion in the past, so we give that action a low evaluation and consequently choose cereal. On that basis, Soar might learn a new rule stating that whenever there are two breakfast options, and one of the options results in indigestion, then choose the other option. One complication that Soar never fully resolved (probably because there is no definite solution) is the level of generalization in the new rule. We might also learn a rule that prefers cereal over bacon, or a rule that prefers anything over bacon, and so on.

A different approach to skill acquisition, and one that does not involve rules, is Logan's instance theory (Logan, 1988). Instance theory assumes that people start with a general-purpose algorithm to solve the problem, and that each correct solution is stored in memory as a so-called *instance*. When a new problem is presented, there is a potential race between instances in memory and the general-purpose algorithm: whichever is first determines the action. Instance retrieval is generally faster than the algorithm, so accumulating instances makes it increasingly likely that the answer is determined by an instance. For example, the sum $3+4=7$ might be found by retrieving the answer from memory, or by counting 4 steps from 3. Instance theory is another incarnation of the idea that skill acquisition involves transforming general knowledge into specialized knowledge.

In the introduction to this chapter, we claimed that within-thread learning is sufficient to model learning in multitasking. Kieras, Meyer, Ballas and Lauber (2000; see also Kieras, 2007) have proposed a contrary account that covers multitask learning in the context of the EPIC cognitive architecture (Meyer & Kieras, 1997). According to Kieras et al., a specialized executive—a process that allocates cognitive resources to tasks—is needed to account for expert multitasking behavior. The executive is specialized in the sense that it incorporates specific knowledge of the particular tasks that are interleaved. To model novice multitasking, they propose a *general executive*—a resource allocation algorithm that operates on any set of tasks. The general executive is far from optimal in assigning resources to tasks, which explains the increased interference evidenced in novice data. They also propose several executives of intermediate specialization that can bridge the gap between a fully general executive and the optimal specialized executive. The main theoretical difference between the EPIC account of learning multitasking and threaded cognition is that in EPIC, the interleaving of tasks itself has to be learned, while threaded cognition asserts that this interleaving arises naturally, without the need for learning. The EPIC account raises a few major challenges with respect to learning, most importantly that general-executive scheduling may turn out to be infeasible or intractable (Garey & Johnston, 1979), and that there is currently no account of how special-ized executives might evolve from a general executive. Experimental work by Ruthruff, van Selst, and Johnston (2006) also supports the idea that learning in multitasking is within the individual threads. In a set of dual-choice PRP experiments, subjects received either single-task or dual-task training before a dual-task test phase. The results showed that dual-task training provided no advantage over single-task training on dual-task performance in the testing phase.

The idea of a specialized executive controller that explicitly interleaves and prioritizes tasks is also part of other, less explicit theories, like Norman and Shallice's *supervisory attentional system* (1986) and Baddeley's *central executive* (1986). The EPIC work has gone a long way in formalizing these ideas into working computational models. However, this work also illus-trates how the resulting models can be very complex, perhaps suggesting that, as posited by threaded cognition, explicit resource allocation is the exception rather than the norm.

The Big Picture

The textbook wisdom about skill acquisition is that experts can multi-task, but novices cannot. In this chapter we have offered an explanation for this claim, along with some subtle nuance. Novice behavior is charac-terized by a heavy reliance on declarative memory, and therefore a nov-ice's difficulty in doing multiple new things at the same time can best be attributed to declarative-memory interference. As novices gain experi-ence, this interference decreases because declarative knowledge is gradu-ally compiled into task-specific productions. The nuance arises in that not all declarative memory access can be eliminated from every task: only pat-terns that recur with a certain frequency are picked up by the production-learning process. This explains why, for example, language interpretation never becomes a truly autonomous skill. Declarative memory access can probably be proceduralized to the extent of handling particular stock phrases and frequently recurring patterns, but most of the time, words are combined in new and unique ways that require the lexical access and declarative manipulation required by the Lewis and Vasishth (2005) model (and, likely, any other linguistic model).

As a consequence, language interpretation is a poor candidate for multitasking, even more so than language generation, because at least language generation is self-paced. In general, to know whether interference between two tasks can be overcome by practice, the demands on different cognitive resources would need to be analyzed. In particular, if interference is primarily due to demands on a resource other than declarative memory, the interference is unlikely to disappear with training. One caveat is that the ACT-R theory does not have an account for motor learning, and the assumption in ACT-R models is generally that motor learning does not contribute to the results. This is probably true for the limited set of motor actions that ACT-R currently supports, but is not true in general (e.g., learning to play the piano). Nevertheless, even novice behavior for a skill with high motor demands like playing a musical instrument is probably characterized by heavy demands on declarative memory.

But is multitasking helpful or harmful for learning? The Ruthruff et al. (2006) study found no advantage or disadvantage of training one or two tasks at a time. But what about children doing homework while listening to or watching various forms of multimedia (Rosen, 2008)? In an experiment by Foerde, Knowlton, and Poldrack (2006), subjects had to learn a classification task, in which they had to predict the weather on the basis of cards with abstracts patterns, either as a single task or in combination with a tone-counting task. Although the learning improvements were similar between the single- and the dual-task group, there were also profound differences. The dual-task group performed at chance level on a post-experiment questionnaire, contrary to the single-task group. Moreover, the single-task group's learning could be localized in the medial temporal lobe of the brain, which is associated with declarative memory, while the dual-task group's learning took place in the striatum, more associated with procedural learning. A possible explanation is that the counting task needs declarative memory on a fairly continuous basis, interfering with the storage of episodic knowledge for the classification task. Instead, utility learning in the procedural system is used, but this knowledge cannot be reported, explaining the poor performance on the post-experiment questionnaire. More generally, we can conclude that learning in a multitasking situation will be disrupted if the interfering task taxes declarative memory, but not otherwise.

The research strategy of letting models learn the task instead of encoding expert knowledge directly into production rules puts more constraints on cognitive models. The models have to predict not only expert performance, but also the gradual improvement in performance with training. Threaded cognition fits this paradigm particularly well, because it does not presuppose a central executive that has to modify its strategy as individual skills go through the learning process, as the nonperfect to perfect time-sharing model shows. The next chapter further explores this idea in the context of more complex tasks.

7

Complex Tasks and the Challenge of Monotasking

One of the key hypotheses of this book is that threaded cognition is part of a person's underlying cognitive architecture. At the behavioral level, this means that multitasking itself does not require learning, or any particular effort. As we have seen in Chapters 4 and 5, errors in multitasking do not arise directly out of doing multiple things at the same time, but out maintaining the integrity of single tasks. For example, if another thread interrupts the current thread, it may replace the contents of the problem state, thus requiring rehearsal to ensure later recovery of the original thread's problem state. If multitasking is indeed easy, but maintaining a single thread is sometimes hard, we may need to rethink the way people organize complex tasks. Complex tasks are often analyzed by assuming a hierarchical structure, in which the overall goal is decomposed into subgoals, and possibly even smaller subgoals. This may require an elaborate internal representation of the state of a complex task, something at which people are not particularly good. Threaded cognition's alternative is to break up a larger goal into several parallel threads that are optimized to require as little internal representation as possible. This can be achieved by relying on the environment, rather than an internal representation, to provide the right cues for control.

In this chapter, we focus on what we call monotasking, modeling behavior and learning on complex single tasks by decomposing them into separate threads. When desired, a person can focus on particular threads and perhaps delay lower-priority threads for a later time; for example, the driver model in Chapter 3 can be augmented with threads that monitor the environment and decide when to change lanes, but these additional threads can be suspended in difficult conditions to focus on steering and speed control. In this chapter, we will show that decomposing a task into several threads is often necessary to explain human data, and, in addition, the decomposition leads to more robust and flexible behavior. At the same time, this idea introduces a new challenge: how the different threads coordinate among themselves for overall complex-task behavior. For this purpose, some means of cognitive control is sometimes necessary (similar to the PRP example in Chapter 2), although it is desirable to keep this extra control as minimal as possible. We now explore these ideas beginning with a discussion of the challenge of monotasking.

The Challenge of Monotasking

In modeling and understanding complex skills, task analysis (Diaper & Stanton, 2003) plays a central role in providing a detailed description of the cognitive, perceptual, and motor actions required to do a task, and often describes the relationships among these actions in a hierarchical representation. Cognitive models based on task analysis are typically constructed to account only for expert behavior, and thus are poorly equipped to account for the types of variability and errors observed in novice behavior. One example arises in the model of a simplified air traffic control task by Taatgen and Lee (2003), which nicely accounts for the transition from novice to expert behavior, but also demonstrates the shortcomings of a strictly hierarchical task structure derived in a straightforward way from task analysis.

Example: Simplified Air Traffic Control

In a simplified air traffic control task (the Kanfer-Ackermann Air Traffic Control, or KA-ATC task; Ackermann, 1988), participants kept track of planes waiting in a holding pattern and landed the planes onto one of four runways. A crucial aspect of the task was to properly assign waiting planes to a small set of available runways, observing weather constraints that could interact with the size of the plane and the length of a runway. Taatgen and Lee (2003) used a hierarchical task analysis to construct

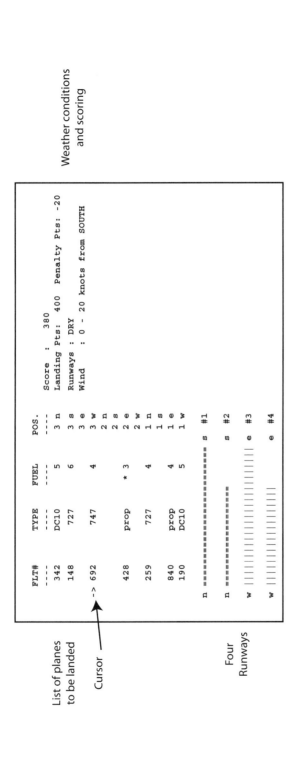

List of planes to be landed

Cursor

Four Runways

```
        FLT#    TYPE   FUEL   POS.
        ----    ----   ----   ----        Score    :    380
        342     DC10    5       3 n        Landing Pts:  400    Penalty Pts: -20
        148     727     6       3 s        Runways : DRY
                        3 e        Wind    : 0 - 20 knots from SOUTH
    ->  692     747     4       3 w
                        2 n
                        2 s
        428     prop  * 3       2 e
                        2 w
        259     727     4       1 n
                        1 s
        840     prop    4       1 e
        190     DC10    5       1 w

n ============================= s  #1

n =================== s  #2

w |||||||||||||||||||||||||||||||| e  #3

w ||||||||||||||||||||| e  #4
```

Weather conditions and scoring

Scan Hold Level 1 → Attend a Plane → Look at weather → Determine right runway → Is runway empty? → Move cursor to Plane → Press Enter → Move cursor to Runway → Press Enter

Figure 7.1. Illustration of the ATC task and some of the declarative instructions.

declarative instructions for this task. Each of these instructions specified an action and was linked into a list of other actions. Figure 7.1 shows a task screen and a small portion of the instructions used to decide which plane to land on which runway. Because of the constraints on plane/runway combinations, the task required some visual search. The model first attended a waiting plane, then determined on what runway it could land, given the weather. If that runway was available, the model would start landing the plane on that runway by moving the arrow cursor to that plane; if the runway was occupied, the model would attend another plane.

The model of this task uses the position in the list of instructions to determine the next action to retrieve. If the model has just attended a plane, the instruction to attend the plane serves as cue to retrieve the next instruction to look at the weather, which would then serve as a cue for the instruction to determine the runway, and so on. The consequence of this representation is that each instruction acts as an internal control state once production compilation has replaced retrieval by rules. For example, the learned production to attend the weather requires (as a condition) that the previous action attended a plane. This is a very brittle rule, because it is not conditioned on when information about the weather is actually needed, but only on what action was just performed.

The model proved to be quite successful in fitting how, with practice, overall score increases and time needed to land a plane decreases. However, at a finer level of detail, the model was much less successful, as illustrated in Figure 7.2. Before making the first keystroke, the model tries to find an appropriate plane/runway combination according to the instructions in Figure 7.1. Then, it moves a cursor to the plane using the arrow keys. Figure 7.2 shows that the model's estimate for the time before the first keystroke is just over 5 seconds in the first session, decreasing to slightly over 2 seconds in the tenth session (each session has a duration of 5 minutes). The improvement in time is mainly due to production compilation (i.e., the elimination of retrievals of declarative instructions). By the tenth session, this time stabilizes because perception limits further improvement.

The participants showed a similar learning curve, but were much faster, They initially needed only 3 seconds before the first keystroke, and eventually improved to just over 1 second. Given the number of perceptual actions needed to choose a plane and a runway (which involves several eye movements) and to check the weather, it is impossible for the model

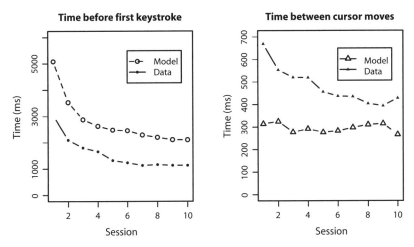

Figure 7.2. Keystroke timing in landing a plane: time before the first keystroke and inter-key time to move the cursor to the desired plane.

to accomplish what people learn to do in 10 sessions. The model fit cannot be improved by changing the parameters, unless parameters that scale perception are manipulated to implausibly low values. The clue to why the model is so far off can be found in examining some of the subsequent keystrokes. To select the plane, a cursor has to be moved to the plane, requiring a sequence of arrow keystrokes. The model performs these key-strokes with an interkey time of approximately 300 ms (right panel of Figure 7.2), for a very plausible estimate of human performance. There is no learning, because the model does not assume participants become faster typists in the course of the experiment. However, looking at the human data, participants were much slower than the model and showed a clear and pronounced learning curve in moving the cursor.

Lee and Taatgen (2002) found a solution to this puzzle. It appeared that participants did not wait until they had found both a plane and a runway before moving the cursor, but started moving the cursor after attending to the first plane. This is not always a good strategy, because it may be impossible to land that first plane, making it necessary to make additional cursor movements to other planes that *can* be landed. Thus, whereas the model places the entire problem-solving time (finding a plane and runway) into the first keystroke time, the human participants partially distributed that time over several keystrokes, explaining the slower interkey times and the presence of a learning effect. From the perspective of classical task analysis, this strategy is quite complex. It is necessary to determine whether two steps can be carried out in parallel at all, how to plan the actions, and how to switch to a different plane if the primary plane is not selected in the first place—a challenging feat on top of the demands of the core air traffic control task. However, if we assume that doing multiple things in parallel is easy, and is handled by threaded cognition, then the strategy is quite clever: As soon as a candidate plane is determined, the cursor is moved to it, obviating the need to remember which plane is considered (because the cursor is already in the right place for the next action); any extra costs of moving the cursor again if another plane is considered is a small price to pay.

Example: Robotics

Another example of the challenge of monotasking arises in robotics, a field in which this challenge has been acknowledged and addressed for some time. When robots were programmed using classical intelligent planning algorithms (Fikes & Nilsson, 1971), they were unable to handle any disturbances or uncertainty in the world. This proved disastrous, because robot sensors and motors are notoriously noisy and unreliable. Moreover, in the case of a large disturbance—such as someone picking up a robot and turning it around—the robot would often no longer be able to function at all.

To make robot behavior more robust, researchers found it necessary to split up complex tasks into multiple parallel behaviors that operate semi-independently (Brooks, 1991; Steels, 1994). An example of how single tasks can be combined into a complex task comes in a robot experiment by Steels (1994), illustrated in Figure 7.3. In the setup, robots did "work" by repeatedly bumping into energy poles and then driving to a recharge station to collect the results of that "work." The room contained various scattered obstacles that the robot had to avoid. For our example, we can simplify Steels' robot controller and reduce it to two aspects: driving to the energy poles, and avoiding obstacles. The energy poles had colored lights that indicated whether or not they contained energy. The robot could detect the lights with two light sensors (Figure 7.3(a)), which in turn influenced the speed of the two motors that controlled the two wheels of the robot. If the left light sensor detected more light than the right sensor, it would let the right wheel spin faster, resulting in a left turn, and vice versa for a right turn. As a consequence, this very simple setup

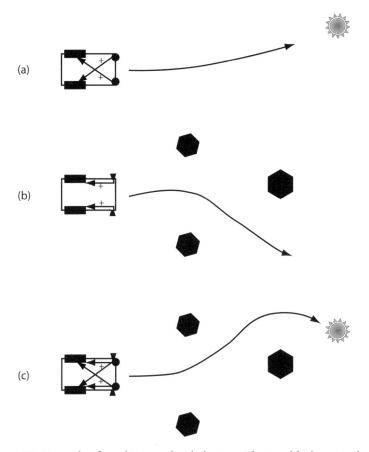

Figure 7.3. Example of combining robot behaviors. The two black rectangles at the left of the robot represent wheels that can be controlled independently. (a) Behavior to drive towards a light source. The two circles on the front of the robot are light sensors that control the speed of the two wheels, steering the robot towards the light. (b) Obstacle avoidance behavior. The two trapezoids represent sonar sensors that steer the robot away from obstacles. (c) Combining the two behaviors steers the robot towards the light while avoiding obstacles.

steered the robot toward the light. Obstacle avoidance (Figure 7.3(b)) was achieved by sonar that influenced motor speed by increasing the speed of the motor on the same side as the obstacle. When these two behaviors are added together, the resulting composite steers towards the light while avoiding obstacles (Figure 7.3(c)). According to Steels, parallel behaviors such as these are much more robust than serialized behaviors.

Even if the robot were picked up and turned away, or if its wheels were to slip, the robot would still eventually reach its desired destination.

What is striking about this example is not just the synergy produced by multiple parallel behaviors, but also the lack of planning or internal representations. In the microecology of the environment, the lights on the energy poles and charging station changed intensity to indicate their current status, ensuring that the robot was always attracted by the right target. This setup of the world conveniently makes it unnecessary for the robots to maintain any problem or control state, because the world already provides this representation. By breaking up the task into several parallel behaviors, this aspect of the world is fully exploited. Before returning to the issue of maintaining an internal state, we will first discuss an example of a task that is not very complex, but can nevertheless be modeled best by separating it into multiple threads.

Multiple Threads in the Attentional Blink Task

As a first step in examining how threaded cognition can combine and sequence task steps, we turn to a category of laboratory tasks called Rapid Serial Visual Presentation (RSVP) tasks and an associated phenomenon known as the *attentional blink*. In RSVP tasks, participants are presented with a rapid stream of visual stimuli, typically at a rate of 100 ms/item. The task is to identify and report target items in this stream. In many experiments, targets are letters, distractors are digits, and the number of targets is between zero and two. The RSVP task entails a combination of two basic cognitive skills: detecting visual targets that satisfy some criterion, and memorizing the targets as they are seen in the RSVP stream. Proper sequencing of these two steps is not trivial, because multiple targets may show up in rapid succession. Indeed, people performing the task often exhibit a particular behavior: they identify the first target correctly, but have difficulty reporting the second target if the interval between the two targets is between 200 and 500 ms—a phenomenon often called the *attentional blink*. A possible explanation for the attentional blink is that our cognitive system is not up to this task; specifically, that it is not capable of handling information at such a fast rate. However, this explanation is contradicted in two ways. First, studies have shown that if two targets are approximately 100 ms apart, the report of the second target is not impaired (Raymond, Shapiro, & Arnell, 1992). Second, studies have shown that people are capable of reporting even longer sequences of three or more targets without any attentional blink, as long as the targets appear close enough together (Di Lollo, Kawahara, Ghorashi, & Enns, 2005; Nieuwenstein & Potter, 2006).

A model by Taatgen, Juvina, Schipper, Borst and Martens (2009) uses two steps to model this task—one that detects targets and one that consolidates targets—and each of these steps is modeled by a separate thread. The target-detection step uses the visual resource to identify the items in the visual stream, and makes requests to declarative memory to determine the category of the item (digit or letter) and decide whether or not the item is a target. If the declarative retrieval reveals that the item is a target, the memory-consolidation step is triggered. Memory consolidation simply places the memory chunk representing the item into ACT-R's problem-state buffer, which takes 200 ms (Anderson, 2007). A sample process timeline is shown in Figure 7.4.

The complexity of the task lies not so much in the basic steps involved, but in the speed at which the input has to be processed, making synchronization of the two threads nontrivial. The model therefore assumes that people add a control step to coordinate the sequencing. This control step, a single production, suspends target detection for as long as the problem state resource is consolidating the target (which takes 200 ms, on average). If a target enters the visual stream while target detection is suspended, it will go undetected, producing an attentional blink. Figure 7.5(a) shows an example of attentional blink in what is termed the "Lag-3" case (300 ms between target presentations). As soon as the first target (the letter "A") is detected, it is consolidated into the problem state. Meanwhile, the target detection thread retrieves the category of distractor "3." This combination triggers the control production that temporarily suspends the target detection stream until problem state is no longer busy. Items that are presented during this period (distractor "8" and target "B") are perceived by the visual system, but are not processed by the target detection thread. Figure 7.5(b) shows an example of success in the Lag-1 case (100 ms between target presentations). Before the control production can suspend target detection, a second target is detected. Indeed, if more targets would follow the second target, they would be detected as well, consistent with human data (Di Lollo et al., 2005).

Figure 7.6 shows the results of the model compared to the human data reported by Taatgen et al. (2009). Consistent with the human data, accuracy on Lag 1 and on Lags 6 and higher, is the same for the first and the

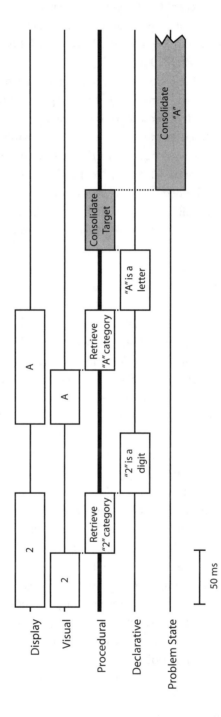

Figure 7.4. The two steps in the attentional blink model: target detection (white boxes) and memory consolidation (gray boxes).

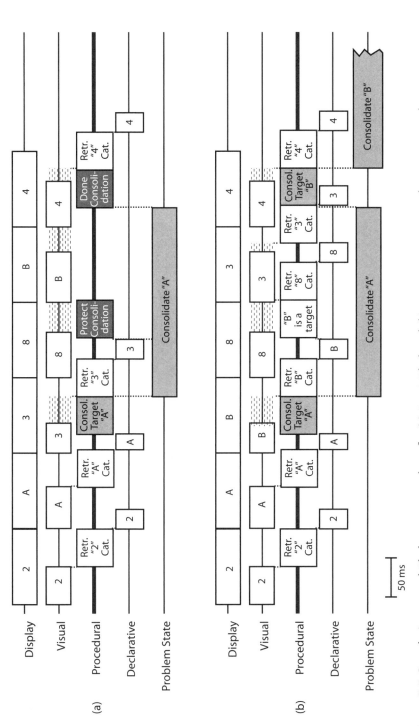

Figure 7.5. Sample Attentional Blink process timelines for (a) Lag 3 Blink and (b) Lag 1 success. Target detection is in white, memory consolidation in light gray and control in dark gray.

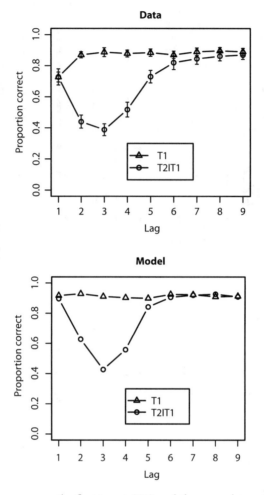

Figure 7.6. Accuracy on the first target (T1) and the second target given that the first target is reported correctly (T2|T1) for the different Lags. From Taatgen et al. (2009), Copyright 2009 Elsevier. Reprinted with permission.

second target, but for Lags 2-5, the accuracy for the second target is much lower, bottoming out at Lag 3.

The threaded cognition model shares similarities with other models that attribute the attentional blink to control (e.g., Bowman & Wyble, 2007; Olivers & Meeter, 2008). The model also accounts for a set of other phenomena related to attentional blink (see Taatgen et al., 2009, for details). However, because the threaded cognition model is grounded in a cognitive architecture (ACT-R), it is in a unique position to make predictions that would be difficult or impossible to make with other models. More specifically, the model can make predictions about what happens with attentional blink if a secondary task is added to the RSVP task. In Experiment 3 in Taatgen et al. (2009), the RSVP task was modified in two ways. One modification was to rotate the first target 180°, thus requiring people to mentally rotate this target. This type of mental rotation is generally associated with processing in the parietal cortex, which, in ACT-R theory, is associated with the problem state resource. The assumption of the model is that the problem state requires 100 ms to rotate the target, in addition to 200 ms to consolidate the target. The second modification involved adding a dot-detection task. While the stream of targets and distractors was presented in the center of the screen, a gray dot would circle around the target stream. In some of the trials this dot would turn red for 100 ms. Participants not only had to report the targets, but also whether the dot had turned red. This secondary task was modeled with one additional thread that monitors the visual–location resource, to detect red items in peripheral vision. This check requires a production rule firing every time the dot moves, or every 100 ms. These extra productions produce additional procedural interference.

These two manipulations—rotated first target and addition of the dot task—increase potential interference in the problem state resource and the procedural resource, respectively. As a consequence, their effects are quite different. Rotation increases the time needed to process the target in the problem state. This increases the time that the problem state is unavailable for the second target and, therefore, the probability of an attentional blink. In contrast, in the dot condition the procedural resource is overloaded, and as a consequence some productions that would normally fire, never do. This means that the dot is not always tracked (explaining why accuracy is not 100%). It also decreases the probability that the control production fires, along with decreasing the probability of a blink. Adding a task, therefore, has the counterintuitive effect of improving performance. Figure 7.7 shows examples of processing in the two conditions. In Figure 7.7(a), the dot task is added as a new thread that monitors the dot in peripheral vision, represented in the visual–location buffer. In the example the dot stays gray, but nevertheless produces considerable procedural interference, preventing the control production from firing. Figure 7.7(b) shows the effect of rotation. The model assumes that detecting a rotated character is very fast, represented by the fast declarative retrieval, but de-rotation and consolidation is slow, represented by the longer problem state activity.

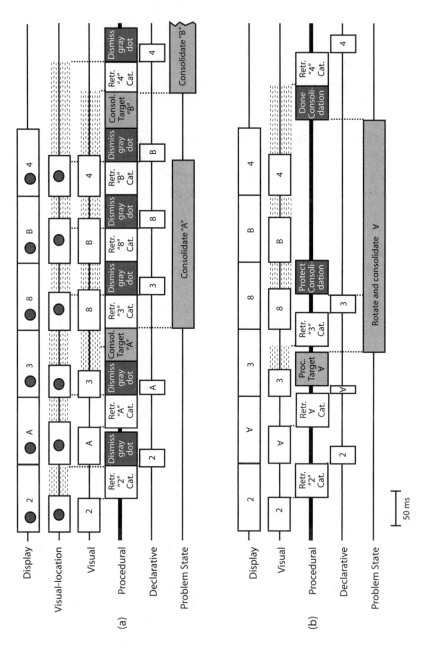

Figure 7.7. Attentional Blink process timelines with (a) addition of the dot detection task, and (b) rotated target 1.

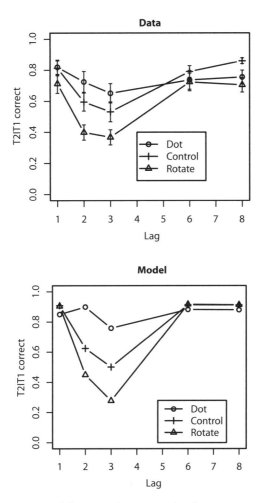

Figure 7.8. Correctness of the second target in the three experimental conditions, data and model. From Taatgen et al. (2009), Copyright 2009 Elsevier. Reprinted with permission.

Figure 7.8 shows the result of the experiment and the model fit. As predicted, participants show a decreased blink when the dot task is added, and an increased blink when the first target is rotated. Participants were quite accurate at the dot task, detecting it in 93% of the cases it was present (the model's accuracy was 81%).

The attentional blink model shows that decomposing tasks into multiple threads is sometimes necessary to explain the phenomena associated with a task. In this particular case, target detection and memory consolidation sometimes partially overlapped, making it difficult if not impossible to model the task with a single thread. However, contrary to most of the other examples of threaded cognition we have seen, there is a dependence between the two threads: memory consolidation can only start once target detection has found a target. The control production that coordinates the sequencing is one of the weakest links in the process, which becomes clear when another task is added. Oddly enough, breaking the link between target detection and memory consolidation actually improves behavior. Why would people introduce this inefficiency into their task representation? One thing to observe is that the problem state resource plays a pivotal role in the sequencing process, just as in the examples of sequential multitasking in Chapter 5. It is, therefore, possible that control productions intended to coordinate sequential multitasking are setting up the sequencing in this task as well.

The Representation of Sequences of Actions

If a sequence of actions is not planned or fixed in advance (as in the unsuccessful model of air traffic control), some other representation or mechanism is necessary to determine when a particular action should be carried out. The Steels (1994) solution is limited to situations in which all the information is accessible through perception, which is not generally true. Clearly a compromise is needed where control is partially external and partially internal. The challenge, then, is to develop ways of representing sequencing in task behavior that is both flexible and robust.

As an example of a fairly long sequence of actions, consider the process of making coffee. Larkin's (1989) analysis shows that when making coffee is considered as a planning problem, it is quite complex and includes approximately 18 actions (when it includes grinding the coffee beans). If these 18 actions were always performed in the same order, making coffee would be a simple matter of memorizing actions, and carrying them out in order. However, some aspects of making coffee can be parallelized, like filling the carafe with water while the grinder is running. Sometimes, additional actions have to be added, like tossing away an old filter in the coffee maker. Or, actions like filling the reservoir can be skipped, if there is still water in it.

Larkin lists six properties of making coffee that a model should be able to explain:

- The process is easy.
- It is largely error free.
- It is not degraded by interruption. The task can be picked up at any stage without extensive problem solving, and it is even possible to complete the coffee-making process when someone else has started it.
- The steps are performed in a variety of orders. The constraints on the task only partially order the subtasks, allowing several orderings of steps and, in theory, even parallel execution of steps.
- The process is easily modified. For example, if there is still water in the reservoir, the plan can effortlessly be modified to skip filling the reservoir, but otherwise carry out all the other steps.
- Performing the task smoothly requires learning—the reasoning process doesn't come "for free." However, experts can adapt a plan in novel ways, so people do not simply cache old solutions.

The balance of flexibility and robustness in coffee-making can be achieved in ways similar to those demonstrated in several earlier models, like the perfect time-sharing model in Chapter 6 and the robot controller described earlier in this chapter. Instead of having an internal representation of the problem, actions are triggered by perception whenever possible. Larkin's solution to the coffee-making problem, and several others, involved what she called *display-based problem solving*. The idea is that a particular action, such as pouring water into the reservoir, is triggered by certain perceptual conditions, such as a full carafe and an empty reservoir. Display-based problem solving is robust because actions are carried out under the circumstances in which they are needed, and not at other times. If the reservoir happens to be already full, the pouring action is not carried out, and instead, the actions that rely on a full reservoir can proceed. Interruptions have no impact on resuming the task, because there is no mental representation (other than the goal itself) to maintain. The task can also be carried out in different orders; for instance, if the grinder takes longer to grind than usual, we may have time to fill the reservoir, while otherwise we would only have filled the carafe.

A representation in which actions are triggered by perception makes parallel processing easier. While the coffee grinder is grinding, the carafe can be filled with water and poured into the reservoir, because its conditions are not dependent on the state of the coffee grounds. This also offers a clue for how to model the simplified air traffic control task

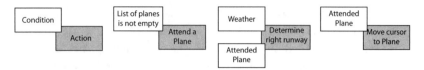

Figure 7.9. Alternative (partial) task representation of the simplified air traffic control task. White boxes represent conditions of actions in gray boxes.

mentioned earlier. The data from that experiment suggest that participants do some of their planning at the same time as moving the cursor—something that is hard to model on the basis of a task analysis like that in Figure 7.1. On the other hand, if task knowledge is structured on the basis of actions triggered by perceptual conditions, we arrive at the representation shown in Figure 7.9. In this representation, determining the appropriate runway can be done on the basis of the weather and the attended plane. At the same time, an attended plane allows the model to move the cursor, which the model can do in parallel with determining the appropriate runway. Thus, many of the steps that prompted the previous model to look up information are now part of the conditions of other instructions.

What all these examples show is that carrying out complex sequential tasks is not just a matter of having an internalized representation of the world, but also of letting the world participate actively in determining the next action. Obviously, we cannot always completely rely on the outside world, because sometimes information is not available, or it is too costly to collect. In the coffee-making example, if the coffeemaker has an opaque reservoir, we have to remember whether or not we put water in it. As another example, if a person is solving a multicolumn subtraction problem, he or she must remember when to borrow from the next column because this information is costly to reconstruct. As outlined in Chapter 4, the problem state resource, along with declarative memory, allows for storage of this type of information during task execution.

More generally, many tasks require some form of internal representation, but the smaller this representation is, the more robust and flexible behavior can be. This is called the *minimal control principle*:

> "People organize their behavior for a task such that the cognitive model that corresponds to this behavior is the model with the minimal number of control states."
>
> (Taatgen, 2007, p. 368)

This principle is a specialized version of an even more general principle in science, going back to Plato, stating that all other things being equal, the simpler explanation is the better explanation (see also Chater & Vitányi, 2002).

Can a Cognitive Model Help Improve Instructions?

The idea that people rely strongly on perceptual conditions to determine next actions has important consequences for the best way to learn task representations. Everyday life is full of instructions: instructions on how to operate a camera or a computer application, directions on how to drive from one place to another, recipes to bake and cook, and so on. The most common format of instructions is a simple list of actions. Take for example the following recipe for baking a cake (from www.foodgeeks.com):

1. Bring egg whites to room temperature, about 1 hour.
2. Meanwhile, sift flour, cocoa, powdered sugar, and cinnamon together three times. Set aside.
3. In a large mixing bowl, beat the egg whites, cream of tartar, and vanilla with an electric mixer on medium speed until soft peaks form. Gradually add the sugar, 2 tablespoons at a time, beating on high speed until stiff peaks form. Transfer to a larger bowl if needed.
4. Sift about 1/4th of the flour mixture over the beaten egg whites. Fold in gently. Repeat, folding in the remaining flour mixture in fourths.
5. Pour into ungreased 10-inch tube pan. Bake on the lowest rack in the oven at 350° F for 40–45 minutes or until the top springs back when touched.
6. Immediately invert cake (leave in pan); cool thoroughly. Loosen sides of cake from pan; remove.

This recipe consists of a considerable number of actions to be carried out in sequence. Although the order is probably not as strict as indicated, only the word *meanwhile* in Step 2 indicates that Steps 1 and 2 may overlap. Moreover, the purpose of the actions are not explained; although the purpose may be obvious in some cases (like baking the cake), other actions are quite opaque. Why do the eggs need to be at room temperature, and will the cake fail to rise if they are too cold? What is the purpose of sifting the flour three times? Is it possible to add ingredients, like raisins, or can certain ingredients be left out? Biochemist and cooking expert Shirley Corriher (2008) has investigated the necessity of sifting flour, and concluded that it is completely unnecessary. Flour from the supermarket does not contain irregularities to remove, and a spoon is more efficient for purposes of mixing ingredients. More fundamentally, cookbook recipes do not help much in making a person a better cook, because recipes do not contain the right building blocks to help the person devise new recipes. A recipe augmented with the purpose of each step would be much more beneficial for novice cooks, and some cookbooks (including Corriher's) go through great lengths to explain these "hows and whys" of cooking.

Several researchers have argued that product designers and manual writers should help people build mental models of the device or software that they have to interact with. Johnson-Laird (1983) and others have used mental models to explain how people perform reasoning tasks without formal logic. Norman (1988) applied this idea to human–computer interaction and design in general, and argued that once a user has an appropriate mental model of a device, they can predict what their actions will do and how the actions should be sequenced to achieve particular goals. Unfortunately, the concept of a mental model was only defined in functional terms, not in any formal way. Perhaps due to this poor definition, mental models have had mixed success in producing better instructions. According to Kieras and Bovair (1984), mental models are only useful insofar as they support exact and specific control actions. Kieras and Bovair found that general principles, metaphors, and analogies generally do not improve performance very much. These observations are consistent with the knowledge representations used by Larkin (1989) and the alternative instructions we proposed for the air traffic control task. If those accounts are right, instructions that are keyed to relevant conditions, either perceptual or cognitive, should provide an advantage over the ubiquitous list-style instructions. In the next section we will discuss a study that tests this theory directly.

Better Instructions in the Flight Management Task

In commercial aviation, instructions in the form of lists are very common— namely, as checklists used to make sure that no steps are forgotten during maintenance, flight preparation, travel, and landing. Modern airplanes use a flight management system (FMS) to help pilots control the airplane.

An FMS offers an additional layer of automation on top of the autopilot, and is capable of flying the airplane for almost the entire flight with the exception of takeoff. Pilots supply the FMS with information and parameters about the flight, including the desired route but also including additional information like the weight of the cargo. The route comprises a list of waypoints connecting the departure airport to the destination airport, together with the altitude and speed at each waypoint. Traditionally, waypoints were radio beacons or visual landmarks, but with advent of global positioning systems (GPS), most are now predefined points on a map. Although the route is programmed into the FMS during flight preparation, pilots often modify it during a flight to accommodate changes in weather or congestion around the destination airport.

Although most planes have an FMS, there is little to no standardization unifying the various available systems; whenever a pilot receives supplementary training to learn to fly a new type of aircraft, the pilot also receives training on the FMS for that aircraft. Training typically consists of learning procedures for the FMS in a classroom, followed by a phase of training in a flight simulator. A procedure consists of a list of actions to be carried out in sequence, and this list must be memorized as part of the classroom training program. For example, the Boeing 777 FMS (detailed shortly) includes 102 different procedures. However, since Federal Aviation Administration (FAA) certification for pilots only tests 25 of these procedures, training is focused on those 25, under the assumption that the pilots will explore and/or discover the other procedures on their own. Unfortunately, this training regimen is not very effective. It is very hard for pilots to memorize all the procedures, hard to retain the ones that are not used very often, and almost impossible to generalize procedures to new situations (Sherry, Polson, Fennell, & Feary, 2002). Effectively, the classroom phase of training is virtually useless, which means that pilots learn procedures primarily during the flight-simulator phase of training—a costly expense in time and money. One of the more lengthy procedures involves entering information into the FMS before the start of the flight, which takes approximately 30 minutes to complete. The instructions dictate that information be entered in a straightforward linear fashion. In practice, however, the situation is very different: The information to be entered arrives at different and not always predictable moments, and pilots are frequently interrupted. Sometimes new data requires that old information be updated; for example, if the pilot is notified that extra cargo is loaded onto the plane, he or she not only has to update the cargo weight, but also the takeoff speed that is dependent on cargo weight.

The problems that pilots encounter during training are analogous to the problems of cookbook recipes, because the steps in the procedures are actions whose purposes are unclear. Based on the previous analyses of making coffee, and of landing planes in the air traffic control task, only a slight augmentation of the procedures should improve performance considerably, especially when the procedures have to be applied in a novel situation. Taatgen, Huss, Dickison, and Anderson (2008) designed an experiment to test this idea. Participants in the study learned procedures for the FMS in two ways: from list instructions identical to those used in airline training programs (adapted from the training manual used by United Airlines), and from context instructions augmented by the

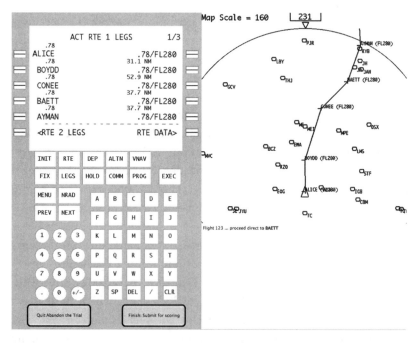

Figure 7.10. Task display and instructions in the FMS task. The Task display consists of the control unit on the left, which consists of a keyboard and a display (the CDU), which is flanked by two rows of keys (the top left of these keys is the 1L key). On the top right the navigational display is shown with the current route. The triangle at the bottom is the plane itself, and the line shows the current route. The bottom row of the CDU is called the scratchpad, which is empty in this example. On the bottom right the task "proceed direct to BAETT" is shown. From Taatgen et al. (2008), Copyright 2008 American Psychological Association. Reprinted with permission.

context in which to use the step—when to do the action, and what it accomplishes. Figure 7.10 shows the task display, and both types of instructions for one of two procedures used in the study. The basic task performed by participants used the only first of these, the direct-to procedure. This procedure changes the waypoint that the plane is currently heading for, and updates the rest of the route to reflect this change. In some of the later problems, participants executed both the direct-to procedure and the second remove-discontinuity procedure. Before the actual experiment, the participants received a general explanation of the task, and the two procedures to memorize in either the list or the context format. They then had to solve trials like the one in Figure 7.10.

Participants solved a series of 36 problems divided in blocks of 12 problems. The first three problems in each block, which we will call *easy problems*, were those that could be solved by literally carrying out the steps in the table in Figure 7.10, thus involving only the first of the two procedures. The next three problems, *medium problems*, required both procedures. The last six problems in each block, *hard problems*, were cases that were not completely covered by the instructions and required some improvisation. For example, in some of the hard problems, a waypoint later in the flight plan had to be changed, even though the instructions only specify how to change the first waypoint.

Figure 7.11 shows the accuracies of the 36 problems for both types of instructions. The context instructions gave a clear advantage over the traditional list instructions. Further analyses revealed that there was an interaction between problem type and instruction: the difference in accuracy became larger as the difficulty of the problems increased. This suggests that list instructions are adequate when actions can be carried out literally, but are worse than context instructions when combining two procedures (in the case of medium problems) or adjusting procedures (in the case of hard problems). These differences were also reflected in the average solution times: 28.7 seconds in the list condition, versus 24.8 seconds in the context condition.

Instruction-Following Model of the FMS Task

Instructions in the model of the FMS task are represented as operators with an action triggered by one or more preconditions, just as in the air traffic control and coffee-making examples (see also Catrambone and Yuasa, 2006). In addition, the operator represents the expected outcome

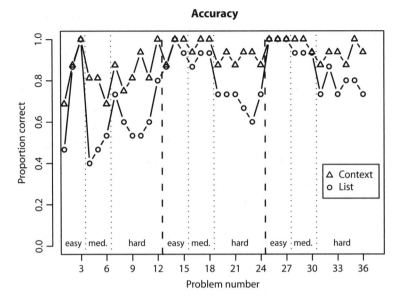

Figure 7.11. Accuracy in the FMS experiment.

of the action. Both preconditions and expected outcomes can refer to external information—that is, information that can be read from the screen, or the internal problem state. When we constructed the model, we wanted it to be identical for both the list and context instruction conditions, with the exception of the instruction representations themselves. For the context instructions, the operators consisted of actions with the preconditions and the expected outcomes that were mentioned in the instructions. Because the list instructions contain no clues about how they are linked to what happens on the screen, we assumed that people mentally keep track of where they are in the list. In the model, this is accomplished by linking the operators together in a list.

Figure 7.12 illustrates the two sets of operators. Each of the operators corresponds to one of the lines in the instructions in Figure 7.10. In the case of the context instructions, the preconditions of each operator refer to items that can be checked against the display, with the exception of "nav check," which is an internal representation of the fact that the navigational display has been checked and is stored in the problem state. Operators also have an expected outcome, which can be used as a cue to retrieve the next operator. Although the current model does not use it, the expected outcomes can, in principle, also be used to check whether a particular action was successful. Figure 7.12 depicts the situation in which the participant has just entered the waypoint into the scratchpad. The model now finds the next operator on the basis of its perceptions (the external state) and its expectations (stored in the problem state). The external state is constructed by a separate thread that scans the display and keeps track of items that change. This external representation is not necessarily complete, because the scanning thread may have missed something, which is particularly true in complex, cluttered displays. The possibly incomplete external state, and the possibly inaccurate problem state, serve as retrieval cues for an operator. Once an operator is retrieved, its conditions are checked against both states. If one of the preconditions refers to the display (e.g., the contents of the scratchpad), and that condition is not yet in the external state, then visual attention is directed to the appropriate location, after which the scanning thread picks up the missing information. An example would be the case illustrated in Figure 7.12 if the visual thread had failed to notice that the scratchpad has changed, and the main thread had retrieved the "Press 1L" operator.

The context-instruction representations include redundancy between the external world and the problem state, and in many cases (though not all) the problem state will match the state of the world. This redundancy has several advantages. First, the consistency of the cue increases the probability that the correct operator is retrieved. More importantly, redundancy provides robustness: if there is an interruption and the problem state is lost, the environment can provide the necessary cues to retrieve the next operator. If the problem state is inaccurate because the problem is different from previous problems, which is the case in the hard problems in the experiment, the difference between external and problem state can trigger a process that tries to determine the right action in the new situation. If, on the other hand, for some reason the external state is incomplete (e.g., because of a display malfunction), the problem state can provide guidance on what to do next.

The list instructions, in contrast, do not provide any references to the external state, forcing the model to rely solely on the problem state to determine its next action. Without the redundancy provided by both the external and problem state, this model's behavior is much more brittle. It does not know what the outcomes of its actions should be, and thus it cannot judge whether it is proceeding toward a solution to the problem.

Participants in the experiment did not solve all initial problems correctly, even though these initial problems required only that they carry

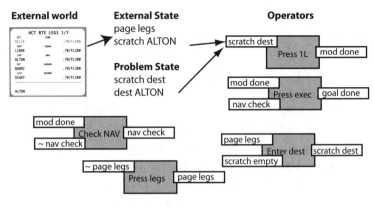

(a) Context instructions

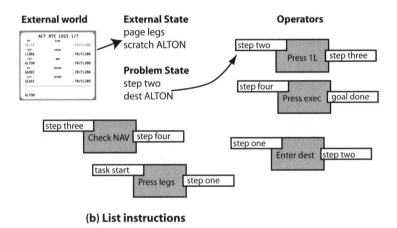

(b) List instructions

Figure 7.12. Illustration of finding the right action in both conditions of the experiment. Each operator consists of one or two preconditions (white boxes on the left), an action (the gray box), and an expected outcome (white box on the right).

out the instructions exactly as they had learned them. The model there-fore assumes that not all instructions have been learned correctly, either because of memory decay or incorrect interpretation of an instruction. As a consequence, every operator is assumed to have a 25% probability of missing (an estimate used to fit the data). Combined with the fact that the model does not have all the knowledge it needs to solve the hard problems, the model needs some method to discover new operators.

We chose a relatively simple method: whenever the model is not able to find the appropriate operator to match the current state, it takes a random guess, tries out this guessed action, and perceives its outcome. If the model then judges that this action brought it closer to the goal, it stores the guessed action with its prior state (both external and problem) and outcome, as a new operator for the task. Given that a guessed action could lead to errors, the model also manages to learn operators that can get it out of trouble—for example, that pressing the "Erase" key puts the FMS back in its original state. The result of this discovery process is that the model learns new context operators. In the case of the context instructions, these new operators fit in seamlessly with the existing ones. With the list instructions, the result is a mixture of both original list instructions and learned context instructions. Although this mixture is not as efficient as the representation consisting of only context instructions, it does enable the list-condition model to solve some of the hard problems, which would have been impossible with list instructions alone. In addition to learning through discovering operators, the model also learns new production rules through production compilation, generating rules that directly recognize the current state and produce the appropriate action. This process is similar to the one discussed in Chapter 6 and illustrated in Figure 6.4.

The model was made to solve the same sets of problems as the participants. A problem was counted as an error if the model reached an unrecoverable error state (e.g., pressing EXEC after an incorrect route modification), or after 120 seconds (i.e., more time than any problem would normally take). Figure 7.13 shows the accuracy results of the model. A first accomplishment of the model is that it could learn the task at all, given the impoverished knowledge it received, but more importantly it also fits the human accuracy data very well. (The model also produced a good fit of the mean solution times, not shown.)

Although the model produces a fine fit to the aggregate data, this does not mean that the details of the model are correct (just as in our earlier air traffic control example). We will now look at three ways to provide further support for the model. The first is to examine a particularly interesting aspect of behavior of the human participants and the model; namely, their use of the task function keys. The second is to test whether the model is capable of making predictions about a new experiment. The third is to examine whether the model can make predictions about eye movements made during task execution.

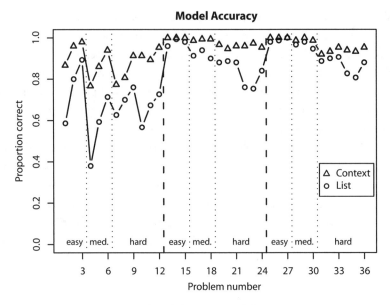

Figure 7.13. Accuracy results of the FMS model.

A Detailed Look at the Use of Function Keys

The use of function keys allows for a more in-depth view of behavior in the FMS task. Two keys play a role in every problem that participants solve: the LEGS key at the start, and the EXEC key at the end. The purpose of the LEGS key is to put the LEGS page on the display, which shows the current flight plan. As the context instructions suggest, this step is only necessary when the Control Display Unit (CDU) is currently not displaying the LEGS page; otherwise it can be omitted. The expectation is, therefore, that participants in the context condition will press the LEGS key only when necessary, but participants in the list condition will always press it. In the experiment, only 11% of the trials required pressing the LEGS key, which means that optimal performance translates to 0.11 LEGS key presses per trial. Figure 7.14 shows that both the participants and model in the context condition press the LEGS key only slightly more often than required. The list participants and model, on the other hand, press the key much more often, approximately every trial.

The function of the EXEC key is to finalize all changes, and should be pressed once at the completion of every trial. However, the procedures as given specify that for medium difficulty problems, the EXEC key should

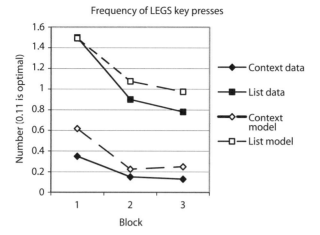

Figure 7.14. LEGS key press frequency. From Taatgen et al. (2008), Copyright 2008 American Psychological Association. Reprinted with permission.

be pressed twice: once at the end of each of the procedures. This is redundant and unnecessary, given the function of the key. Nevertheless, the participants and model in the list condition press the EXEC key more often for a medium problem than in a simple problem, as shown in Figure 7.15. The participants and model in the context condition show no difference between the two types of problems. (Note that the list participants do not always press EXEC twice in a discontinuity problem, which the model predicts if it has discovered the operator that resolves the discontinuity itself.)

Predictive Power of the Model

For a cognitive model to fit a set of data, one might fit parameters, try different solution strategies, and so on. Usually data are collected with a particular qualitative expectation in mind. More ideally, a quantitative prediction should be made before any data is collected, but unfortunately this is not feasible in many cases. A new task often includes uncertainties that cannot be properly put into a model and have to be estimated on the basis of the data. In the FMS task, we do not know the exact level of activation of the declarative task knowledge, because we leave it up to the participants to decide when they are done studying the instructions. A different approach, and a better approach for the FMS task, involves fitting a model to a first experiment, and then using this model to predict behavior

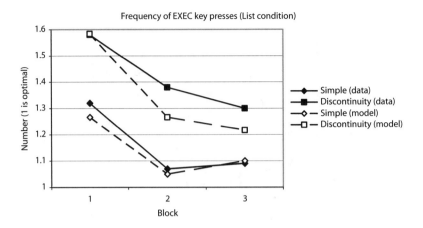

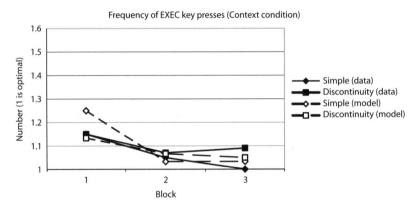

Figure 7.15. EXEC key press frequency. From Taatgen et al. (2008), Copyright 2008 American Psychological Association. Reprinted with permission.

in a second experiment. Under this approach, we ran a second experiment in which new problem types were added to the experimental blocks. These problems concerned partially completed problems—problems in which a number of steps necessary to reach the goal were already carried out. An additional twist was that, in some of these problems, an error had been made in one of the steps that were already carried out. In the case of the partially completed problems, the participant had to first notice the partial completion, then assess what state the problem was in, and subsequently carry out the remaining actions. In addition, in the partially completed problems with an error, the participant first had to repair the error before finishing the problems. In the reality of the cockpit, pilots sometimes have to solve partially completed problems when the copilot has started a procedure and then hands it over to the pilot. This is closely related to a situation in which a task is interrupted and later resumed when the problem state of the task has been forgotten and needs to be reconstructed (see Chapter 5).

The instructions for the second experiment were identical to those for the first experiment. As a consequence, the model of the first experiment should be able to produce a prediction for the outcome of the second, without any changes. We again expected the context instructions to give an advantage over the list instructions, because they offer a way to deduce an action for a certain state even though this state is not produced by an action of the model itself. Figure 7.16 shows the results for both conditions with the model prediction. The results of the experiment show that the context instructions again produced a significant advantage over the list instructions in terms of accuracy. In addition, the model's results proved to be quite accurate, especially given that they are truly *a priori* predictions of performance.

Predictions of Eye Movements

A key aspect of the FMS model as described is that it depends heavily on visual attention to determine its next action. If the model is accurate, then, it should be able to provide reasonable predictions of eye movements in the task—eye movements serving as a surrogate measure of visual attention. To test this idea, Taatgen and Dickison (2008) performed an eye-movement experiment using a design similar to the first FMS experiment discussed in this chapter. To analyze the data, the screen was divided into four regions: the top right region with the CDU (see Figure 7.10), the bottom right region with the keyboard, the top right region with the navigation display (NAV), and the bottom right region with the instructions and feedback. The top left panel of Figure 7.17 shows the proportion of time participants spent looking in a particular region over the course of a problem, aggregated over all medium-difficulty problems solved correctly by participants. The total time needed to solve the problem was divided into ten segments, and for each segment the proportion that the participant looked at a particular region was calculated. The graph includes the average over all participants and all medium problems. Characteristic of medium problems is that participants have to apply two procedures: the basic procedure used for the easy problems, and another procedure to remove so-called discontinuities. In medium

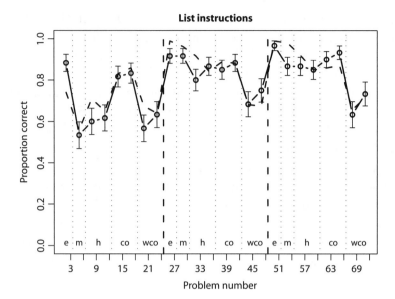

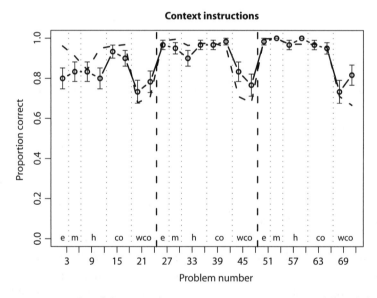

Figure 7.16. Results of the second experiment. Data is represented by solid lines with standard error bars, model predictions by dashed lines. Each point in the graph represents the average of three problems. e = easy, m = medium, h = hard, co = partially completed, wco = partially completed with an error. The e, m and h problems were identical to the problems in the first experiment, but the co and wco problems are new predictions by the model. From Taatgen et al. (2008), Copyright 2008 American Psychological Association. Reprinted with permission.

problems, one of the lines on the CDU will display "discontinuity" after Step 3 in the instructions (see Figure 7.10), and the NAV display will show a disconnected route. When this occurs, the participant should carry out two additional steps to reconnect the route by copying a waypoint into the discontinuity line before resuming the main procedure.

At the start of a trial, participants primarily looked at the instructions, and then gradually shifted their attention to the keyboard to type the waypoint as per the instructions. After entering the waypoint, they shifted attention to the CDU to find and press the 1L key. At this moment, the discontinuity appears, something that can be deduced from either the CDU or the NAV display. The data show a slight increase in eye movements in the NAV area, as can be seen in the detail 1 graph in Figure 7.17. Handling a discontinuity involves entering a second waypoint, and thus participants tended to look back at the instructions. This second waypoint can be entered through a shortcut that only involves the CDU, explaining why eye movements focus on that area. After all modifications have been done, the NAV display has to be checked, and the detail 2 graph indeed indicates participants' increased eye-movement activity in that area. Analysis of individuals, however, shows that only 59% of them actually check the NAV display before pressing EXEC. Pressing EXEC directs the eyes to the keyboard, then back to the instructions area to see the visual feedback from this action.

The model results, shown in the right-hand panels of Figure 7.17, show a reasonably faithful qualitative fit to the data, at least for the trial as a whole. The effects in the detailed graphs are more pronounced (and less spread out) for the model, in part because the human eye-movement measurements include eye-tracking noise (in contrast to the "perfect eye tracking" of the model). In addition, participants' behavior was more variable than that of the model. In the case of detail 1, the model seemed to prefer checking the NAV display to deduce whether there was a discontinuity, while participants preferred checking the CDU. Both participants and model looked back at the instructions noting a discontinuity. Towards the end of a problem, the model always checked the NAV display, producing a pronounced peak in eye-movement activity in that area.

In summary, the model is reasonably accurate in predicting eye movements, but not perfect. It does support the notion that people use visual information in deciding their next action, even though the model may not always accurately predict exactly what information is used. This is probably no surprise, given that there are redundancies in the display

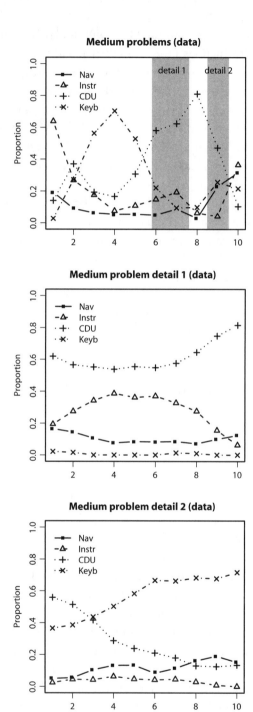

Figure 7.17. (continued)

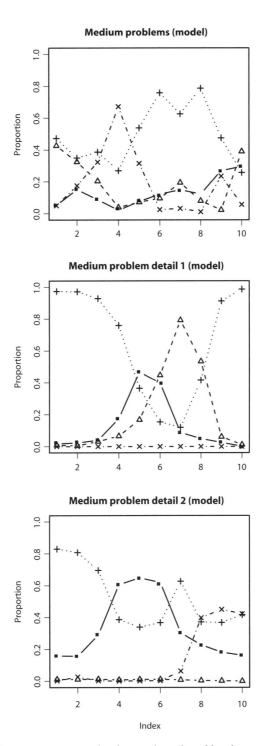

Figure 7.17. Eye-movements in the data and produced by the model. The top two panels show the trial as a whole, while the bottom four panels show the details of the two areas indicated in gray.

information, so the participants may or may not use particular cues to decide on their next action. Nevertheless, the present model selects actions based on what it expects and what it perceives in the world, and offers a significant improvement over classical models in its ability to behave in, and adapt to, the changing conditions of a complex task.

Research Connections

Models of complex tasks have always been among the main goals of the cognitive-architecture approach, not least because they involve many different areas of cognition. The General Problem Solver (GPS: Newell & Simon, 1963) was one of the first attempts to create an algorithm that could perform any type of task. The Soar cognitive architecture (Laird, Newell, & Rosenbloom, 1987) is a modern incarnation of GPS that sees problem solving as the basis for cognition. The early motivation for modeling complex tasks was that any model that could perform such a task would give insights into the underlying cognitive components. Newell (1973) himself, for example, proposed to study everything there is to know about playing chess as a means to gaining a broader understanding of human problem solving. The ACT-R architecture, on the other hand, takes a more bottom-up approach, which is also more consistent with EPIC (Meyer & Kieras, 1997) and many neural-network approaches. In this approach, the first order of business is to get the basic components of the architecture right, and only when they have been faithfully modeled can we use them as building blocks for models of complex cognitive tasks. Both approaches have their merits, and although the models presented in this chapter use ACT-R, many of the ideas on how to derive and evaluate new actions, and how to become faster by proceduralization, have been inspired by Soar's approach. The proper sequencing of actions in routine tasks is often not the topic of study in cognitive architectures, with some exceptions (notably Cooper & Shallice, 2000, and Botvinick & Plaut, 2004).

Research on embodied cognition that started with the robot work by Brooks and Steels has also embraced the idea that the environment is partially (or completely) in control of cognition, and that the traditional view of perception–cognition–action is misleading (Clark, 1997). For example, Prinz (1997) found that perception can activate corresponding actions directly, and Roelfsema, Lamme, and Spekreijse (1998) showed that motor cells corresponding to candidate eye movements are activated directly by perception. In a more applied setting, Kirsh (1995) argued that people tend to organize their world to facilitate performance. In the game of Tetris, for instance, players rotate pieces physically (by pressing keys) instead of mentally, because the former is faster and less effortful (Kirsh & Maglio, 1994). Detailed eye-movement studies of making tea (Land, Mennie, & Rusted, 1999) and sandwiches (Hayhoe, Shrivastava, Mruczek, & Pelz, 2003) also demonstrated the strong involvement of visual perception in carrying out tasks, similarly to the study of eye movements in the FMS task presented here.

The Big Picture

In this chapter we have turned from multitasking to monotasking, and have looked at issues that are usually taken for granted. In the symbolic tradition of cognitive modeling, proper sequencing of actions is often trivial because symbolic representations lock in the proper sequence with little chance of errors. As we have seen, this approach is characterized by a lack of robustness and flexibility, which leads to failure for even the smallest change or disturbance in the task. Moreover, in the air traffic control example, a traditional model was not even able to model the key-stroke-level aspects of the data. An alternative is to no longer consider steps in sequential behavior as an inflexible list, but as parallel candidates for execution as soon as they are applicable. Such a solution puts a much larger burden on what is usually called executive control. Control can, however, be minimized by relying on the environment to cue the right steps at the right time. Offloading control to the environment as much as possible—what we call the *minimal control principle*—not only alleviates this problem, but also improves both robustness and flexibility.

The example of learning in the Flight Management System (FMS) task shows how these theoretical ideas can be tested in a very practical situation. Instructions that encourage relying on the environment for control produce better performance in both speed and accuracy, and especially in problems that require extra flexibility. Procedural instructions are very common in complex task environments like the FMS, but also in everyday life—for example, recipes from a cookbook, driving directions produced by online services, instructions for various consumer electronics, and for using software. In many of these instructions, list-style formats are used that could easily be extended to context instructions. The theory developed in this chapter implies that instructions should always make sure to specify the context of the instructed actions, both in terms of the conditions under which the action applies, and the expected results of the specific action. In doing so, knowledge is not only more flexible and robust for execution of a single task, but also more amenable to flexibility and robustness in a multitasking environment.

8

Designing for Multitasking

We have, to this point, outlined three major components of our theory of threaded cognition—concurrent multitasking, sequential multitasking, and learning in multitasking (Chapters 2, 4, 6)—and more detailed studies of each, in applied domains (Chapters 3, 5, 7). In this chapter, we step back from the theory to analyze and discuss the theory's implications for the design of real systems, primarily computer-based systems as well as "off-the-desktop" portable devices such as portable digital assistants, smartphones, navigation devices, and so on. We first develop a set of design guidelines grounded in the theory to aid designers in developing better systems for use in a multitasking context. We then discuss how the computational framework and models representing the theory can be integrated into design tools that facilitate understanding and prediction of multitasking behavior.

Guidelines for Designers

Guidelines for design of computer-based systems have been popular for several decades in the fields of human–computer interaction, human factors and ergonomics, and industrial engineering (e.g., Dix, Finlay, Abowd, & Beale, 2003; Norman, 1988; Sharp, Rogers, & Preece, 2007; Shneiderman, 1998). Most of these efforts have not focused on multitasking as a central factor in design, although some notable exceptions (Gonzalez & Mark, 2004; Iqbal & Horvitz, 2007; Norman, 2007; Trafton & Monk, 2008) have made progress in this direction. In this section, we explore the implications of our multitasking theory and extrapolate them to broader recommendations for design.

An Overarching Guideline

Multitasking is often characterized in the media as the bane of modern society (e.g., Kirn, 2007; Rosen, 2008; Thompson, 2005). But this one-sided view ignores the many benefits of multitasking, not to mention its central and important role in human cognition. Multitasking allows us to walk while monitoring our surroundings, to type words while forming ideas, to listen to lectures while writing notes or formulating questions. In fact, not multitasking can sometimes be dangerous: imagine a driver focused solely on steering her/his vehicle without ever looking around to check for nearby vehicles. The benefits of multitasking cannot and should not be dismissed; instead, we should strive to better understand its strengths and limitations, and take both into account in the design of interactive systems.

As a general principle, then, designers should not eliminate or discourage multitasking. Instead, they should facilitate multitasking, with an important caveat: that users can control their level of multitasking for themselves, and adapt it dynamically as they see fit. We have discussed several examples of the differences between forced and user-controlled multitasking; for instance, Chapter 5 discussed the disruptive effects of interrupting a user at points of higher workload, and also how users tend to switch at points of lower workload when interruptions are user-controlled. As another example, Microsoft's now-defunct Office Assistant, the animated paper clip that offered advice to users, continually forced users into concurrent multitasking. Its animation drew attention away from the primary task, and its well-meaning recommendations were, in fact, additional distractions. Not surprisingly, users often alleviated this problem by exercising control over the system and simply turning off the assistant (Associated Press, 2001). When designers provide functionality that can be used broadly across the multitasking continuum, users can utilize the functionality however they see fit. For example, a modern operating system allows for multiple active running applications, but a user can open as few or as many applications as they wish in order to achieve their goals. Similarly, a calendar application can provide information on an hourly, daily, or monthly basis, leaving it to the user to decide how to utilize its functions (e.g., whether to set alarms for meetings, etc.).

Nevertheless, there is no doubt that in some task domains, users may decide to push past the limits of acceptable multitasking. Driver distraction is a salient example: drivers often choose to engage in secondary tasks while driving, ignoring the potential safety risks to themselves and those around them. Thus, we arrive at our first guideline, emphasizing the positive traits of multitasking, with the understanding that (1) multitasking should generally be user controlled, and (2) certain situations and task environments are exceptions to this general case, as we flesh out in the guidelines and prescriptions that follow.

- **DG–1:** *Encourage and facilitate user-controlled multitasking— except as noted in later guidelines.*

To specify further constraints on this general case, it is important to first consider the context of the system being designed. We can define context here to incorporate all aspects of the user experience when interacting with the system. For example, although a designer may be developing a single-user computer interface, there may be particular interfaces that will likely be used in particular contexts: a word-processing application used on an office desktop, a database interface used by telephone operators at a busy switchboard, or a medical PDA interface used by a nurse roaming the hospital hallways. Although he/she often has little control over the context beyond the system itself, the designer needs to keep this context in mind, and ensure that the system is usable in the associated context.

Given the system and context, the next step is determining whether these fall more on the concurrent or sequential end of the multitasking continuum. Figure 8.1, derived from the earlier Figure 4.1 in Chapter 4, shows, along with labels, the (more) concurrent and (more) sequential ranges of the continuum. Many designs would align primarily with one of these ranges. For instance, a telephone operator using a database interface must converse with the client while looking up information, which involves concurrent multitasking with subsecond task switches. On the other hand, an office worker using a word-processing application may be expected to focus on this task for at least a few minutes at a time, thus falling primarily in the range of sequential multitasking. As seen in the figure, each range involves different potential sources of interference.

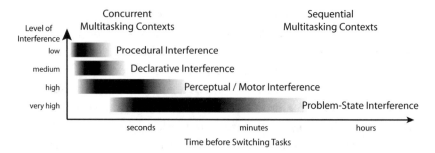

Figure 8.1. The multitasking continuum with ranges for concurrent and sequential multitasking.

The sources of interference differ in the typical duration of use of the corresponding resources and, therefore, have different impacts on the magnitude of interference: roughly 50 ms for procedural, 100–200 ms for declarative, 100–1000 ms for perceptual–motor, and up to tens of seconds for the problem state. We will find it useful to describe the guidelines for each range separately, in order to best address issues at the corresponding time scales. It should be noted, however, that some systems and tasks span across these ranges—for example, a note-taking tool might involve concurrent multitasking for writing while listening, but might also involve sequential multitasking for writing every few minutes after hearing and understanding a section of material.

Concurrent Multitasking Contexts

In contexts involving concurrent multitasking, procedural, declarative, and perceptual–motor interference can all affect user behavior, and thus should be understood in guiding system design. In cases of very rapid interleaving of tasks, threaded cognition and ACT-R theory posit that almost any combination of tasks can, in theory, lead to multitasking interference. Each task thread involves procedural steps that initiate processes in the mind's various resources, and the procedural resource, like all other resources, can only be used by a single thread at a given time. Thus, any task can, in principle, experience procedural interference with some other concurrent task. (Perfect time-sharing with no interference only occurs when the procedural steps line up exactly, such that they do not overlap.) Given that a procedural step lasts 50 ms, procedural interference generally results in occasional task delays on the order of 50 ms.

Unfortunately, not much can be done by designers (or users) to mitigate procedural interference; even behaviors with the highest degree of expertise require procedural rules for executing the behaviors. Nevertheless, the magnitude of the temporal delays caused by procedural interference is rather small. Thus, a designer is faced with a critical question: Might even occasional 50 ms delays result in unacceptable decreases in performance? We have seen that in high-paced tasks, such as the manual tracking task analyzed in Chapters 2 and 4, even these small delays negatively affect performance. Moreover, in a safety-critical domain such as driving, the smallest degradation in performance can have dangerous consequences. (Consider that a vehicle traveling at highway speeds takes only 100 ms to travel 10 feet—potentially, the difference between a collision and near miss.) At the same time, as noted earlier, multitasking in service of the safety-critical task (e.g., monitoring other cars while driving) cannot and should not be discouraged. Thus, we derive our next guidelines in terms of safety-critical and high-paced systems:

- **DG–2**: *For safety-critical systems, discourage and/or eliminate any multitasking not relevant to the primary task.*
- **DG–3**: *For high-paced systems, determine whether short (50 ms) delays cause unacceptable degradation in performance, and if so, eliminate any multitasking not relevant to the primary task.*

Memory-based (declarative) interference can also affect concurrent multitasking. In fact, memory plays a critical role in our theory in at least three ways. First, because it is needed by many individual tasks for information storage and retrieval, memory use is often a source of contention among multiple task threads. Second, memory rehearsal and recall of a task problem state is a critical step in dealing with task interruptions. Third, memory is central to learning, in that memorized task instructions transform to procedural knowledge over time, thus predicting additional memory load at early stages in the learning process. Not surprisingly, then, designers should minimize memory load as one avenue toward alleviating these sources of multitasking interference.

There are two key ways to attempt to minimize memory load. The first involves taking knowledge "in the head" and putting it "in the world"—a good guideline for all contexts (Larkin & Simon, 1987; Norman, 1988), but especially so for multitasking contexts. Instead of relying on the user to remember commands and other information, this information can be placed in the system environment to make it as visible and available as possible. For example, whereas command-line user interfaces force a user to recall and type the next command, graphical user interfaces typically include menus and toolbars that represent the same functionality onscreen: The user can simply click on a menu or toolbar button to immediately activate the function, and if its location is not known, a brief visual search usually suffices to find the function. It should be noted, however, that users sometimes rely on imperfect knowledge in the head over perfect knowledge in the world, depending on the effort required to access the information (Gray & Fu, 2004). The greatest interference from knowledge "in the head" would arise in early stages of learning, when the pieces of information are not easily recalled, and thus take more time to retrieve (or relearn).

The second way to minimize memory load is to minimize the training needed to achieve expert performance. The learning theory presented in Chapter 6 suggests that early stages of learning require additional memory use, and create more potential for interference from the recall of task instructions. While well-learned skills are fully procedural and only make use of the procedural resource to execute steps, the early stages of learning require retrieval of a task instruction for each procedural step—a heavy load on the memory resource. Minimizing necessary training time also minimizes the time during which memory experiences this higher load. Also, it reinforces the importance of utilizing already-learned interface skills that the user could transfer from other tasks—for example, keeping a consistent interaction style for pulldown menus, lists, or other complex graphical interface components. Because the skills involved in such subtasks would be already well known from other contexts, transferring these skills to a new task (as opposed to changing the interaction style to define a new skill) helps to further minimize learning and memory usage. Another consequence of threaded cognition and the learning theory is that it is better to train new skills separately. If two new skills have to be learned concurrently, declarative memory interference will slow down the process considerably; when two practiced skills are combined, no further learning is necessary and threaded cognition can more easily interleave these skills.

- **DG–4:** *Maximize "knowledge in the world" to reduce memory load.*
- **DG–5:** *Maximize use of well-learned skills and procedures.*
- **DG–6:** *Train separable skills one at a time, until they are well learned and fully proceduralized.*

The third major source of interference during concurrent multitasking comes from perceptual–motor interference—when the primary task shares one or more perceptual or motor modalities with a concurrent task. For very widely used computer-based systems, like a generic office program (e.g., word processor, mail application, etc.), common distractions may be unpredictable and/or unavoidable (e.g., an office worker talking to a colleague). However, systems that tend to be used in particular contexts may call for more constraints on design; namely, trying to minimize perceptual–motor conflicts with expected concurrent tasks.

Consider a typical smartphone with communication capabilities for voice, email, instant messaging, and so on. The portable nature of these devices makes them highly amenable to use in multitasking environments, and indeed, one can easily find people walking, cycling, and driving while using these devices. Because vision is heavily used for walking, cycling, and driving, this guideline suggests that the design of these devices should minimize the need for vision in operating the device. For example, a menu-driven interface, where a user clicks a button to scroll down and select an option, is highly dependent on vision and can lead to significant distraction (Salvucci & Macuga, 2002). Audio feedback during scrolling may alleviate this dependence, especially when used together with alternative techniques for interaction (e.g., Zhao, Dragicevic, Chignell, Balakrishnan, & Baudisch, 2007). An especially good solution is the inclusion of redundant functionality, allowing functions that normally require vision (e.g., manual dialing) to be performed with another modality (e.g., voice dialing).

In the above case, the designer may know little about expected concurrent tasks because of the highly portable nature of the system. However, some systems are grounded specifically in a particular environment, and thus provide even further constraints on design. In-vehicle systems are one such category. Knowing that a particular radio, climate control system, navigation device, etc. will be installed in a vehicle makes these systems amenable to closer analysis for their potential to distract drivers (as in Salvucci, 2009). As another example, US Navy researchers have been investigating and developing multiple-display, multimodal "watchstations" in which a single operator juggles several mission-relevant tasks (Brock, Stroup, & Ballas, 2002). The system interface on each screen can be designed with the other watchstation interfaces in mind, such that the designer for one particular task interface can minimize the contention for perceptual–motor resources in the overall system. Thus, designers should make use of all available knowledge about the expected multitasking context to best constrain designs and avoid perceptual–motor conflicts.

When perceptual–motor conflicts are unavoidable, the theory suggests that small chunks of perceptual or motor activity, which are easily broken up, are much more amenable to multitasking than solid, continuous blocks of activity. Sustained perception (e.g., listening to an interesting radio program) tends to keep the perceptual resource busy without pauses; thus, the associated thread may not release the resource and may block other threads from acquiring it. (For example, a very interesting radio program may engage a listener so much that, if another person tries to interrupt, the listener may raise a hand to implicitly ask that person to wait until the segment is over.) In contrast, threads that use a resource in a more piecemeal fashion—acquiring and releasing it frequently—allows other threads to interleave their own processing. Thus, designers should aim for perceptual and/or motor processing that can be broken in a way that facilitates interleaving with other concurrent tasks.

It should also be noted that favoring more piecemeal activity extends beyond perceptual and motor actions. Sustained cognitive attention—continuous cognitive processing devoted to a single task—may interfere with other threads, just as continuous perceptual or motor processing would. For some tasks, sustained cognitive attention is an unavoidable aspect of the task, such as reading or writing a difficult passage of text. Such tasks lead to a tendency to monotask, because only through sustained attention can the task be successfully completed. This makes it even more critical that other tasks that may appear in the same context allow for piecemeal cognitive activity, allowing tasks that truly require sustained attention to receive it.

- **DG–7**: Minimize perceptual–motor conflicts with expected concurrent tasks.
- **DG–8:** Avoid the necessity of sustained attention where possible; instead, favor more piecemeal activity in perceptual, motor, and even cognitive resources.

Sequential Multitasking Contexts

In sequential multitasking environments, the dominant source of interference is problem-state interference—that is, the conflict that arises from switching the problem state context of the current task to another task.

The other sources of interference, notably perceptual–motor and declarative memory, can also have effects on sequential multitasking, especially when switching between tasks roughly every few seconds (see Figure 8.1). The guidelines above for alleviating these types of interference would then still apply. Nevertheless, the central factor in suspending and resuming a task during sequential multitasking is the ability to switch problem state and task context more generally.

As discussed in Chapters 4 and 5, suspending and resuming a task can be based primarily on either memory-based or reconstruction-based processes. Memory-based processes are dominant for shorter interruptions (tens of seconds to a few minutes) and/or when the problem state is very simple (e.g., a single piece of information, like a name or number). In this case, when users are interrupted they take time to rehearse the current state of the task in memory. Unfortunately, forced interruptions—in which a person is immediately transported to a new task without warning—can interfere with the rehearsal process and slow down resumption of the original task, especially when the interruption is a memory-intensive task, or one that is not well learned (and thus relies on memorized instructions). Instead, a warning of an imminent interruption allows for a short time to reflect upon and rehearse the current problem state. For example, a ringing phone provides the perfect opportunity for a person to stop actively performing the task and to reflect upon the state of the task before answering the phone and starting the interrupting conversation. Similarly, an audible alert for a chat message allows a user to self-interrupt at a convenient point in time. Note that the warning need not occur too far in advance of the interruption: our analysis suggests that memory rehearsal of only 2–3 seconds can be sufficient to significantly reduce resumption time after interruption.

It should also be noted that users want, and need, precise control over system interruptions. First, users exhibit a strong tendency to self-interrupt at points of lower workload (Czerwinski, Cutrell, & Horvitz, 2000; Iqbal & Horvitz, 2007; Salvucci & Bogunovich, 2010; Wiberg & Whittaker, 2005), so systems should facilitate this tendency and allow users to manage when they switch tasks. Second, users should be able to turn interruptions on and off as they wish, not only to ensure better task performance but also to reduce feelings of difficulty and the annoyance of switching (Czerwinski, Horvitz, & Wilhite, 2004; Iqbal & Bailey, 2005).

- **DG–9:** *Avoid forced interruptions; instead, provide allowances for user self-interruption.*

- **DG–10:** *When interruptions are necessary, warn users of the interruption at least 2–3 seconds before the start of the interruption.*
- **DG–11:** *Allow users to enable and disable system interruptions as desired.*

When interruptions last a few minutes or more, and/or the task's problem state is fairly complex, users typically cannot rely on memory to resume the suspended task. Instead, users perform a process of reconstruction, whereby they examine the task environment to rebuild problem-state information; for example, a user interrupted while ordering a product online may resume the task by scanning the web page for the first unfilled text field. At the same time, even this reconstruction process relies on memory to some extent; consider a user interrupted while reading online news, scanning the news headlines (reconstruction) and recalling whether or not he or she has read that article (memory).

The theory's account of reconstructing and recalling problem state suggests several additional guidelines. First, designers should aim to encourage task behaviors that do not require maintenance of problem state, or at least include many points of execution at which no problem state is necessary. The chat-interruption study in Chapter 5 provides an example of this, whereby users have access to relevant information onscreen. Second, when problem-state information is simple and compact, that information can be stored onscreen (a close cousin of the earlier guideline of keeping knowledge in the world). Third, systems can provide visual cues for the most recent actions in the environment, such as highlighting a recently pressed button or recently filled-in text field (Trafton, Altmann, & Brock, 2005).

- **DG–12:** *Encourage task behaviors that minimize a user's need to maintain problem-state information.*
- **DG–13:** *Place problem-state information onscreen whenever possible.*
- **DG–14:** *Provide visual cues for recent actions in the task environment.*

The way in which users mentally represent a task can have a strong impact on the robustness of performance and the ability to apply multitasking skills. As we have seen in Chapter 7, knowledge of what a particular action accomplishes, and under which circumstances it applies, helps users to fill in gaps in knowledge they need to deal with unfamiliar situations (Taatgen, Huss, Dickison & Anderson, 2008). This guideline is related to the more general recommendation to provide users with a mental model of a device (Norman, 1988). However, mental models have not always been successful in improving performance. Kieras and Bovair (1984) concluded that mental models are only useful when they support exact and specific control actions, and the Taatgen et al. (2008) experiment in Chapter 7 demonstrated that specific context instructions can lead to significant improvements in performance, whereas general mental models sometimes do not. Thus, we add one final guideline to reflect these ideas:

- **DG–15:** *Provide task instructions that explain under what circumstances each action has to be carried out, and what its expected outcome should be.*

Design Tools for Multitasking Contexts

The guidelines above are intended to be general guidelines that a designer can keep in mind while creating new systems for multitasking contexts. On the one hand, general guidelines allow for applicability to a wide variety of task domains. On the other hand, they do not provide specific predictions as to how user performance may change as a function of specific design choices, and they do not provide us with practical tools we can use to evaluate and compare designs. Fortunately, the grounding of our theory in a computational cognitive architecture allows for exactly these types of predictions when embedded into computer-based design tools. Such design tools provide an excellent complement to the set of general design guidelines.

While there have been many tools developed to aid designers in their work, there have been relatively few grounded in psychological theory, and even fewer aimed specifically at multitasking environments. The most notable theory-based systems have been integrated with rapid prototyping systems that allow for specification of both the task environment and the possible behaviors in this environment. For example, recent tools have allowed users to create behavioral models as textual specifications (Kieras, Wood, Abotel, & Hornof, 1995) and by task demonstration (Hudson et al., 1999; John, Prevas, Salvucci, & Koedinger, 2004; see also Myers, McDaniel, & Wolber, 2000, Paganelli & Paternò, 2003, and St. Amant, Lieberman, Potter, & Zettlemoyer, 2000, for related work). The resulting models, which typically interact in some way with the prototyped task interface, provide predictions of specific measures of behavior (e.g., time on task) that a designer might use to compare prototype designs. However, only one of these systems, CogTool (John et al., 2004; John & Salvucci, 2005), has attempted to account for behavior in a multitasking context. (See Pettitt, Burnett, & Stevens, 2007, however, for related modeling work.)

We now present a new system, called *Distract-R*, that demonstrates how threaded cognition itself can be integrated into a practical tool to facilitate design in multitasking environments.

The Distract-R System

Distract-R (Salvucci, 2009) is an integrated system for rapid prototyping and evaluation of in-vehicle devices—that is, user interfaces intended for use in a vehicle. The system's focus on driving and driver distraction allows for very detailed predictions. As opposed to a desktop user interface, for which measures like time-on-task are most often analyzed, the driving domain requires detailed analysis of measures related to driving performance. Distract-R is based on a validated model of driver behavior—in fact, the driver model described in detail in Chapter 3. However, the system is intended for use by designers with little to no experience in behavioral or cognitive modeling—the cognitive models operate solely "under the hood," taking a behavioral model specified by task demonstration and generating robust, theory-based predictions of performance.

Distract-R allows a user to prototype and evaluate new designs in five stages, corresponding to stages of specifying interfaces, tasks, drivers, scenarios, and a final stage of generating and analyzing simulation results. In the Interfaces stage, the user creates new interface designs by dropping components onto a simple canvas, such as the phone example in Figure 8.2. Components such as buttons, knobs, and displays can be combined with a microphone and/or speaker to create straightforward representations of the new interfaces. The screen in Figure 8.2 shows the phone interface with a standard numeric keypad, speaker and microphone. The user can create a number of possible designs and add them to the full list of prototyped interfaces. Figure 8.3 shows three other sample prototypes for an alternative phone interface, as well as a heating control interface and a stereo interface.

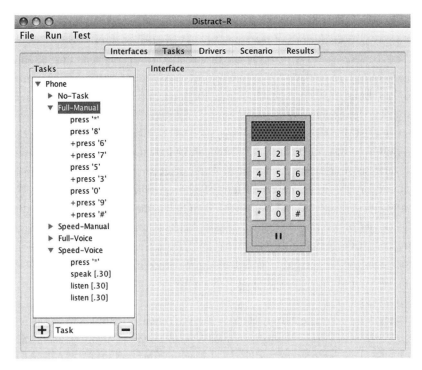

Figure 8.2. Distract-R interface. From Salvucci (2009), Copyright 2009 Association for Computing Machinery. Reprinted with permission.

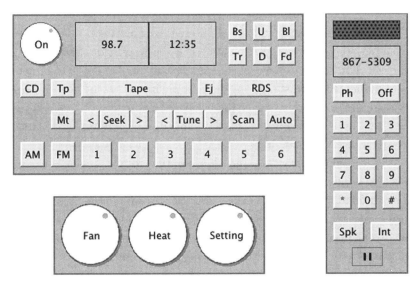

Figure 8.3. Sample Distract-R interfaces. From Salvucci (2009), Copyright 2009 Association for Computing Machinery. Reprinted with permission.

In the *Tasks* stage, the user specifies task behavior on the interfaces by simple demonstration. When a new task is created, each click on an interface component adds a step to the task related to the clicked component. For example, a click on a button denotes pressing the button, a click on a microphone denotes speaking into the microphone, and a click on a speaker denotes listening to a sound. A right-click on a component provides a list of more specific options, such as the time needed to speak the required phrase, or the angular distance to rotate a knob. Figure 8.2 shows several possible tasks (in the leftmost tree structure) related to the sample phone, notably the four conditions of phone dialing by manual or voice interaction discussed in Chapter 3 (from Salvucci, 2001). The most critical aspect of the tasks stage is that task demonstration creates an underlying cognitive model of the task behavior. Through a process of compilation (see Salvucci, 2009; Salvucci & Lee, 2003), the steps of the task behavior are translated into a working ACT-R computational model to be used in simulation.

The *Drivers* stage allows users to dictate certain attributes of the drivers with which to evaluate the interfaces and tasks. Currently, users can specify three factors: the age of the driver (younger or older), the driver's steering aggressiveness, and the driver's urge to maintain a stable path, especially when interacting with a secondary task. Each of these factors has a direct correlate to the underlying cognitive model of driving (Salvucci, 2006), and thus affects behavior when run in simulation. (The final chapter will discuss individual differences in behavior, as well as one example related to age-related differences between older and younger drivers.) The *Scenarios* stage lets the user specify the driving environment for simulating behavior. Options for these environments include the type of road (e.g., curvy or straight), the presence or absence of a lead vehicle, and the time characteristics of the simulation (total time, and time between secondary-task behaviors).

In the final *Results* stage, users click a button to run simulations of all possible combinations of the interfaces and tasks, drivers, and scenarios. The simulations rely on threaded cognition to interleave the interface task behaviors with the primary-task driving behavior, along with a modified version of the core ACT-R engine for simulating production rules for both tasks. The simulations run roughly 1000 times faster than real time; for example, Distract-R can simulate 15 minutes of driving in less than 1 second of real time. Thus, in just a few seconds, the system can run the various combinations and collect the model's predicted behavioral data related to each interface and task. Figure 8.4 shows one way in which a user can view these results, as a graph of average task time (dialing time) for each interface. The user can also view results for other common measures of driver performance, such as lateral deviation or velocity, lane violations, speed deviation, brake response time, and so on. The system thus provides the user with quantitative measures with which to compare the interface prototypes. If the user would like to see the behavior in greater detail, Distract-R can replay the simulations in real time, as shown in Figure 8.5, including a forward view of the roadway and an inside-the-vehicle view of the driver's interaction with the interface. Viewing the full graphical simulations allows the user to see exactly when and how the driver becomes distracted by the secondary task, and how performance is affected at a moment-by-moment level.

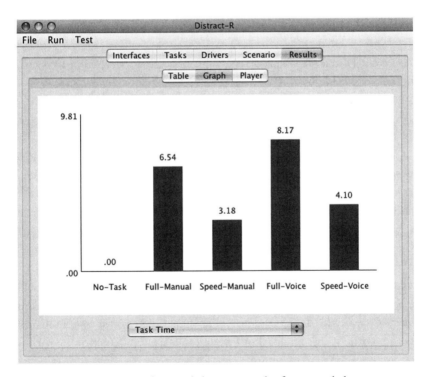

Figure 8.4. Distract-R results panel showing graph of average dialing time (in seconds) for prototyped interfaces. From Salvucci (2009), Copyright 2009 Association for Computing Machinery. Reprinted with permission.

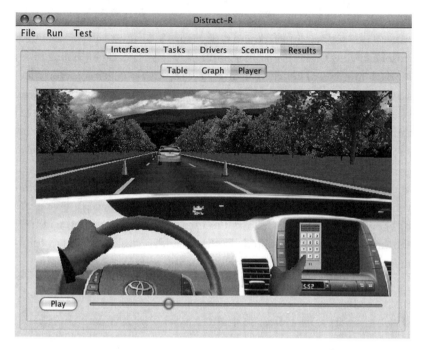

Figure 8.5. Distract-R simulation environment to allow for real-time viewing of simulated behavior. From Salvucci (2009), Copyright 2009 Association for Computing Machinery. Reprinted with permission.

Distract-R thus balances a reliance on rigorous cognitive models with designers' ease of use. The underlying models have been validated in several ways—the driver model itself has been well studied (see Chapter 3), and the integrated predictions for a few interesting interfaces have been separately validated using experimental data from a high-fidelity driving simulator (Greenberg et al., 2003). These validations provide some level of confidence that the system's predictions are reasonably good approximations of behavior. At the same time, the complexities of the modeling engine, including threaded cognition and ACT-R, are hidden away from users. Overall, the designers get the benefits of the rigorous psychological theory without the drawbacks of having to learn the details of the theory or computational architecture.

The entire Distract-R design cycle, from prototyping to demonstration to simulation and analysis, takes only a few minutes to complete (less than 20 minutes for the most complex study described in Salvucci, 2009). This rapid cycle enables designers to easily test out new ideas with respect to other ideas, and with respect to their potential effects on driver performance. Given the fact that Distract-R has a single simulation engine, and that empirical results are obtained in many ways (e.g., simulators versus real driving), some differences between Distract-R's predictions and observed results would not be surprising. However, our experience thus far with the system indicates that the system's qualitative predictions, especially rank-order predictions between multiple interfaces and tasks, generally correspond very well to empirical results. This is extremely important in a domain where human experiments can be costly and hazardous. Distract-R allows a user to rapidly reduce the design space from many options to the best few, avoiding costly tests on less promising designs, and focusing on the most promising designs for detailed experimentation.

9

Reflections and Future Directions

As a unifying theory, threaded cognition intends to account for all aspects of multitasking. In this book, we have demonstrated that threaded cognition accounts for several major types of multitasking that have traditionally been studied separately, and that the theory also extends to areas that are traditionally not considered multitasking. Nevertheless, there are certain aspects of multitasking that we have largely left out of our analysis to this point, yet should be recognized as critical to a unifying view of multitasking. This chapter highlights three important such areas: individual differences, brain realization, and metacognition. We explore the implications of our currently developed theory in each of these areas, as well as speculating on future research directions that may serve to flesh out the theory into more rigorous accounts of these and other important multitasking phenomena.

Individual Differences

It likely comes as no surprise that individuals exhibit differences with respect to their multitasking behavior. In fact, the news media and Internet "blogosphere" often speak of multitasking in terms of differences—discussing, for example, whether women are better multitaskers than men, or whether young and old people differ in their multitasking abilities.

But threaded cognition states that multitasking is a fundamental cognitive skill that allows all people to perform multiple tasks at the same time. How, then, can threaded cognition account for the variability in behavior that arises from individual differences?

The first important observation is that individual differences arise in many aspects of cognition, and all these sources of differences ultimately have an impact on multitasking behavior. One can broadly characterize differences in terms of what Meyer, Glass, Mueller, Seymour, & Kieras (2001) have called hardware and software differences. Hardware differences arise from fundamental differences in the human system—differences in cognitive processing, visual or motor systems, etc. In modeling terms, the hardware corresponds to the cognitive architecture itself, and its core abilities and characteristics. Software differences arise from differences in (declarative and procedural) knowledge, which may in turn arise from different experiences, such as exposure to particular task domains. For example, twins with essentially the same cognitive hardware may have vast differences in knowledge and ability based simply on differences in training (e.g., one trained as a nurse, the other as an air traffic controller). In modeling terms, this software refers to the knowledge, added to the core architecture, that specifies the skills for a particular task domain.

Our theory posits that threaded cognition is based in the cognitive architecture at the hardware level of cognition. Thus, people are born with the ability to execute and interleave multiple threads, and this ability is central to our overall multitasking ability. Threaded cognition on its own leaves no room for individual differences: the mechanics of the theory always work the same way, and there are no parameters that can influence it directly. However, our account, along with ACT-R theory, also includes a theory of skill acquisition by which people translate memorized knowledge to procedural skills. This process of production compilation is also an architectural, hardware aspect of cognition. The combination of these two core mechanisms can, in fact, produce an array of differences due to differences in knowledge (software). In fact, we have described many examples in which expertise in a task can affect not only performance in that task (which would be expected), but also affect performance in a concurrent task due to multitasking interference.

Consider individual differences related to gender. The research literature on gender-related differences in multitasking has not settled on an answer to the question of whether women, men, or neither are better multitaskers. The informal conclusion of several experts in the field (see Mahany, 2005; Seven, 2004) suggests that there are no significant differences in core multitasking ability between the sexes. Our theory would concur with this view; we see no reason to believe that the ability to interleave multiple threads would differ based on gender. However, different individuals may have very different abilities in particular tasks, and thus any gender-related differences in these tasks would manifest themselves as differences in task performance while multitasking. Thus, any such differences would come not from innate differences in multitasking performance, but from differences in people's skills and abilities in the individual task domains. In the movie "Kramer vs. Kramer," having been left by his wife played by Meryl Streep, Dustin Hoffman's character makes breakfast for himself and his young son. He tries to make French toast and coffee while keeping his son happy, who comments that Daddy does it all wrong, because he forgets the milk and puts too much coffee in the coffeemaker. The son then asks for orange juice, and while Dustin Hoffman fetches the juice from the refrigerator, the toast burns. Dustin loses his temper, drops the hot pan on the floor, and the boy starts crying. What does this example say about whether men are poor multitaskers? The movie answers that question by showing the same scene towards the end of the movie, in which father and son make the perfect breakfast. The movie's take on this issue is essentially the explanation threaded cognition offers: carrying out concurrent novel tasks is very hard because of declarative interference, but much easier as expertise in one or both tasks is acquired. According to the theory, any perceived gender differences are, therefore, not due to innate differences in multitasking ability, but to differences in proficiency in the individual skills as determined by the individual's practice and experience with those skills.

While threaded cognition posits that a person's "multitasking hardware" is fixed, there are other aspects of the human hardware that may differ between individuals. A salient example is that of age-related differences. Meyer et al. (2001) found that one of the most robust hardware differences between younger (roughly 20–30 years of age) and older (roughly 60–70) adults comes in the speed of their cognitive processing. They found that cognitive processing for older adults slows down by roughly 13%—which, in ACT-R terms, translates to a 13% increase in the production-firing time (from 50 to 56.5 ms).

Salvucci (2009) transferred this idea to multitasking in a modeling study of driver distraction comparing older and younger drivers. The study modeled empirical data collected by Reed and Green (1999), in which both groups dialed 10-digit phone numbers while navigating a simulated driving environment. The Distract-R system (see Chapter 8) was used to simulate driver performance, with the only difference between the age groups being the 13% slowdown in production-firing time. The empirical results and Distract-R predictions for the lateral velocity (a measure of the vehicle's stability) are shown in Figure 9.1. In the human results, younger and older drivers exhibited identical performance when driving alone without a secondary task. As expected, both sets of drivers exhibit decreased performance in the presence of a secondary task; however, the older drivers exhibited significantly worse performance as indicated by the significantly higher level of lateral velocity. The model's predictions reproduce these two effects. When driving as a single task, the 13% increase effectively adds only tens of milliseconds to the time between control updates, which in itself is not large enough to affect downstream performance. However, when dialing while driving, this increase becomes magnified—the additional time stretches from tens to hundreds of milliseconds, and thus causes the "older" model to experience more significant effects of driver distraction than the "younger" model.[1]

Of course, this analysis provides only a glimpse of how such differences can affect behavior. Differences related to age, like other types of differences, permeate many aspects of the human hardware (e.g., potential declines in visual and motor abilities). Also, the hardware and software are closely interrelated, and changes to cognitive and perceptual-motor systems often go hand-in-hand with adaptations of knowledge and skill. For example, an older driver that is aware of changes to his/her own visual or motor skills would likely drive differently to compensate, perhaps driving at a slower speed or leaving more headway to a lead vehicle. These software adaptations are often more difficult to quantify, and a significant challenge for future models of human multitasking arises in understanding the complex interaction between these sources of differences.

Another explanation for individual differences in multitasking may be found in how people carry out single tasks—consistent with the conclusion

---

1. It should be noted that the youngest drivers, namely teenage drivers, are in fact much more likely to experience fatal crashes due to multitasking than more experienced drivers (Lee, 2007). This phenomenon seems likely rooted in their relative lack of expertise, as well as other complex factors (e.g., desire to engage in multitasking activities).

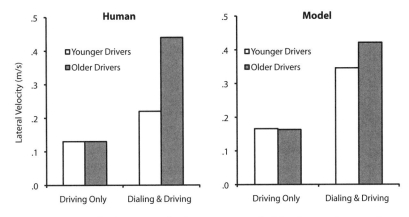

Figure 9.1. Lateral velocity results for younger and older drivers, human data and model simulations. From Salvucci (2009), Copyright 2009 Association for Computing Machinery. Adapted with permission.

of Chapter 7 that multitasking is easy, but monotasking is hard. We carried out a series of experiments (Dickison & Taatgen, 2007; Juvina, Taatgen, & Dickison, 2007; Taatgen, Juvina, Herd, Jilk, & Martens, 2007) supporting this line of reasoning. To assess individual differences in multitasking, participants were given several tasks:

- the dual-task timing (DTT) task (Taatgen, van Rijn, & Anderson, 2007) in which participants perform two choice-reaction tasks in parallel while estimating a time interval;
- the Abstract Decision Making (ADM) task (Josslyn & Hunt, 1998), designed to measure multitasking ability;
- the N-back task (McElree, 2001), where, in a sequence of letters, the current letter has to be compared to the letter N items back in the list (see also Chapter 4); and
- the Attentional Blink task (see Chapter 7).

We found medium to strong correlations in performance on the four tasks: The DTT, ADM and N-back correlated positively, but, interestingly, these tasks correlated negatively with the attentional blink task. In the subsequent models constructed of these tasks, we found that the best explanation for the individual differences in all tasks was one that centered on task strategy. For the ADM task, we constructed two models: one that tried to deduce what the right decision should be, and another that tried to guess the right decision by relying on perceptual cues, activating the right element in declarative memory (Dickison & Taatgen, 2007). The former model required more active elements in working memory and more reasoning steps, but also led to better performance. Better performance, therefore, was characterized by a strategy with a higher degree of top-down control. This high-control model produced a good fit for the participants who performed well on the task, while the more reactive, low-control model produced a good fit for the lower performing participants.

Similarly, we constructed high-control and low-control models of the N-back task (Juvina, Taatgen, & Dickison, 2007). The high-control model rehearsed the last N presented letters, and could therefore compare the currently presented letter and the letter N positions back. The low-control model did not actively try to rehearse letters, instead using a recognition strategy in which it assessed whether it had seen the current presented letter before. If it did, the model tried to estimate how long ago the earlier presentation was, and whether that was approximately N positions ago (using ACT-R's theory of temporal estimation). The high-control model provided a good fit with the participants who performed well on the task, while again, the low-control model fit the poor performers better.

Finally, the counterintuitive finding that poor performers on all the other tasks actually performed better on the attentional blink task can also be explained from the perspective of high versus low control. In Chapter 7 we saw that the attentional blink is produced by a production rule that suspends target detection during memory consolidation. Several researchers have found that decreased control leads to a decrease in blink magnitude (Arend, Johnston, & Shapiro, 2006; Olivers & Nieuwenhuis, 2005, 2006). A low-control model of the task, therefore, consists of the model discussed in Chapter 7 without the control production, and does not exhibit an attentional blink—fitting participants with no or almost no attentional blink quite well (Taatgen, Juvina, Herd, Jilk, & Martens, 2007).

A cross-comparison of all the experiments showed that if a participant fit the high-control model on one task, then their behavior would often also be consistent with the high-control model for the other tasks, including the attentional blink task where high control produces worse performance. Given that one task (the ADM task) has been identified in the literature as testing multitasking ability, and one of the others (the dual-task timing task) explicitly involves multitasking, this result strongly suggests that individual differences in multitasking may be attributable to individual differences in the quality of control in monotasking.

A similar theory-based approach can also be used to account for differences in behavior from the same individual, such as those that may occur from fatigue. Gunzelmann, Moore, Salvucci, and Gluck (2009) conducted a modeling study to test specifically how fatigue may affect driver performance. They integrated a mathematical model of sleep deprivation and its effects on attention (Gunzelmann, Gross, Gluck, & Dinges, 2009) with an existing model of driver behavior (Salvucci, 2006), and simulated driving in various stages of sleep deprivation. Figure 9.2 compares the model predictions with empirical results obtained in roughly the same sleep-deprivation conditions (Peters, Kloeppel, & Alicandri, 1999). The leftmost graph shows the number of lane violations (when the vehicle crosses a lane line) in the human experiment, and the rightmost graph shows the proportion of lane violations to all simulations exhibited by the model. The human drivers exhibited only a slight performance decrease in the first day of sleep deprivation, but a fairly large decrease in the next two days. The model exhibited a similar pattern, because fatigue-related lapses in attention to driving become longer and more frequent over time.

The above work notwithstanding, a great deal more research—empirical and theoretical—is needed to better understand the complex relationship between individual differences and multitasking. Nevertheless, all these examples (involving age, memory, and fatigue) suggest that our approach to modeling multitasking in a cognitive architecture offers significant promise in addressing individual differences. As the community gains further understanding of these types of differences, and develops accounts for them within a cognitive architecture, our theory immediately benefits, allowing threaded cognition to predict how differences

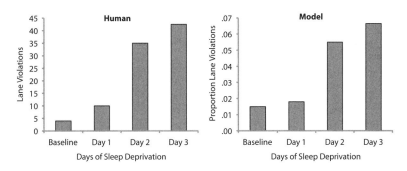

Figure 9.2. Lane violations as a function of sleep deprivation, human (Peters, Kloeppel, & Alicandri, 1999) and model (Gunzelmann et al., 2009).

may affect multitasking behavior. In other words, by modeling in a unified architecture, an understanding of individual differences can be translated qualitatively (by general analysis) and quantitatively (by model simulation) to an understanding of more general differences in multitasking ability.

Threaded Cognition in the Brain

We have largely stayed away from discussing multitasking in terms of neural processing in the brain, in favor of presenting a computational theory with an emphasis on processing resources and the interaction of these resources as task threads. We believe that the latter level of analysis is a more useful one for the many multitasking phenomena addressed in this book. Nevertheless, any theory of cognitive processing should be grounded as much as possible in our understanding of the brain, at the very least to ensure that the proposed computational mechanisms could in fact be "implemented" in terms of realistic neural structures.

A grounding of threaded cognition in the brain begins with the grounding of the underlying ACT-R architecture in brain processing. Over the past decade, Anderson and colleagues (e.g., Anderson, 2007; Anderson, Bothell, Byrne, Douglass, Lebiere, & Qin, 2004; Anderson, Qin, Sohn, Stenger, & Carter, 2003) have established a rigorous mapping between ACT-R processing resources and brain regions. The validation of this mapping has come primarily from fMRI studies of various tasks. One example is a study by Anderson, Qin, Jung, and Carter (2007) in which participants were presented by a sequence of three names (e.g., "Tom Dick Fred") followed by a probe of either two digits or two letters. The probe served as an instruction on whether and how to change the order of the sequence. For example, "23" would signify that names 2 and 3 should be swapped. If one of two digits was higher than 3 (e.g., "24"), no transformation was needed. When the probe was a string of two letters, participants recalled the association between those two letters and two digits that they then had to use to change the order. For example, subjects had learned before the actual experiment that "AT" maps onto "23," meaning that for the probe "AT" they were required to swap the second and third words. Stimuli were presented either aurally or visually, and responses had to be given by either speaking or typing. A final manipulation was the presence or absence of a delay between the presentation of the sequence and the probe. Each component of the task was associated with an ACT-R resource: swapping names with the problem state, retrieving a letter/digit mapping with declarative memory, reading the stimuli with the visual resource, hearing stimuli with the aural resource, typing answers with the manual resource, and speaking the answer with the vocal resource. Because the actual task condition could either include or omit each of these task components, the experiment provided a strong test of the mapping between ACT-R resources and brain regions.

Figure 9.3 shows the results in two of these regions: parietal, corresponding to the problem state, and prefrontal, corresponding to declarative memory. What is displayed is the *Blood Oxygen Level Dependent* (BOLD) response, an indication of activity in a region over time. The human results (dotted lines) show that there is more parietal activity in trials where the order of the sequence has to be changed, and that this activity shifts in time if there is a delay between the sequence and the probe. This result is consistent with ACT-R (solid lines), because the change of order in the sequence requires a manipulation in the problem state. A similar result is present in the prefrontal activity: increased activity and the shift due to the presentation delay is associated with the presence of a mapping task (e.g., remembering "AT" means "23"). To recall such a mapping, ACT-R requires declarative memory, and thus exhibits this pattern of activity in the prefrontal area.

The work grounding ACT-R in the brain also allows us to define a thread in terms of the brain. A thread is simply the processing distributed across brain structures that is devoted to the thread's task goal. However, the ACT-R work with the BOLD response does not provide a direct test of threaded cognition itself. Borst, Taatgen, van Rijn, Stocco, and Fincham (2009) designed an fMRI experiment with that goal. In the study, participants alternated between solving subtraction problems and entering text, identical to the experiment discussed in Chapter 4, with the exception that participants did both tasks by clicking with the mouse on the appropriate buttons on the screen. As discussed in Chapter 4, the critical aspect of this experiment is that participants were slower and made more errors if both tasks required maintenance of a problem state. In the model, this was explained by the fact that with each task switch, the current problem state had to be saved in declarative memory and the problem state of the new task had to be retrieved. The fMRI experiment allowed us to directly study the two resources involved in this process; namely, declarative memory and the problem state.

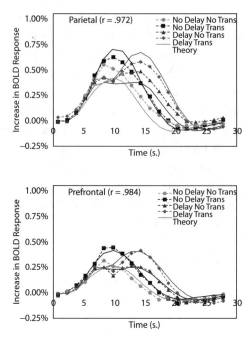

Figure 9.3. Bold response curves for parietal and prefrontal regions. From Anderson et al. (2007), Copyright 2009 Elsevier. Reprinted with permission.

Based on the model for the original experiment and the mapping of ACT-R resources on the brain, a prediction for the BOLD response was made, shown in Figure 9.4. Figure 9.4(a) is the activity in the motor cortex. Given that the same number of responses are required in each experimental condition, the model predicted that the activity in that area would be the same across conditions. However, because the harder versions of the task take longer to complete, the activity is spread out over a longer period of time. The area under each of the curves is, however, the same. For the fusiform gyrus associated with the visual resource (Figure 9.4(b)), the model did predict a difference because the easy text-entry task generates more visual activity than the hard text-entry task. (In the easy version of the task, each letter has to be looked up separately, while in the hard version, the whole word is read in one action.)

The more interesting areas are the problem state and declarative memory, shown in Figure 9.4(c) and 9.4(d) respectively. If neither task requires a problem state (the easy/easy condition), no activity is predicted in the part of the parietal cortex that is associated with the problem state

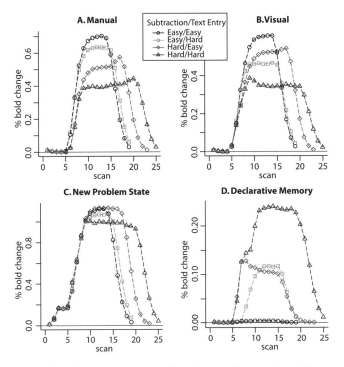

Figure 9.4. Predicted BOLD responses for the visual, manual, problem-state and declarative-memory resources (Borst et al., 2009). Each scan is 2 seconds.

resource (Figure 9.4(c)). If one of the tasks requires a problem state, the model predicts moderate activity in that area. In the hard/hard condition, when both tasks require maintenance of a problem state, high activity is predicted in the problem state area, because the problem state has to be swapped in and out of declarative memory with each change in task. A similar prediction can be made for declarative memory. In the easy subtraction task, declarative memory is only needed for very simple subtraction facts, which produce barely any changes in the BOLD prediction. In the hard subtraction task, multiple subtraction facts of a higher difficulty have to be retrieved, producing some activity. While easy text entry does not require declarative memory at all, in the hard text entry the model has to determine which letter is in what position in a word, and then has to increment the position marker. Declarative retrievals are necessary to complete this step. However, when both tasks are hard, declarative memory is also used to store the problem state of the currently inactive task, producing over-additive, extra activation.

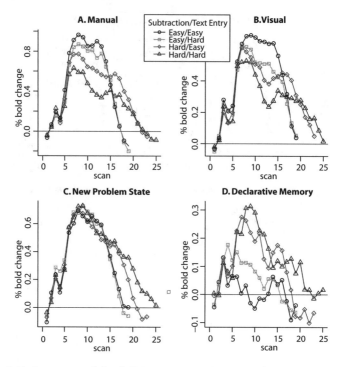

Figure 9.5. Outcomes of the fMRI experiment (Borst et al., 2009).

Figure 9.5 shows the BOLD results from the human experiment. The predictions for the visual and motor areas turned out to be reasonably accurate. In the motor area, the surface under the curve is indeed approximately equal for all four areas, but in the visual area there is more activity if the text entry task is easy. The declarative outcome appears to conform to the prediction to some extent, although the effect is not as large as predicted. There is indeed little activity in the easy/easy condition, but the hard subtraction tasks appears to tax declarative memory more than the model predicted. The problem state area appears to produce the largest discrepancy between prediction and outcome, even though the hard/hard condition does produce an over-additive amount of total activation as predicted. But, whereas the model predicts no activation in the easy/easy condition, the results show a strong activation even in that condition. A possible explanation for this discrepancy is that the area associated with the problem state, a part of the parietal cortex, is likely also involved in visual perception with regard to the location of the visual stimulus. (A simple reaction-time experiment, in which a participant simply presses a button when a light comes on, also produces activity in the parietal area: Kao & Anderson, personal communication, cited in Borst et al., 2009) Using this assumption, Borst et al. (2009) were able to produce a good fit of the parietal area.

These first attempts to find evidence for threaded cognition in the brain are encouraging, but by no means conclusive, and further evidence needs to be gathered to produce a more complete picture of how threads interact in the brain. Another open question is what threaded cognition would predict for activity in ACT-R's goal resource, which has been associated with the brain's anterior cingulate. A possible prediction would be that the activity increases with the number of goals, but it is also possible that such activity is only affected by changes to the set of represented goals (i.e., when a goal is added or removed). Again, more empirical and modeling studies are needed to better understand the relationship between threaded cognition and the brain.

Metacognition and Task Priorities

Threaded cognition is based on the premise that, when people want to perform tasks together, they "just do it"—start task threads, and rely on threaded cognition to interleave them. One may have the sense, however, that sometimes people explicitly think about their multitasking behavior and adapt it to optimize performance, safety, or some other aspect of behavior. For example, a person that needs to finish three tasks in the next hour—say, compose an email, call a friend, and grab lunch—may reflect for a moment and plan out the best way to accomplish these tasks. Another person that realizes he or she is stuck on the current task may actively decide to put aside that task to do another, in the hope that some time away from the original task may help organize thoughts and overcome the block. How would such behavior be accounted for in the context of threaded cognition?

The term *metacognition* is often used to refer to this type of behavior, namely the monitoring and control of one's own cognitive processes. More specifically, in the context of multitasking, we can consider metacognition to mean reasoning about one's own multitasking behavior and performance. Our theory to this point has addressed what we feel is by far the more common scenario, that people needing to perform multiple tasks simply execute them using threaded cognition. Nevertheless, our theory does not preclude the existence of explicit metacognitive processes. In fact, threaded cognition offers a new way to think about metacognition— as distinct metacognitive threads that monitor task performance and potentially manage the execution of other task threads.

To illustrate this idea, consider again the example of driving. Chapter 3 described a driver model (Salvucci, 2006) that has the ability to monitor its surrounding vehicles and change lanes when necessary. Although the original version of this model was developed before threaded cognition, we revised the model to utilize threads in a natural way. One thread is strictly devoted to control of the vehicle, looking at the road ahead and handling the necessary steering, acceleration, and braking. Another thread continually monitors the environment, noting the position and relative speed of other vehicles ahead and behind, including adjacent lanes. When the control thread decides to change lanes (based on the fact that the lead vehicle is traveling too slowly), it starts a third thread devoted to deciding when to change lanes; this thread uses the information obtained by the monitoring thread about surrounding vehicles (stored in declarative memory), and also double-checks the adjacent lane to make sure this information is accurate. (The thread even knows of vehicles in its blind spot, based on position and speed information for vehicles seen earlier.) When it is safe to change lanes, the decision-making thread places this information in a buffer for the control thread to read, and the control thread switches its attention to the destination lane to enact the lane change. In this example, the decision-making thread can be viewed as a metacognitive thread: it monitors the environment, as well as other threads (namely, the monitoring thread), and can direct the execution of other threads (the control thread) to alter their behavior.

This type of metacognitive thread can serve many purposes in control-ling task execution. One possible purpose involves prioritizing tasks: Can one task be given priority over another, and how would this ultimately change multitasking behavior? Brumby and colleagues (Brumby, Howes, Salvucci, 2007; Brumby, Salvucci, Mankowski, & Howes, 2007; Brumby, Salvucci, & Howes, 2009) have been exploring this issue in the context of driver distraction, focusing on how drivers break up a sequence of secondary-task actions, and how this affects performance in both tasks. In one study (Brumby, Salvucci, & Howes, 2009), they examined the effects of dialing a 10-digit cell phone number when given differing priorities. In one segment, participants were instructed to "focus on steering" to drive as safely as possible; in another segment, they were instructed to "focus on dialing" to dial as quickly as possible. Brumby et al. performed an analysis using a cognitive constraint model (Howes, Vera, & Lewis, 2007) that predicted the driving lateral deviation and total dialing time for possible multitasking strategies. Between each pair of digits, the model could either interleave driving or continue with dialing, thus generating many possible ways to interleave dialing and driving.

Figure 9.3 shows the empirical and model results with driving lateral deviation plotted against total dialing time. Several representative strategies are plotted as black dots at their predicted deviation–time points, along with variants of these strategies (based on varied time spent driving) as gray dots. The model points clearly show the inherent speed–accuracy tradeoff in the combined task (see Navon & Gopher, 1979; Norman & Bobrow, 1975)—namely, the speed of dialing versus the accuracy in driving. The two white triangles show the points for the human drivers on this speed–accuracy curve, for both the "focus on dialing" and "focus on steering" conditions. When focusing on dialing, performance most closely matched the strategy of simply dialing all digits consecutively and allowing the vehicle to drift far from the lane center. When focusing on steering, performance most closely matched that of breaking up dialing by the representational chunks of a standard North American phone number (xxx-xxx-xxxx). Note that drivers did not exhibit the most conservative strategy of interleaving driving after each digit; breaking up dialing by chunks allowed them to achieve a balanced point on the speed–accuracy curve, maintaining roughly the same driving performance as the most conservative strategy, yet allowing for reasonably fast dialing times.

How might we account for different priorities and corresponding behavioral changes in threaded cognition, and how might metacognitive threads adapt these priories dynamically? Although some cognitive models have incorporated explicit representation of priorities as a simple numerical value (e.g., Freed, 1998), this approach does not explain the origin of these values and how they might be learned or adapted over time (e.g., assuming that the priority of safe driving is extremely large, why would people ever dial a phone while driving?). Instead, a better approach for threaded cognition is to allow task threads themselves to manage their own requirements for resource processing time. In the dialing and driving example above, the "focus on dialing" model could keep the visual resource across chunk boundaries, in contrast to the "focus on driving" model which releases this resource at chunk boundaries (as seen

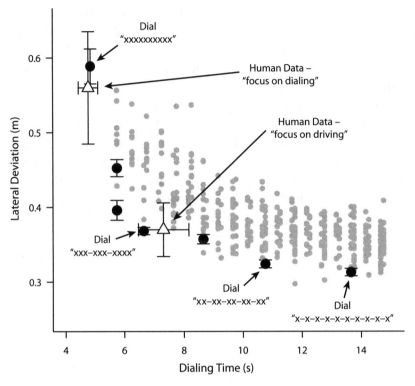

Figure 9.6. Lateral deviation plotted with dialing time, showing the speed-accuracy tradeoff curve for dialing while driving. From Brumby, Salvucci, & Howes (2009), Copyright 2009 Association for Computing Machinery. Adapted with permission.

in Chapter 3). As a more subtle example, the driver model allows for a short delay (about 500 ms) before another steering update is needed; by changing this delay as task demands change, the model can adapt its processing requirements dynamically (Salvucci, Taatgen, & Kushleyeva, 2006) and allow other threads to occupy more or less processing time during these delays.

Balanced, prioritized processing across threads can be realized as meta-cognitive threads that monitor other threads and direct them to increase or decrease processing based on external and internal demands. In turn, metacognition and priorities are also related to individual differences, in that—as seen in the Brumby et al. example above—even the same individual can adapt his or her behavior based on desired goals. The work highlighted here can be considered the first tentative steps to extend threaded cognition to account for task priorities and metacognition more generally.

A Final Word

Multitasking is a fixture in our present world, and there is no doubt that it will be a fixture in our future world. With this in mind, we have strived in this book to present a theory of multitasking that accounts for a range of laboratory and applied phenomena that elucidate the complexities of our multitasking behavior. The word "unifying" in the title of the first chapter hints at our view of the current state of affairs. We have not reached a truly "unified" theory for human multitasking, but we believe that the current theory is beginning to bring together previously disparate areas of multitasking research, and hope that it will continue to do so.

References

Aasman, J. (1995). *Modelling driver behaviour in Soar*. Leidschendam, The Netherlands: KPN Research.

Accot, J. & Zhai, S. (2003). Refining Fitts' law models for bivariate pointing. In *Proceedings of the SIGCHI Conference on Human Factors in Computing Systems: CHI 2003* (pp. 193–200). New York: ACM Press.

Ackerman, P. L. (1988). Determinants of individual differences during skill acquisition: Cognitive abilities and information processing. *Journal of Experimental Psychology: General, 117*, 288–318.

Adamczyk, P. D. & Bailey, B. P. (2004). If not now, when? The effects of interruptions at different moments within task execution. In *Proceedings of the SIGCHI Conference on Human Factors in Computing Systems: CHI 2004* (pp. 271–278). New York: ACM Press.

Alm, H. & Nilsson, L. (1994). Changes in driver behaviour as a function of handsfree mobile phones—a simulator study. *Accident Analysis & Prevention, 26*, 441–451.

Alm, H. & Nilsson, L. (1995). The effects of a mobile telephone task on driver behaviour in a car following situation. *Accident Analysis & Prevention, 27*, 707–715.

Altmann, E. M. (2004). Advance preparation in task switching: what work is being done? *Psychological Science, 15*, 616–622.

Altmann, E. M. & Gray, W. D. (2002). Forgetting to remember: the functional relationship of decay and interference. *Psychological Science, 13*, 27–33.

Altmann, E. M. & Gray, W. D. (2008). An integrated model of cognitive control in task switching. *Psychological Review, 115*, 602–639.

Altmann, E. M. & Trafton, J. G. (2002). Memory for goals: An activation-based model. *Cognitive Science, 26*, 39–83.

Altmann, E. M. & Trafton, J. G. (2007). Timecourse of recovery from interruption: data and a model. *Psychological Bulletin & Review, 14*, 1079–1084.

Anderson, J. R. (1982). Acquisition of cognitive skill. *Psychological Review, 89*, 369–403.

Anderson, J. R. (1983). *The architecture of cognition*. Cambridge, MA: Harvard University Press.

Anderson, J. R. (1987). Skill acquisition: Compilation of weak-method problem solutions. *Psychological Review, 94*, 192–210.

Anderson, J. R. (2002). Spanning seven orders of magnitude: A challenge for cognitive modeling. *Cognitive Science, 26*, 85–112.

Anderson, J. R. (2005). Human symbol manipulation within an integrated cognitive architecture. *Cognitive Science, 29*, 313–341.

Anderson, J. R. (2007). *How can the human mind occur in the physical universe?* New York: Oxford University Press.

Anderson, J. R., Bothell, D., Byrne, M. D., Douglass, S., Lebiere, C., & Qin, Y. (2004). An integrated theory of the mind. *Psychological Review, 111*, 1036–1060.

Anderson, J. R., Bothell, D., Lebiere, C., & Matessa, M. (1998). An integrated theory of list memory. *Journal of Memory and Language, 38*, 341–380.

Anderson, J. R., Corbett, A. T., Koedinger, K., & Pelletier, R. (1995). Cognitive tutors: Lessons learned. *The Journal of the Learning Sciences, 4*, 167–207.

Anderson, J. R. & Fincham, J. M. (1994). Acquisition of procedural skills from examples. *Journal of Experimental Psychology: Learning, Memory, and Cognition, 20*, 1322–1340.

Anderson, J. R. & Matessa, M. (1997). A production system theory of serial memory. *Psychological Review, 104*, 728–748.

Anderson, J. R., Qin, Y., Jung, K. J., & Carter, C. S. (2007). Information-processing modules and their relative modality specificity. *Cognitive Psychology, 54*, 185–217.

Anderson, J. R., Taatgen, N. A., & Byrne, M. D. (2005). Learning to achieve perfect timesharing: architectural implications of Hazeltine, Teague, & Ivry (2002). *Journal of Experimental Psychology: Human Perception and Performance, 31*, 749–761.

Arend, I., Johnston, S., & Shapiro, K. (2006). Task-irrelevant visual motion and flicker attenuate the attentional blink. *Psychonomic Bulletin & Review, 13*, 600–607.

Associated Press (2001). Microsoft banks on anti-Clippy sentiment. *USA Today*, May 3, 2001.

Baddeley, A. D. (1986). *Working memory*. Oxford, England: Oxford University Press.

Baddeley, A. D. (2003). Working memory: Looking back and looking forward. *Nature Reviews Neuroscience, 4*, 829–839.

Baddeley, A. D. & Della Sala, S. (1996). Working memory and executive control. *Philosophical Transactions of the Royal Society of London, 351B,* 1397–1404.

Baddeley, A. D., Thomson, N., & Buchanan, M. (1975). Word length and the structure of short-term memory. *Journal of Verbal Learning and Verbal Behavior, 14,* 575–589.

Bailey, B. P. & Iqbal, S. T. (2008). Understanding changes in mental workload during execution of goal-directed tasks and its application for interruption management. *ACM Transactions on Computer-Human Interaction, 14,* 1–28.

Best, B. J. & Lebiere, C. (2006). Cognitive agents interacting in real and virtual worlds. In R. Sun (Ed.). *Cognition and Multi-agent Interaction: From Cognitive Modeling to Social Simulation* (pp. 186–218). Cambridge, UK: Cambridge University Press.

Boer, E. R. (1999). Car following from the driver's perspective. *Transportation Research, Part F, 2,* 201–206.

Borst, J. P. & Taatgen, N. A. (2007). The costs of multitasking in threaded cognition. In *Proceedings of the Eighth International Conference on Cognitive Modeling* (pp. 133–138).

Borst, J. P., Taatgen, N. A., & Van Rijn, H. (2008). Problem representations in multitasking: An additional cognitive bottleneck. In *Proceedings of the 30th Annual Conference of the Cognitive Science Society.*

Borst, J.P., Taatgen, N.A., & Van Rijn, H. (2010). The problem state: A cognitive bottleneck in multitasking. *Journal of Experimental Psychology: Learning, Memory, & Cognition, 36*(2), 363–382.

Borst, J.P., Taatgen, N.A., Van Rijn, H., Stocco, A., & Fincham, J.M. (2009). Testing fMRI Predictions of a Dual-Task Interference Model. In *Proceedings of the 9th International Conference on Cognitive Modeling.*

Botvinick, M., Braver, T., Barch, D. Carter, C. & Cohen, J. (2001). Conflict monitoring and cognitive control. *Psychological Review, 108,* 624–652.

Botvinick, M. & Plaut, D. C. (2004). Doing without schema hierarchies: A recurrent connectionist approach to routine sequential action and its pathologies. *Psychological Review, 111,* 395–429.

Bovair, S., Kieras, D. E., & Polson, P. G. (1990). The acquisition and performance of text-editing skill: A cognitive complexity analysis. *Human-Computer Interaction, 5,* 1–48.

Bowman H. & Wyble B. (2007). The simultaneous type, serial token model of temporal attention and working memory. *Psychological Review, 114,* 38–70.

Brackstone, M. & McDonald, M. (1999). Car-following: A historical review. *Transportation Research Part F, 2,* 181–196.

Broadbent, D. E. (1958). *Perception and communication.* Elmsford, NY: Pergamon Press.

Brock, D., Stroup, J. L., & Ballas, J. A. (2002). Effects of 3D Auditory Display on Dual Task Performance in a Simulated Multiscreen Watchstation Environment. In *Proceedings of the Human Factors and Ergonomics Society 46th Annual Meeting,* (pp. 1570–1573). Santa Monica, CA: Human Factors and Ergonomics Society.

Brookhuis, K. A., De Vries, G., & De Waard, D. (1991). The effects of mobile telephoning on driving performance. *Accident Analysis & Prevention, 23,* 309–316.

Brooks, R.A. (1991). Intelligence without representation. *Artificial Intelligence, 47,* 139–159.

Brown, I. D., Tickner, A. H., & Simmonds, D. C. V. (1969). Interference between concurrent tasks of driving and telephoning. *Journal of Applied Psychology, 53,* 419–424.

Brumby, D.P., Howes, A., & Salvucci, D.D. (2007). A cognitive constraint model of dual-task trade-offs in a highly dynamic driving task. In *Proceedings of the SIGCHI Conference on Human Factors in Computing Systems: CHI 2007* (pp. 233–242). New York: ACM Press.

Brumby, D.P., Salvucci, D.D., & Howes, A. (2009). Focus on driving: How cognitive constraints shape the adaptation of strategy when dialing while driving. In *Proceedings of the SIGCHI Conference on Human Factors in Computing Systems: CHI 2009* (pp. 1629–1638). New York: ACM Press.

Brumby, D.P., Salvucci, D.D., Mankowski, W., & Howes, A. (2007). A cognitive constraint model of the effects of portable music-player use on driver performance. In *Proceedings of the Human Factors and Ergonomics Society 51st Annual Meeting* (pp. 1531–1535). Santa Monica, CA: Human Factors and Ergonomics Society.

Byrne, M. D. & Anderson, J. R. (2001). Serial modules in parallel: The psychological refractory period and perfect time-sharing. *Psychological Review, 108,* 847–869.

Byrne, M. D. & Kirlik, A. (2005). Using computational cognitive modeling to diagnose possible sources of aviation error. *International Journal of Aviation Psychology, 15,* 135–155.

Card, S. K., Moran, T. P., & Newell, A. (1980). The keystroke-level model for user performance time with interactive systems. *Communications of the ACM, 23,* 396–410.

Card, S. K., Moran, T. P., & Newell, A. (1983). *The psychology of human-computer interaction.* Hillsdale, NJ: Lawrence Erlbaum Associates.

Catrambone, R. & Yuasa, M. (2006). Acquisition of procedures: The effects of example elaborations and active learning exercises. *Learning and Instruction, 16,* 139–153.

Chater, N. & Vitányi, P. (2003). Simplicity: A unifying principle in cognitive science? *Trends in Cognitive Sciences, 7,* 19–22.

Chisholm, C. D., Dornfeld, A. M., Nelson, D. R., & Cordell, W. H. (2001). Work interrupted: A comparison of workplace interruptions in emergency departments and primary care offices. *Annals of Emergency Medicine, 38*, 146–151.

Choi, D., Konik, T., Nejati, N., Park, C., & Langley, P. (2007). A believable agent for first-person shooter games. In *Proceedings of the Third Annual Artificial Intelligence and Interactive Digital Entertainment Conference* (pp. 71–73). Stanford, CA: AAAI Press.

Chong, R. S. (1998). Modeling dual-task performance improvement: Casting executive process knowledge acquisition as strategy refinement (Tech. Rep. No. CSE-TR-378–98). Unpublished doctoral dissertation, Department of Computer Science and Engineering, University of Michigan, Ann Arbor.

Clark, A. (1997). *Being there: Putting brain, body and world together again.* Cambridge, MA: MIT Press.

Cohen, J. D., Dunbar, K., & McClelland, J. L. (1990). On the control of automatic processes: A parallel distributed processing account of the Stroop effect. *Psychological Review, 97*, 332–361.

Cooper, R. & Shallice, T. (2000). Contention scheduling and the control of routine activities. *Cognitive Neuropsychology, 17*, 297–338.

Corriher, S. O. (2008). *Bakewise: The Hows and Whys of Successful Baking with over 200 Magnificent Recipes.* New York: Scribner.

Crossman, E. R. F. W. (1959). A theory of the acquisition of speed-skill. *Ergonomics, 2*, 153–156.

Cutrell, E. B., Czerwinski, M., & Horvitz, E. (2000). Effects of instant messaging interruptions on computing tasks. In *Proceedings of CHI 2000 Extended Abstracts* (pp. 99–100). New York: ACM Press.

Czerwinski, M., Chrisman, S., & Schumacher, B. (1991). The effects of warnings and display similarity on interruption in multitasking environments. *ACM SIGCHI Bulletin, 23*, 38–39.

Czerwinski, M., Cutrell, E., & Horvitz, E. (2000). Instant messaging: Effects of relevance and timing. In Turner, S. & Turner, P. (eds.), *People and Computers XIV: Proceedings of HCI 2000* (pp. 71–76). Sutherland, UK: British Computer Society.

Czerwinski, M., Horvitz, E., & Wilhite, S. (2004). A diary study of task switching and interruptions. In *Proceedings of the SIGCHI Conference on Human Factors in Computing Systems: CHI 2004* (pp. 175–182). New York: ACM Press.

DeJong, G. F. & Mooney, R. (1986). Explanation-based learning: An alternative view. *Machine Learning, 1*, 145–176.

Diaper, D. & Stanton, N. A. (eds.), (2003). *Handbook of task analysis for human-computer interaction.* Mahwah, NJ: Lawrence Erlbaum Associates.

Dickison, D. & Taatgen, N.A. (2007). ACT-R models of cognitive control in the abstract decision making task. In *Proceedings of the Eighth International Conference on Cognitive Modeling* (pp. 79–84). New York: Psychology Press.

Di Lollo, V., Kawahara, J., Ghorashi, S. M. S., & Enns, J. T. (2005). The attentional blink: Resource depletion or temporary loss of control? *Psychological Research, 69,* 191–200.

Dingus, T. A., Klauer, S. G., Neale, V. L., Petersen, A., Lee, S. E., Sudweeks, J., et al. (2006). The 100-car naturalistic driving study; Phase II- Results of the 100-car field experiment. Contract No. DTNH22-00-C-07007 (Task Order No. 06). Blacksburg, VA: Virginia Tech Transportation Institute.

Dismukes, K. & Nowinski, J. (2007). Prospective memory, concurrent task management, and pilot error. In A. Kramer, D. Wiegmann, & A. Kirlik (eds.), *Attention: From Theory to Practice* (pp. 225–236). New York: Oxford University Press.

Dismukes, K., Young, K., & Sumwalt, R. (1998). Cockpit interruptions and distractions: Effective management requires a careful balancing act. *ASRS Directline, 10,* 4–9.

Dix, A., Finlay, J., Abowd, G. D., & Beale, R. (2003). *Human-Computer Interaction* (3rd ed.). London: Prentice Hall.

Dixon, S. R., Wickens, C. D., & Chang, D. (2005). Mission control of multiple unmanned aerial vehicles: A workload analysis. *The Journal of the Human Factors and Ergonomics Society, 47,* 479–487.

Doane, S. M. & Sohn, Y. W. (2000). ADAPT: A predictive cognitive model of user visual attention and action planning. *User Modeling and User-Adapted Interaction, 10,* 1–45.

Donges, E. (1978). A two-level model of driver steering behavior. *Human Factors, 20,* 691–707.

Drews, F. A., Pasupathi, M., & Strayer, D. L. (2008). Passenger and cell phone conversations during simulated driving. *Journal of Experimental Psychology: Applied, 14,* 392–400.

Fajen, B. R. & Warren, W. H. (2003). Behavioral dynamics of steering, obstacle avoidance, and route selection. *Journal of Experimental Psychology: Human Perception and Performance, 29,* 343–362.

Fikes, R. E. & Nilsson, N. J. (1971). STRIPS: A new approach to the application of theorem proving to problem solving. *Artificial Intelligence, 2,* 189–208.

Fitts, P. M. (1964). Perceptual-motor skill learning. In A. W. Melton (Ed.), *Categories of Human Learning* (pp. 243–285). New York: Academic Press.

Fitts, P. M. & Posner, M. I. (1967). *Learning and skilled performance in human performance.* Belmont, CA: Brock-Cole.

Foerde, K., Knowlton, B. J., & Poldrack, R. A. (2006). Modulation of competing memory systems by distraction. *Proceedings of the National Academy of Sciences, 103,* 11778–11783.

Fogarty, J., Ko, A., Aung, H. H., Golden, E., Tang, K., & Hudson, S. (2005). Examining task engagement in sensor-based statistical models of human interruptibility. In *Proceedings of the SIGCHI Conference on Human Factors in Computing Systems: CHI 2005* (pp. 331–340). New York: ACM Press.

Freed, M. (1998). Managing multiple tasks in complex, dynamic environments. In *Proceedings of the 1998 National Conference on Artificial Intelligence* (pp. 921–927). Menlo Park, CA: AAAI Press.

Fu, W.-T., Bothell, D., Douglass, S., Haimson, C., Sohn, M.-H, & Anderson, J. R. (2004). Learning from real-time over-the-shoulder instructions in a dynamic task. In *Proceedings of the Sixth International Conference on Cognitive Modeling* (pp. 100–105). Pittsburgh, PA: Carnegie Mellon University.

Fu, W.-T. & Pirolli, P. (2007). SNIF-ACT: A cognitive model of user navigation on the World Wide Web. *Human-Computer Interaction, 22,* 355–412.

Garey, M. R. & Johnson, D. S. (1979). *Computers and intractibility, a guide to the theory of NP-completeness.* San Francisco, CA: Freeman.

Gluck, K. A., Ball, J. T., Krusmark, M. A., Rodgers, S. M., & Purtee, M. D. (2003). A computational process model of basic aircraft maneuvering. In *Proceedings of the Fifth International Conference on Cognitive Modeling* (pp. 117–122). Bamberg, Germany: Universitats-Verlag Bamberg.

Gluck, K. A. & Pew, R. W. (eds.), (2005). *Modeling human behavior with integrated cognitive architectures: Comparison, evaluation, and validation.* Mahwah, NJ: Lawrence Erlbaum Associates.

GMAC (2006). Study: 18 million Americans may be unfit for roads. GMAC Insurance, May 26, 2006. Retrieved November 7, 2009, from http://www. gmacinsurance.com/SafeDriving/2006/NDT2006_PressRelease.asp

Godthelp, H. (1986). Vehicle control during curve driving. *Human Factors, 28,* 211–221.

Gonzalez, V. M. & Mark, G. (2004). "Constant, constant, multi-tasking craziness": Managing multiple working spheres. In *Proceedings of the SIGCHI Conference on Human Factors in Computing Systems: CHI 2004* (pp. 113–120). New York: ACM Press.

Gray, W. D. (Ed.) (2007). *Integrated models of cognitive systems.* New York: Oxford University Press.

Gray, W. D. & Fu, W. (2004). Soft constraints in interactive behavior: The case of ignoring perfect knowledge in-the-world for imperfect knowledge in-the-head. *Cognitive Science, 28,* 359–382.

Gray, W. D., John, B. E., & Atwood, M. E. (1993). Project Ernestine: A validation of GOMS for prediction and explanation of real-world task performance. *Human-Computer Interaction, 8,* 237–309.

Gray, W. D. & Schoelles, M. J. (2003). The nature and timing of interruptions in a complex cognitive task: Empirical data and computational cognitive models. In *Proceedings of the 25th Annual Meeting of the Cognitive Science Society.* Austin, TX: Cognitive Science Society.

Greenberg, J. A., Tijerina, L., Curry, R., Artz, B. A., Cathey, L., Kochhar, D., et al. (2003). Driver distraction: Evaluation with event detection paradigm. *Transportation Research Record, 1843,* 1–9.

Groeger, J. A. (2000). *Understanding driving: Applying cognitive psychology to a complex everyday task.* Philadelphia, PA: Psychology Press.

Gunzelmann, G., Gross, J. B., Gluck, K. A., & Dinges, D. F. (2009). Sleep deprivation and sustained attention performance: Integrating mathematical and cognitive modeling. *Cognitive Science, 33,* 880–910.

Gunzelmann, G., Moore, L. R., Salvucci, D. D., & Gluck, K. A. (2009). Fluctuations in alertness and sustained attention: Predicting driver performance. In *Proceedings of the Ninth International Conference on Cognitive Modeling.* Manchester, UK.

Hancock, P. A., Lesch, M., Simmons, L. (2003). The distraction effects of phone use during a crucial driving maneuver. *Accident Analysis & Prevention, 35,* 501–514.

Hankey, J. M., Dingus, T. A., Hanowski, R. J., Wierwille, W. W., & Andrews, C. (2000). In-vehicle information systems behavioral model and design support: Final report. Tech. Report No. FHWA-RD-00-135, Federal Highway Administration, U. S. Department of Transportation.

Hayhoe, M. M., Shrivastava, A., Mruczek, R., & Pelz, J.B. (2003). Visual memory and motor planning in a natural task. *Journal of Vision, 3,* 49–63.

Hazeltine, E., Teague, D., & Ivry, R. B. (2002). Simultaneous dual-task performance reveals parallel response selection after practice. *Journal of Experimental Psychology: Human Perception and Performance, 28,* 527–545.

Hendricks, D. L., Freedman, M., Zador, P. L., & Fell, J. C. (2001). The relative frequency of unsafe driving acts in serious traffic crashes. Report for Contract No. DTNH22-94-C-05020, National Highway Traffic Safety Administration, U. S. Department of Transportation.

Hess, R. A. & Modjtahedzadeh, A. (1990). A control theoretic model of driver steering behavior. *IEEE Control Systems Magazine, 8,* 3–8.

Hildreth, E. C., Beusmans, J. M. H., Boer, E. R., & Royden, C. S. (2000). From vision to action: Experiments and models of steering control during driving. *Journal of Experimental Psychology: Human Perception and Performance, 26,* 1106–1132.

Hodgetts, H. M. & Jones, D. M. (2006a). Interruption of the tower of London task: Support for a goal-activation approach. *Journal of Experimental Psychology: General, 135,* 103–115.

Hodgetts, H. M. & Jones, D.M. (2006b). Contextual cues aid recovery from interruption: The role of associative activation. *Journal of Experimental Psychology: Learning, Memory & Cognition, 32,* 1120–1132.

Holden, K. L. & O'Neal, M.R. (1992). The utility of various windowing capabilities for single-task and multi-task environments. In *Proceedings of CHI'92 Conference on Human Factors in Computing Systems, Extended Abstracts* (p. 52). New York: ACM Press.

Holyoak, K. J. & Thagard, P. (1989). Analogical mapping by constraint satisfaction. *Cognitive Science, 13,* 295–355.

Horrey, W. J. & Lesch, M.F. (2009). Driver-initiated distractions: Examining strategic adaptation for in-vehicle task initiation. *Accident Analysis & Prevention, 41*, 115–122.

Horrey, W. J. & Wickens, C. D. (2004). Driving and side task performance: The effects of display clutter, separation, and modality. *Human Factors, 46*, 611–624.

Horrey, W. J. & Wickens, C. D. (2006). Examining the impact of cell phone conversations on driving using meta-analytic techniques. *Human Factors, 48*, 196–205.

Horrey, W. J., Wickens, C. D., & Consalus, K. P. (2006). Modeling drivers' visual attention allocation while interacting with in-vehicle technologies. *Journal of Experimental Psychology: Applied, 12*, 67–78.

Horvitz, E., Apacible, J., & Subramani, M. (2005). Balancing awareness and interruption: Investigation of notification deferral policies. In *Proceedings of the Tenth Conference on User Modeling* (pp. 433–437). Berlin: Springer-Verlag.

Howes, A., Vera, A., Lewis, R. L. (2007). Bounding rational analysis: Constraints on asymptotic performance. In W. D. Gray (Ed.) *Integrated Models of Cognitive Systems* (pp. 403–413). New York: Oxford University Press.

Hudson, S. E., Fogarty, J., Atkeson, C. G., Avrahami, D., Forlizzi, J., Kiesler, S., et al. (2003). Predicting human interruptibility with sensors: A Wizard of Oz feasibility study. In *Proceedings of the SIGCHI Conference on Human Factors in Computing Systems: CHI 2003* (pp. 257–264). New York: ACM Press.

Hudson, S. E., John, B. E., Knudsen, K., & Byrne, M. D. (1999). A tool for creating predictive performance models from user interface demonstrations. In *Proceedings of the 12th Annual ACM Symposium on User Interface Software and Technology* (pp. 93–102). New York: ACM Press.

Iqbal, S. T., Adamczyk, P. D., Zheng, S. X., & Bailey, B. P. (2005). Towards an index of opportunity: Understanding changes in mental workload during task execution. In *Proceedings of the SIGCHI Conference on Human Factors in Computing Systems: CHI 2005* (pp. 311–320). New York: ACM Press.

Iqbal, S. T. & Bailey, B. P. (2005). Investigating the effectiveness of mental workload as a predictor of opportune moments for interruption. In *Proceedings of the SIGCHI Conference on Human Factors in Computing Systems: CHI 2005* (pp. 1489–1492). New York: ACM Press.

Iqbal, S. T. & Bailey, B. P. (2006). Leveraging Characteristics of task structure to predict costs of interruption. In *Proceedings of the SIGCHI Conference on Human Factors in Computing Systems: CHI 2006* (pp. 741–750). New York: ACM Press.

Iqbal, S. T. & Horvitz, E. (2007). Disruption and recovery of computing tasks: Field study, analysis and directions. In *Proceedings of the SIGCHI Conference on Human Factors in Computing Systems: CHI 2007* (pp. 677–686). New York: ACM Press.

Jin, J. & Dabbish, L. A. (2009). Self-interruption on the computer: A typology of discretionary task interleaving. In *Proceedings of the SIGCHI Conference on Human Factors in Computing Systems: CHI 2009* (pp. 1799–1808). New York: ACM Press.

John, B. E. (1990). Extensions of GOMS analyses to expert performance requiring perception of dynamic visual and auditory information. In *Proceedings of the SIGCHI Conference on Human Factors in Computing Systems: CHI 1990* (pp. 107–116). New York: ACM Press.

John, B. E. & Kieras, D. E. (1996). The GOMS family of user interface analysis techniques: Comparison and contrast. *ACM Transactions on Computer-Human Interaction, 3,* 320–351.

John, B. E., Prevas, K., Salvucci, D. D., & Koedinger, K. (2004). Predictive human performance modeling made easy. In *Proceedings of the SIGCHI Conference on Human Factors in Computing Systems: CHI 2004* (pp. 455–462). New York: ACM Press.

John, B. E. & Salvucci, D. D. (2005). Multi-purpose prototypes for assessing user interfaces in pervasive computing systems. *IEEE Pervasive Computing, 4,* 27–34.

Johnson-Laird, P. N. (1983). *Mental models: Towards a cognitive science of language, inference, and consciousness.* Cambridge, MA: Harvard University Press.

Jones, R. M., Laird, J. E., Nielsen P. E., Coulter, K., Kenny, P., & Koss, F. (1999). Automated intelligent pilots for combat flight simulation. *AI Magazine, 20,* 27–42.

Joslyn, S. L., Hunt, E. (1998). Evaluating individual differences in response to emergency situations. *Journal of Experimental Psychology: Applied, 4,* 16–43.

Just, M. A. & Carpenter, P. A. (1992). A capacity theory of comprehension: Individual differences in working memory. *Psychological Review, 99,* 122–149.

Just, M. A., Carpenter, P. A., & Varma, S. (1999). Computational modeling of high-level cognition and brain function. *Human Brain Mapping, 8,* 128–136.

Juvina, I. & Taatgen, N. A. (2007). Modeling control strategies in the N-back task. In *Proceedings of the Eighth International Conference on Cognitive Modeling* (pp. 73–78). New York: Psychology Press.

Juvina, I., Taatgen, N. A., Dickison, D. (2007). Cognitive control as alternation of activation and suppression in the Stroop task. In *Proceedings of the Twenty-Ninth Annual Meeting of the Cognitive Science Society* (pp. 1133–1138). New York: Lawrence Erlbaum Associates.

Kaber, D. B. & Endsley, M. R. (2004). The effects of level of automation and adaptive automation on human performance, situation awareness and workload in a dynamic control task. *Theoretical Issues in Ergonomics Science, 5,* 113–153.

Kahneman, D. (1973). *Attention and effort.* Englewood Cliffs, NJ: Prentice-Hall.

Kantowitz, B. H. & Casper, P. A. (1988) Human workload in aviation. In E. L. Wiener & D.C. Nagel (eds.), *Human Factors in Aviation*. Academic Press. San Diego, CA.

Keele, S. W. (1973). *Attention and human performance*. Pacific Palisades, CA: Goodyear.

Kelley, T. D. & Scribner, D. R. (2003). Developing a predictive model of dual task performance. Technical Report No. ARL-MR-0556, U.S. Army Research Laboratory, Aberdeen, MD.

Kieras, D. E. (2007). Control of cognition. In W. D. Gray (Ed.). *Integrated Models of Cognitive Systems* (pp. 327–355). New York: Oxford University Press.

Kieras, D. E. & Bovair, S. (1984). The role of a mental model in learning to operate a device. *Cognitive Science, 8,* 191–219.

Kieras, D. E. & Meyer, D.E. (1997). An overview of the EPIC architecture for cognition and performance with application to human-computer interaction. *Human-Computer Interaction, 12,* 391–438.

Kieras, D. E., Meyer, D. E., Ballas, J. A., & Lauber, E. J. (2000). Modern computational perspectives on executive mental processes and cognitive control: Where to from here? In S. Monsell & J. Driver (Eds.), *Control of Cognitive Processes: Attention and Performance XVIII* (pp. 681–712). Cambridge, MA: MIT Press.

Kieras, D. E., Wood, S. D., Abotel, K., & Hornof, A. (1995). GLEAN: A computer-based tool for rapid GOMS model usability evaluation of user interface designs. In *UIST'95 Proceedings of the 8th Annual ACM Symposium on User Interface Software and Technology* (pp. 91–100). New York: ACM Press.

Kirn, W. (2007). The autumn of the multitaskers. *The Atlantic Online,* November 2007.

Kirsh, D. (1995). The intelligent use of space. *Artificial Intelligence, 73,* 31–68.

Kirsh, D. & Maglio, P. (1994). On distinguishing epistemic from pragmatic action. *Cognitive Science, 18,* 513–549.

Kramer, A. F., Wiegmann, D. A., & Kirlik, A. (2007). *Attention: From theory to practice*. New York: Oxford University Press.

Kucera, H. & Francis, W. N. (1967). *Computational analysis of present-day American English*. Providence, RI: Brown University Press.

Laird, J. E. & Duchi, J. C. (2000). Creating human-like synthetic characters with multiple skill levels: A case study using the Soar Quakebot. In *AAAI Technical Report SS-01-02* (pp. 54–58). Menlo Park, CA: AAAI Press.

Laird, J. E., Newell, A., & Rosenbloom, P. S. (1987). Soar: An architecture for general intelligence. *Artificial Intelligence, 33,* 1–64.

Lallement, Y. & John, B. E. (1998). Cognitive architecture and modeling idiom: An examination of three models of the Wickens task. In M. A. Gernsbacher & S. J. Derry (Eds.), *Proceedings of the Twentieth Annual Conference of the Cognitive Science Society* (pp. 597–602). Hillsdale, NJ: Lawrence Erlbaum Associates.

Land, M. & Horwood, J. (1995). Which parts of the road guide steering? *Nature*, 377, 339–340.

Land, M., Mennie, N., & Rusted, J. (1999). The roles of vision and eye movements in the control of activities of daily living. *Perception*, 28, 1311–1328.

Langer, G. (2005). Traffic in the United State: A Look Under the Hood of a Nation on Wheels. ABC News. Retrieved November 9, 2009, from http://abcnews.go.com/print?id=485098

Larkin, J. H. (1989). Display-based problem solving. In D. Klahr & K. Kotovsky (Eds.), *Complex Information Processing: The Impact of Herbert A. Simon* (pp. 319–341). Hillsdale, NJ: Lawrence Erlbaum Associates.

Larkin, J. H. & Simon, H. A. (1987). Why a diagram is (sometimes) worth 10,000 words. *Cognitive Science*, 11, 65–100.

Latorella, K. A. (1999). Investigating Interruptions: Implications for Flight-deck Performance. Technical Report NASA/TM-1999-209707, NASA, Washington, DC.

Lebiere, C. & Anderson, J. R. (1993). A connectionist implementation of the ACT-R production system. In *Proceedings of the Fifteenth Annual Meeting of the Cognitive Science Society* (pp. 635–640). Hillsdale, NJ: Lawrence Erlbaum Associates.

Lebiere, C., Wallach, D., & West, R. L. (2000). A memory-based account of the prisoner's dilemma and other 2x2 games. In *Proceedings of the Third International Conference on Cognitive Modeling* (pp. 185–193). Veenendaal, Netherlands: Universal Press.

Lee, F. J. & Taatgen, N. A. (2002). Multi-tasking as skill Acquisition. In *Proceedings of the Twenty-Fourth Annual Conference of the Cognitive Science Society* (pp. 572–577). Mahwah, NJ: Lawrence Erlbaum Associates.

Lee, J., Forlizzi, J., & Hudson, S. E. (2008). Iterative design of MOVE: A situationally appropriate vehicle navigation system. *International Journal of Human-Computer Studies*, 66, 198–215.

Lee, J. D. (2007). Technology and the teen driver. *Journal of Safety Research*, 38, 203–213.

Lee, J. D., Caven, B., Haake, S., & Brown, T. L. (2001). Speech-based interaction with in-vehicle computers: The effect of speech-based e-mail on drivers' attention to the roadway. *Human Factors*, 43, 631–640.

Lee, J. D., Hoffman, J. D., & Hayes, E. (2004). Collision warning design to mitigate driver distraction. In *Proceedings of the SIGCHI Conference on Human Factors in Computing Systems: CHI 2004* (pp. 65–72). New York: ACM Press.

Lee, J. D., McGehee D. V., Brown T. L., & Reyes, M. L. (2002). Collision warning timing, driver distraction, and driver response to imminent rear-end collisions in a high fidelity driving simulator. *Human Factors*, 44, 314–334.

Lee, J. D. & Moray, N. (1994). Trust, self-confidence, and operators' adaptation to automation. *International Journal of Human-Computer Studies*, 40, 153–184.

Levison, W. H. & Cramer, N. L. (1995). Description of the integrated driver model (Tech. Rep. No. FHWA-RD-94-092). McLean, VA: Federal Highway Administration.

Levy, J., Pashler, H., & Boer, E. (2006). Central interference in driving: Is there any stopping the psychological refractory period? *Psychological Science, 17,* 228–235.

Lewis, R. L. & Vasishth, S. (2005). An activation-based model of sentence processing as skilled memory retrieval. *Cognitive Science, 29,* 375–419.

Li, S. Y. W., Cox, A. L., Blandford, A., Cairns, P., Young, R. M., & Abeles, A. (2006). Further investigations into post-completion error: The effects of interruption position and duration. In *Proceedings of the 28th Annual Meeting of the Cognitive Science Conference* (pp. 471–476). Austin, TX: Cognitive Science Society.

Liu, Y., Feyen, R., & Tsimhoni, O. (2006). Queueing Network-Model Human Processor (QN-MHP): A computational architecture for multitask performance in human-machine systems. *ACM Transactions on Computer-Human Interaction, 13,* 37–70.

Logan, G. D. (1979). On the use of a concurrent memory load to measure attention and automaticity. *Journal of Experimental Psychology: Human Perception and Performance, 5,* 189–207.

Logan, G. D. (1985). Executive control of thought and action. *Acta Psychologica, 60,* 193–210.

Logan, G. D. (1988). Toward an instance theory of automatization. *Psychological Review, 95,* 492–527.

Lovett, M. C., Daily, L. Z., & Reder, L. M. (2000). A source activation theory of working memory: Cross-task prediction of performance in ACT-R. *Journal of Cognitive Systems Research, 1,* 99–118.

MacKenzie, I. S. (1992). Fitts' law as a research and design tool in human-computer interaction. *Human-Computer Interaction, 7,* 91–139.

Mahany, B. (2005). The trouble with multitasking. *Chicago Tribune,* Nov 17, 2005.

Mark, G., Gonzalez, V. M., & Harris, J. (2005). No task left behind?: Examining the nature of fragmented work. In *Proceedings of the SIGCHI Conference on Human Factors in Computing Systems: CHI 2005* (pp. 321–330). New York: ACM Press.

Mark, G., Gudith, D., & Klocke, U. (2008). The cost of interrupted work: more speed and stress. In *Proceedings of the SIGCHI Conference on Human Factors in Computing Systems: CHI 2008* (pp. 107–110). New York: ACM Press.

Martin-Emerson, R. & Wickens, C. D. (1992). The vertical visual field and implications for the head-up display. In *Proceedings of the Thirty-Sixth Annual Symposium of the Human Factors Society* (pp. 1408–1412). Santa Monica, CA: Human Factors Society.

McClelland, J. L. (1979). On the time relations of mental processes: An examination of systems of processes in cascade. *Psychological Review, 86*, 287–330.

McCrickard, D. S., Chewar, C. M., Somervell, J. P., & Ndiwalana, A. (2003). A model for notification systems evaluation—assessing user goals for multitasking activity. *ACM Transactions on Computer-Human Interaction, 10*, 312–338.

McElree, B. (2001). Working memory and focal attention. *Journal of Experimental Psychology: Learning, Memory & Cognition, 27*, 817–835.

McFarlane, D. C. (1997). Interruption of people in human-computer interaction: A general unifying definition of human interruption and taxonomy. Technical Report #NRL/FR/5510-97-9870, Naval Research Laboratory, Washington, DC.

McFarlane, D. C. & Latorella, K. A. (2002). The scope and importance of human interruption in human-computer interaction design. *Human-Computer Interaction, 17*, 1–61.

McKnight, A. J. & McKnight, A. S. (1993). The effect of cellular phone use upon driver attention. *Accident Analysis & Prevention, 25*, 259–265.

McRuer, D. T., Allen, R. W., Weir, D. H., & Klein, R. H. (1977). New results in driver steering control models. *Human Factors, 19*, 381–397.

Meyer, D. E., Glass, J. M., Mueller, S. T., Seymour, T. L., & Kieras, D. E. (2001). Executive-process interactive control: A unified computational theory for answering twenty questions (and more) about cognitive ageing. *European Journal of Cognitive Psychology, 13*, 123–164.

Meyer, D. E. & Kieras, D. E. (1997). A computational theory of executive cognitive processes and multiple-task performance: Part 1. Basic mechanisms. *Psychological Review, 104*, 3–65.

Mitchell, D. K. (2000). Mental workload and ARL workload modeling tools. Technical Report No. ARL-TN-161, Army Research Laboratory, Aberdeen, MD.

Miyata, Y. & Norman, D. (1986). Psychological issues in support of multiple activities. In Norman, D.A. & Draper, S. W. (Eds.), *User-Centered Design* (pp. 265–284). Mahwah, NJ: Lawrence Erlbaum Associates.

Monk, C. A., Boehm-Davis, D. A. & Trafton, J. G. (2004). Recovering from interruptions: Implications for driver distraction research. *Human Factors, 46*, 650–663.

Monk, C. A., Trafton, J. G., & Boehm-Davis, D. A. (2008). The effect of interruption duration and demand on resuming suspended goals. *Journal of Experimental Psychology: Applied, 14*, 299–313.

Monsell, S. (2003). Task switching. *Trends in Cognitive Sciences, 7*, 134–140.

Myers, B., McDaniel, R., & Wolber, D. (2000). Programming by example: Intelligence in demonstrational interfaces. *Communications of the ACM. 43*, 82–89.

Navon, D. & Gopher, D. (1979). On the economy of the human-processing system. *Psychological Review, 86,* 214–255.

Neale, V.L., Dingus, T.A., Klauer, S.G., Sudweeks, J., & Goodman, M. (2005). An overview of the 100-car naturalistic study and findings. In *Proceedings of the 19th International Technical Conference on Enhanced Safety of Vehicles* (paper #05-0400-W). Washington, DC: National Highway Traffic Safety Administration.

Newell, A. (1973). You can't play 20 questions with nature and win: projective comments on the papers of this symposium. In W. G. Chase (Ed.), *Visual Information Processing* (pp. 283–308). New York: Academic Press.

Newell, A. (1990). *Unified theories of cognition.* Cambridge, MA: Harvard University Press.

Newell, A. & Rosenbloom, P. S. (1981). Mechanisms of skill acquisition and the law of practice. In J. R. Anderson (Ed.), *Cognitive Skills and Their Acquisition* (pp. 1–51). Hillsdale, NJ: Lawrence Erlbaum Associates.

Newell, A. & Simon, H. A. (1963). GPS: A Program that Simulates Human Thought. In E. A. Feigenbaum & J. Feldman (Eds.), *Computers and Thought* (pp. 279–296). New York: McGraw-Hill.

Newell, A. & Simon, H. A. (1972). *Human problem solving.* Englewood Cliffs, NJ: Prentice-Hall.

Nieuwenstein, M. & Potter, M. (2006). Continuous target input overrides the attentional blink in rapid serial visual presentation. *Psychological Science, 17,* 471–475.

Norman, D. A. (1988). *The psychology of everyday things.* New York, NY: Basic Books.

Norman, D. A. (2007). *The design of future things.* New York, NY: Basic Books.

Norman, D. A. & Bobrow, D. G. (1975). On data-limited and resource-limited processes. *Cognitive Psychology, 7,* 44–64.

Norman, D. A. & Shallice, T. (1986). Attention to action: Willed and automatic control of behavior. In R. J. Davidson, G. E. Schwartz, & D. Shapiro (Eds.), *Consciousness and Self-Regulation* (pp. 1–18). New York: Plenum.

Olivers, C. N. L. & Meeter, M. (2008). A boost and bounce theory of temporal attention. *Psychological Review, 115,* 836–863.

Olivers, C. N. L. & Nieuwenhuis, S. (2005). The beneficial effect of concurrent task-irrelevant mental activity on temporal attention. *Psychological Science, 16,* 265–269.

Olivers, C. N. L. & Nieuwenhuis, S. (2006). The beneficial effects of additional task load, positive affect, and instruction on attentional blink. *Journal of Experimental Psychology: Human Perception and Performance, 32,* 364–379.

O'Reilly, R. C. & Frank, M. J. (2006). Making working memory work: A computational model of learning in the prefrontal cortex and basal ganglia. *Neural Computation, 18,* 283–328.

Paganelli, L. & Paternò, F. (2003). A tool for creating design models from web site code. *International Journal of Software Engineering and Knowledge Engineering, 13*, 169–189.

Parasuraman, R., Sheridan, T. B., & Wickens, C. D. (2000). A model of types and levels of human interaction with automation. *IEEE Transactions on Systems, Man and Cybernetics, 30*, 286–297.

Pashler, H. (1984). Processing stages in overlapping tasks: Evidence for a central bottleneck. *Journal of Experimental Psychology: Human Perception and Performance, 10*, 358–377.

Pashler, H. (1994). Dual-task interference in simple tasks: Data and theory. *Psychological Bulletin, 116*, 220–244.

Pavlik, P. I., Jr. & Anderson, J. R. (2005). Practice and forgetting effects on vocabulary memory: An activation-based model of the spacing effect. *Cognitive Science, 29*, 559–586.

Peters, R. D., Kloeppel, E., & Alicandri, E. (1999). Effects of partial and total sleep deprivation on driving performance. Publication No. FHWA-RD-94-046, Washington, DC: Federal Highway Administration, US Department of Transportation.

Pettitt, M., Burnett, G. & Stevens, A. (2007). An extended keystroke-level model for predicting the visual demand of in-vehicle information systems. In *Proceedings of the SIGCHI Conference on Human Factors in Computing Systems: CHI 2007* (pp. 1515–1524). New York: ACM Press.

Pew, R. W. (1974). Levels of analysis in motor control. *Brain Research, 71*, 393–400.

Pew, R. W. & Mavor, A. S. (2007). *Human-system integration in the system development process: a new look*. Washington, DC: National Academies Press.

Polson, P. G. & Kieras, D. E. (1985). A quantitative model of the learning and performance of text editing knowledge. In *Proceedings of the SIGCHI Conference on Human Factors in Computing Systems: CHI 1985* (pp. 207–212). New York: ACM Press.

Posner, M. I. & Petersen, S. E. (1990). The attention system of the human brain. *Annual Review of Neuroscience, 13*, 25–42.

Prinz, W. (1997). Perception and action planning. *European Journal of Cognitive Psychology, 9*, 129–154.

Pylyshyn, Z. W. & Storm, R. W. (1988). Tracking multiple independent targets: Evidence for a parallel tracking mechanism. *Spatial Vision, 3*, 179–197.

Qin, Y., Sohn, M.-H., Anderson, J. R., Stenger, V. A., Fissell, K., Goode, A., & Carter, C. S. (2003). Predicting the practice effects on the blood oxygenation level-dependent (BOLD) function of fMRI in a symbolic manipulation task. *Proceedings of the National Academy of Sciences, 100*, 4951–4956.

Raymond, J. E., Shapiro, K. L, & Arnell, K. M. (1992). Temporary suppression of visual processing in an RSVP task: An attentional blink? *Journal of Experimental Psychology: Human Perception and Performance, 18*, 849–860.

Rayner, K. & Pollatsek, A. (1989). *The psychology of reading.* Englewood Cliffs, NJ: Prentice-Hall.

Reed, M. P. & Green, P. A. (1999). Comparison of driver performance on-road and in a low-cost simulator using a concurrent telephone dialing task. *Ergonomics, 42*, 1015–1037.

Regan, M. A., Lee, J. D., & Young, K. L. (Eds.) (2008). *Driver distraction: Theory, effects and mitigation.* Boca Raton, FL: CRC Press.

Ricard, G. L. (1994). Manual control with delays: A bibliography. *ACM SIGGRAPH Computer Graphics, 28*, 149–154.

Ritter, F. E., Van Rooy, D., St. Amant, R., & Simpson, K. (2006). Providing user models with direct access to computer interfaces: An exploratory study of a simple human-robot interface. *IEEE Transactions on Systems, Man, and Cybernetics, 36*, 592–601.

Ritter, F. E. & Wallach, D. P. (1998). Models of two-person games in ACT-R and Soar. In *Proceedings of the Second European Conference on Cognitive Modelling* (pp. 202–203). Thrumpton: Nottingham University Press.

Ritter, F. E. & Young, R. M. (2001). Embodied models as simulated users: Introduction to this special issue on using cognitive models to improve interface design. *International Journal of Human-Computer Studies, 55*, 1–14.

Roelfsema, P.R., Lamme, V.A.F. & Spekreijse, H. (1998). Object-based attention in the primary visual cortex of the macaque monkey. *Nature, 395*, 376–381.

Rogers, R. D. & Monsell, S. (1995). Costs of a predictable switch between simple cognitive tasks. *Journal of Experimental Psychology: General, 124*, 207–231.

Rosen, C. (2008). The myth of multitasking. *The New Atlantis, 20*, 105–110.

Rosson, M. B. (1983). Patterns of experience in text editing. In *Proceedings of the SIGCHI Conference on Human Factors in Computing Systems: CHI 1983* (pp. 171–175). New York: ACM Press.

Rubinstein, J. S., Meyer, D. E., & Evans, J. E. (2001). Executive Control of Cognitive Processes in Task Switching. *Journal of Experimental Psychology: Human Perception and Performance, 27*, 763–797.

Rumelhart, D. E., McClelland, J. L., & the PDP research group. (1986). *Parallel distributed processing—Volume 1: Foundations.* Cambridge, MA: MIT Press.

Ruthruff, E., van Selst, M., & Johnston, J. C. (2006). How does practice reduce dual-task interference: integration, automatization, or just stage-shortening? *Psychological Research, 70*, 125–142.

Salvucci, D. D. (2001a). Predicting the effects of in-car interface use on driver performance: An integrated model approach. *International Journal of Human-Computer Studies, 55*, 85–107.

Salvucci, D. D. (2001b). An integrated model of eye movements and visual encoding. *Cognitive Systems Research, 1*, 201–220.

Salvucci, D. D. (2005). A multitasking general executive for compound continuous tasks. *Cognitive Science, 29*, 457–492.

Salvucci, D. D. (2006). Modeling driver behavior in a cognitive architecture. *Human Factors, 48*, 362–380.

Salvucci, D. D. (2009). Rapid prototyping and evaluation of in-vehicle interfaces. *ACM Transactions on Human-Computer Interaction.*

Salvucci, D. D. (2010). On reconstruction of task context after interruption. In *Proceedings of the SIGCHI Conference on Human Factors in Computing Systems: CHI 2010.* New York: ACM Press.

Salvucci, D. D. & Anderson, J. R. (2001). Integrating analogical mapping and general problem solving: The path-mapping theory. *Cognitive Science, 25*, 67–110.

Salvucci, D. D. & Beltowska, J. (2008). Effects of memory rehearsal on driver performance: Experiment and theoretical account. *Human Factors, 50*, 834–844.

Salvucci, D. D., Boer, E. R., & Liu, A. (2001). Toward an integrated model of driver behavior in a cognitive architecture. *Transportation Research Record, 1779*, 9–16.

Salvucci, D. D. & Bogunovich, P. (2010). Multitasking and monotasking: The effects of mental workload on deferred task interruptions. In *Proceedings of the SIGCHI Conference on Human Factors in Computing Systems: CHI 2010.* New York: ACM Press.

Salvucci, D. D. & Gray, R. (2004). A two-point visual control model of steering. *Perception, 33*, 1233–1248.

Salvucci, D. D. & Lee, F. J. (2003). Simple cognitive modeling in a complex cognitive architecture. In *Proceedings of the SIGCHI Conference on Human Factors in Computing Systems: CHI 2003* (pp. 265–272). New York: ACM Press.

Salvucci, D. D. & Macuga, K. L. (2002). Predicting the effects of cellular-phone dialing on driver performance. *Cognitive Systems Research, 3*, 95–102.

Salvucci, D. D., Markley, D., Zuber, M., & Brumby, D. P. (2007). iPod distraction: Effects of portable music-player use on driver performance. In *Proceedings of the SIGCHI Conference on Human Factors in Computing Systems: CHI 2007* (pp. 243–250). New York: ACM Press.

Salvucci, D. D., Monk, C. A., & Trafton, J. G. (2009). A process-model account of task interruption and resumption: When does encoding of the problem state occur? In *Proceedings of the Human Factors and Ergonomics Society 53rd Annual Meeting* (pp. 799–803). Santa Monica, CA: Human Factors and Ergonomics Society.

Salvucci, D. D. & Taatgen, N. A. (2008). Threaded cognition: An integrated theory of concurrent multitasking. *Psychological Review, 115*, 101–130.

Salvucci, D. D., Taatgen, N. A., & Borst, J. P. (2009). Toward a unified theory of the multitasking continuum: from concurrent performance to task switching, interruption, and resumption. In *Proceedings of the SIGCHI Conference on Human Factors in Computing Systems: CHI 2009* (pp. 1819–1828). New York: ACM Press.

Salvucci, D. D., Taatgen, N. A., & Kushleyeva, Y. (2006). Learning when to switch tasks in a dynamic multitasking environment. In *Proceedings of the Seventh International Conference on Cognitive Modeling* (pp. 268–273). Trieste, Italy: Edizioni Goliardiche.

Schneider, W. & Chein, J.M. (2003). Controlled and automatic processing: Behavior, theory, & biology. *Cognitive Science, 27*, 525–559.

Schneider, W. & Shiffrin, R. M. (1977). Controlled and automatic human information processing. I. Detection, search, and attention. *Psychological Review, 84*, 1–66.

Schoppek, W. (2002). Examples, rules, and strategies in the control of dynamic systems. *Cognitive Science Quarterly, 2*, 63–92.

Schumacher, E. H., Seymour, T. L., Glass, J. M., Fencsik, D. E., Lauber, E. J., Kieras, D. E., et al. (2001). Virtually perfect time sharing in dual-task performance: uncorking the central cognitive bottleneck. *Psychological Science, 12*, 101–108.

Senders, J. W., Kristofferson, A. B., Levison, W. H., Dietrich, C. W., and Ward, J. L. (1967). The Attentional Demand of Automobile Driving, Highway Research Record # 195, Washington, D.C.: National Academy of Sciences, Transportation Research Board, 15–33.

Seven, R. (2004). Life interrupted: Plugged into it all, we're stressed to distraction. *The Seattle Times: Pacific Northwest Magazine*, November 28, 2004.

Sharp, H., Rogers, Y., & Preece, J. (2007). *Interaction design: Beyond human-computer interaction*. New York: John Wiley & Sons.

Sheridan, T. B. (1970). On how often the supervisor should sample. *IEEE Transactions on Systems Science and Cybernetics, SSC-6*, 140–145.

Sheridan, T. B. (1992). *Telerobotics, automation, and human supervisory control*. Cambridge, MA: MIT Press.

Sherry, L., Polson, P., Fennell, K., & Feary, M. (2002). Drinking from the Fire Hose: The over-reliance on memorized action sequences for MCDU operation. Honeywell Publication # C69-5370-022.

Shiffrin, R. M. & Schneider, W. (1977). Controlled and automatic human information processing. II. Perceptual learning, automatic attending and a general theory. *Psychological Review, 84*, 127–190.

Shinar, D., Rotenberg, E., & Cohen, T. (1997). Crash reduction with an advance brake warning system: A digital simulation. *Human Factors, 39*, 296–302.

Shneiderman, B. (1998). *Designing the user interface* (3rd ed.). Reading, MA: Addison Wesley.

Siegler, R. S. & Shrager, J. (1984). Strategy choices in addition and subtraction: How do children know what to do? In C. Sophian (Ed.), *The Origins of Cognitive Skills* (pp. 229–293). Hillsdale, NJ: Lawrence Erlbaum Associates.

Singley, M. K. & Anderson, J. R. (1987). A keystroke analysis of learning and transfer in text editing. *Human-Computer Interaction, 3*, 223–274.

Sodhi, M., Reimer, B., & Llamazares, I. (2002). Glance analysis of driver eye movements to evaluate distraction. *Behavior Research Methods, Instruments and Computing, 34*, 529–538.

Sohn, M. H. & Anderson, J. R. (2001). Task preparation and task repetition: Two-component model of task switching. *Journal of Experimental Psychology: General, 130*, 764–778.

Sohn, M. H. & Carlson, R. A. (2000). Effects of repetition and foreknowledge in task-set reconfiguration. *Journal of Experimental Psychology: Learning, Memory, and Cognition, 26*, 1445–1460.

Spelke, E., Hirst, W., & Neisser, U. (1976). Skills of divided attention. *Cognition, 4*, 215–230.

Spink, A., Park, M., Jansen, B. J., & Pederson, J. (2006). Multitasking during Web search sessions. *Information Processing and Management, 42*, 264–275.

St. Amant, R., Lieberman, H., Potter, R., & Zettlemoyer, L. (2000). Visual generation in programming by example. *Communications of the ACM, 43*, 107–114.

Stanton, N. A. & Young, M. S. (1998). Is utility in the mind of the beholder? A review of ergonomics methods. *Applied Ergonomics, 29*, 41–54.

Steels, L. (1994). A case study in the behavior-oriented design of autonomous agents. In *Proceedings of the Third International Conference on Simulation of Adaptive Behavior* (SAB-94). Cambridge, MA: MIT Press.

Strayer, D. L. & Drews, F. A. (2004). Profiles in driver distraction: Effects of cell phone conversations on younger and older drivers. *Human Factors, 46*, 640–649.

Strayer, D. L. & Johnston, W. A. (2001). Driven to distraction: Dual-task studies of simulated driving and conversing on a cellular telephone. *Psychological Science, 12*, 462–466.

Sutton, R. S. & Barto, A. G. (1998). *Reinforcement learning: An introduction.* Cambridge, MA: MIT Press.

Taatgen, N. A. (2005). Modeling parallelization and flexibility improvements in skill acquisition: From dual tasks to complex dynamic skills. *Cognitive Science, 29*, 421–455.

Taatgen, N. A. (2007). The minimal control principle. In W. D. Gray (Ed.), *Integrated Models of Cognitive Systems* (pp. 368–379). New York: Oxford University Press.

Taatgen, N. A. & Anderson, J. R. (2002). Why do children learn to say "broke"? A model of learning the past tense without feedback. *Cognition, 86*, 123–155.

Taatgen, N. A. & Dickison, D. (2008). Modeling eye-movement patterns in the flight-management task: combining bottom-up and top-down vision. *Proceedings of the Fifteenth ACT-R workshop.* Pittsburgh PA: Carnegie Mellon University.

Taatgen, N. A., Huss, D., Dickison, D., & Anderson, J. R. (2008). The acquisition of robust and flexible cognitive skills. *Journal of Experimental Psychology: General, 137,* 548–565.

Taatgen, N. A., Juvina, I., Herd, S., Jilk, D., & Martens, S. (2007). Attentional Blink: An internal traffic jam? In *Proceedings of the Eighth International Conference on Cognitive Modeling* (pp. 91–96). New York: Psychology Press.

Taatgen, N. A., Juvina, I., Schipper, M., Borst, J., & Martens, S. (2009). Too much control can hurt: A threaded cognition model of the attentional blink. *Cognitive Psychology, 59,* 1–29.

Taatgen, N. A. & Lee, F. J. (2003). Production compilation: A simple mechanism to model complex skill acquisition. *Human Factors, 45,* 61–76.

Taatgen, N. A., van Oploo, M., Braaksma, J. & Niemantsverdriet, J. (2003). How to construct a believable opponent using cognitive modeling in the game of set. In *Proceedings of the Fifth International Conference on Cognitive Modeling* (pp. 201–206). Bamberg, Germany: Universitätsverlag Bamberg.

Taatgen, N. A., van Rijn, H., & Anderson, J. R. (2007). An integrated theory of prospective time interval estimation: The role of cognition, attention and learning. *Psychological Review, 114,* 577–598.

Telford, C. W. (1931). The refractory phase of voluntary and associative response. *Journal of Experimental Psychology, 14,* 1–35.

Thomas, L. C. & Wickens, C. D. (2001). Visual displays and cognitive tunneling: Frames of reference effects on spatial judgments and change detection. In *Proceedings of Human Factors and Ergonomics Society 45th Annual Meeting* (pp. 336–340). Santa Monica, CA: Human Factors and Ergonomics Society.

Thompson, C. (2005). Meet the life hackers. *New York Times,* October 16, 2005.

Tijerina, L., Johnston, S., Parmer, E., Winterbottom, M. D., & Goodman, M. (2000). Driver distraction with route guidance systems (Technical Report DOT HS 809 069). East Liberty, OH: National Highway Traffic Safety Administration.

Trafton, J. G., Altmann, E. M., & Brock, D. P. (2005). Huh, what was I doing? How people use environmental cues after an interruption. In *Proceedings of the Human Factors and Ergonomics Society 49th Annual Meeting* (pp. 468–472). Santa Monica, CA: Human Factors and Ergonomics Society.

Trafton, J. G., Altmann, E. M., Brock, D. P., & Mintz, F. E. (2003). Preparing to resume an interrupted task: Effects of prospective goal encoding and retrospective rehearsal. *International Journal of Human-Computer Studies, 58,* 583–603.

Trafton, J. G., Bugajska, M. D., Fransen, B. R., & Ratwani, R. M. (2008). Integrating vision and audition within a cognitive architecture to track conversations. In *Proceedings of the 3rd ACM SIGCHI/SIGART Conference on Human-Robot Interaction* (pp. 201–208). New York: ACM Press.

Trafton, J. G. & Monk, C. M. (2008). Task Interruptions. In D. A. Boehm-Davis (Ed.), *Reviews of Human Factors and Ergonomics, Volume 3*.

Trafton, J. G., Schultz, A. C., Perzanowski, D., Bugajska, M. D., Adams, W., Cassimatis, N. L., & Brock, D. P. (2006). Children and robots learning to play hide and seek. In *Proceedings of the 1st ACM SIGCHI/SIGART Conference on Human-Robot Interaction* (pp. 242–249). New York: ACM Press.

Tsimhoni, O. & Liu, Y. (2003). Modeling steering using the Queuing Network—Model Human Processor (QN-MHP). In *Proceedings of the Human Factors and Ergonomics Society 47th Annual Meeting* (pp. 1875–1879). Santa Monica, CA: Human Factors and Ergonomics Society.

Tsimhoni, O., Smith, D., & Green, P. (2004). Address entry while driving: Speech recognition versus a touch-screen keyboard. *Human Factors, 46*, 600–610.

van Rijn, H., van Someren, M., & van der Maas, H. (2003). Modeling developmental transitions on the balance scale task. *Cognitive Science, 27*, 227–257.

van Rijn, H. & Taatgen, N. A. (2008). Timing of multiple overlapping time intervals: How many clocks do we have? *Acta Psychologica, 129*, 365–375.

Venkataraman, G. (1994). *Quantum revolution 1, the breakthrough*. Andhra Pradesh, India: Universities Press.

Welford, A. T. (1952). The "psychological refractory period" and the timing of high speed performance: A review and a theory. *British Journal of Psychology, 43*, 2–19.

Wiberg, M. & Whittaker, S. (2005). Managing availability: supporting lightweight negotiations to handle interruptions. *ACM Transactions on Computer-Human Interaction, 12*, 356–387.

Wickens, C. D. (1976). The effects of divided attention on information processing in tracking. *Journal of Experimental Psychology: Human Perception and Performance, 2*, 1–13.

Wickens, C. D. (1984). Processing resources in attention. In R. Parasuraman, J. Beatty & R. Davies (Eds.), *Varieties of Attention* (pp. 63–101). New York: Wiley.

Wickens, C. D. (2002a). Multiple resources and performance prediction. *Theoretical Issues in Ergonomics Science, 3*, 159–177.

Wickens, C. D. (2002b). Situation awareness and workload in aviation. *Current Directions in Psychological Science, 11*, 128–133.

Wickens, C. D. (2008). Multiple resources and mental workload. *Human Factors, 50*, 449–455.

Wickens, C.D., Dixon, S. R. & Ambinder, M. (2006). Workload and automation reliability in unmanned air vehicles. In N. J. Cooke, H. L. Pringle, H. K. Pederson, & O. Connor (Eds.), *Human Factors of Remotely Operated Vehicles* (pp. 209–222). Amsterdam: Elsevier.

Wickens, C. D. & McCarley, J. A. (2007). *Applied attention theory*. Boca Raton, FL: CRC Press.

Wilkie, R. M. & Wann, J. P. (2003). Controlling steering and judging heading: Retinal flow, visual direction and extra-retinal information. *Journal of Experimental Psychology: Human Perception and Performance, 29,* 363–378.

Woodman, G. F., Vogel, E. K., & Luck, S. J. (2001). Visual search remains efficient when visual working memory is full. *Psychological Science, 12,* 219–224.

Wu, C. & Liu, Y. (2007). Queueing network modeling of driver workload and performance. *IEEE Transactions on Intelligent Transportation Systems, 8,* 528–537.

Wu, C. & Liu, Y. (2008). Queuing network modeling of the Psychological Refractory Period (PRP). *Psychological Review, 115,* 913–954.

Zhao, S., Dragicevic, P., Chignell, M., Balakrishnan, R., & Baudisch, P. (2007). EarPod: Eyes-free Menu Selection using Touch Input and Reactive Audio Feedback. In *Proceedings of the SIGCHI Conference on Human Factors in Computing Systems: CHI 2007* (pp. 1395–1404). New York: ACM Press.

Index

Note: Page numbers followed by "*f*" and "*t*" denote figures and tables, respectively.